China's Nuclear Future

China's Nuclear Future

edited by

Paul J. Bolt & Albert S. Willner

Viva Books

New Delhi | Mumbai | Chennai | Kolkata | Bengaluru | Hyderabad | Kochi | Guwahati

First Indian Edition 2008
Reprinted 2010

VIVA BOOKS PRIVATE LIMITED

- 4737/23 Ansari Road, Daryaganj, New Delhi 110 002
  E-mail: vivadelhi@vivagroupindia.net, Tel. 42242200
- 76, Service Industries, Shirvane, Sector 1, Nerul, Navi Mumbai 400 706
  E-mail: vivamumbai@vivagroupindia.net, Tel. 27721273, 27721274
- Jamals Fazal Chambers, 26 Greams Road, Chennai 600 006
  E-mail: vivachennai@vivagroupindia.net, Tel. 28290304, 28294241
- B-103, Jindal Towers, 21/1A/3 Darga Road, Kolkata 700 017
  E-mail: vivakolkata@vivagroupindia.net, Tel. 22836381, 22816713
- 7, Sovereign Park Apartments, 56-58, K. R. Road, Basavanagudi, Bangalore 560 004
  E-mail: vivabangalore@vivagroupindia.net, Tel. 26607409, 26607410
- 101-102 Mughal Marc Apartments, 3-4-637 to 641, Narayanguda, Hyderabad 500 029
  E-mail: vivahyderabad@vivagroupindia.net, Tel. 27564481, 27564482
- Beevi Towers, First Floor, SRM Road, Kaloor, Kochi 682 018, Kerala
  E-mail: vivakochi@vivagroupindia.net, Tel: 0484-2403055, 2403056
- 232, GNB Road, Beside UCO Bank, Silpukhuri, Guwahati 781 003
  E-mail: vivaguwahati@vivagroupindia.net, Tel: 0361-2666386

www.vivagroupindia.com

Published by arrangement with

Lynne Rienner Publishers, Inc.
1800 30th Street, Suite 314
Boulder, Colorado 80301
USA

ISBN : 978-81-309-0796-3

Published by Vinod Vasishtha for Viva Books Private Limited, 4737/23, Ansari Road, Daryaganj, New Delhi-110 002. Printed and bound by Anand Sons, Delhi - 110 092.

S0000 / S0800 / S0810

To Our Parents

Gordon and Barbara Bolt

Eddie and Johanna Willner

Contents

Acknowledgments

A project of this magnitude requires the assistance of many people. We would first like to thank James Smith, director of the Air Force Institute for National Security Studies, for conceiving of and supporting the project from start to finish, beginning at a conference sponsored by the INSS in July 2003. Participants at the conference, who shaped the book in numerous ways, include Ken Allen, Hal Bidlack, Ron Christman, Dominic DeScisciolo, Hank Gaffney, William Berry, Thomas Drohan, Richard Fisher, John Gibilterra, Lyle Goldstein, Diana Heerdt, Peter Lavoy, Christopher McConnaughay, Robert Gromoll, Donald Henry, Jeffrey Larsen, Jo May, Michael McDevitt, Alex Mosko, Emerson Niou, Don Opperman, Stephen Polk, Terri Olascoaga, Robert Ord, James Przystup, Joel Ryan, Andrew Scobell, Rob Sikorski, William Thomas, Toby Volz, Andrew Yang, Kathleen Walsh, James Wirtz, and Suisheng Zhao. Special thanks also go to David Lai and David Finkelstein for their contributions.

Others from West Point and the Air Force Academy who provided valuable guidance and support include Colonel Russell Howard, Colonel Cindy Jebb, Colonel Jay Parker, Lieutenant Colonel Brenda Vallance, and Colonel Douglas Murray. Jeffrey Larsen of Larsen Consulting made extremely valuable editorial contributions to the book, as well as providing support for the initial conference.

The two anonymous reviewers of our manuscript made numerous valuable suggestions, as did our editor at Lynne Rienner Publishers, Leanne Anderson. Leanne was particularly patient and understanding.

Finally, we would like to thank our families, whose love and support made this all possible.

1

China's Nuclear Future in a Changing Environment

Albert S. Willner and Paul J. Bolt

When China detonated its first atomic bomb on October 16, 1964, the United States and Soviet Union faced a new and potentially destabilizing change in the Cold War balance of power. Both countries, along with Britain, had signed the limited nuclear test ban treaty in 1963. Both countries had reason to fear the consequences of China's possession of the bomb. The United States saw China as an uncompromising adversary, and had threatened to use nuclear weapons against the communist state on more than one occasion.[1] The Soviet Union viewed Mao Zedong, China's leader, as warlike and imprudent. In 1959 it had formally reneged on a promise made in 1957 to give China a prototype atomic bomb.[2] Relations had been deteriorating since that time, and within five years of China's first nuclear explosion, there would be serious border clashes between the former allies.

Nevertheless, the impact of China's nuclear weapons program was smaller than many had anticipated. The number of warheads China deployed was never more than a small fraction of the arsenals of the US and Soviet Union. With a no-first-use policy, China has for a long time been content to maintain fewer than two dozen nuclear-tipped DF-5/5A missiles capable of reaching the United States.[3] China has evidently considered a fairly small nuclear stockpile sufficient for deterrence purposes, following a doctrine often labeled "minimum deterrence" that is sufficient to make a second strike capability at least plausible and thus prevent nuclear blackmail.[4]

However, today there are good reasons to reassess China's nuclear policy. Just as a particular domestic and international context led China to seek atomic and then thermonuclear weapons beginning in 1955, in spite of China's weak economy and the tremendous cost of such an undertaking, so too we must ask if the contemporary environment will lead to changes in China's nuclear posture.[5] The current environment can be broken down into internal and external factors. Domestic factors that affect the nuclear issue include growing wealth coupled with priority given to economic development, increased professionalism in the People's Liberation Army (PLA), space successes, and the transfer of power to the so-called Fourth Generation of Chinese leadership. Important elements of a changing international environment include the global perception of China as a rising power, the war on terrorism, the Taiwan standoff, the reduction in US and Russian nuclear weapons, US antimissile defenses and the US abrogation of the Anti-Ballistic Missile (ABM) Treaty, and continued nuclear proliferation, especially to Pakistan, India, and North Korea. While these factors will be analyzed in more depth in later chapters, it is worthwhile to consider them briefly here.

China's rapid economic growth is by now well known. From 1978–2003, China's real gross domestic product grew at an average rate of 9 percent a year, while foreign trade averaged 15 percent annual growth.[6] The implications of this growth for national power are profound. Along with increased central government tax revenues comes a stronger technological base and more advanced management skills, all important for strengthening the military industrial complex. Nevertheless, such growth is also accompanied by serious problems that demand government attention as well, including environmental degradation, sharpening inequality between provinces and individuals, and, ironically, destabilizing unemployment.

China's economic growth has been enabled by state policies that place first priority on economic development and its antecedent, international stability. As a result, China's overall growth in military expenditures has been comparatively restrained. In particular, China learned from the Soviet Cold War experience that overspending on defense leads to national weakness rather than strength. Thus, Beijing considers any effort to match the US military across a broad range of weapons systems, resulting in an arms race, as foolish. Such an effort would cost too much money and poison the environment necessary for sustained, rapid economic growth. Nevertheless, China's growing gross national product (GNP) has enabled large increases in defense spending, especially after the PLA violently suppressed protests in Beijing in 1989. In the ten years after Tiananmen, China's military spending doubled in real terms.[7] This allows China to devote increased resources to its nuclear weapons systems if it so desires.

Another important domestic factor that affects China's nuclear weapons program is the continuing professionalization of the PLA. The PLA was born as a guerrilla army, fighting against seemingly superior Nationalist and Japanese forces. After the communist victory in 1949, an army imbued with ideology continued to maintain a people's war doctrine that envisioned a retreat into China's interior in the event of invasion, with a slow but sure retaking of territory through guerrilla warfare. Nevertheless, hard lessons from the Korean War, as well as influence from the Soviet military, led many officers to advocate greater professionalism. Thus the Maoist period witnessed tension between those who emphasized the human and ideological factors in warfare and those who advocated a more professional force with modern equipment.[8]

Since Deng Xiaoping's rise to power in the late 1970s, the PLA has steadily become more of a professional military force. The one exception was the period following the Tiananmen Square demonstrations, when there occurred a brief period of politicization of the military and a series of purges based on perceived loyalty to the regime. Nevertheless, the PLA has moved beyond "people's war" to "limited war under high-technology conditions." This has been accompanied by a fervent effort to modernize and become more technically advanced. The lessons from US military operations in the 1990 Gulf War and subsequent US operations have increased the PLA's motivation to transform itself in revolutionary ways. As an example, the PLA has made great efforts to develop capabilities in both offensive and defensive information warfare.[9] Such advances can only benefit China's nuclear forces, the Second Artillery Corps.

Recent successes in China's space program demonstrate the levels of technological sophistication and professionalism of which military programs are capable. In 2003 China became only the third country to send a human into space. China also has launched commercial and government satellites. While some of the expertise for these programs undoubtedly came from Russia and even US companies, China's indigenous contributions should not be downplayed. There is a clear link between China's space rockets and its strategic nuclear missiles program.

The final domestic development we will consider is the shift in power from the so-called Third Generation of leadership to the Fourth Generation, symbolized in 2002 by the transfer of the presidency and the office of general secretary of the Chinese Communist Party from Jiang Zemin to Hu Jintao. In 2004 this was followed by Jiang turning over the reins of the party's Central Military Commission to Hu as well. Currently there is no indication that the Fourth Generation will have radically different perspectives toward the international environment or the United States than the Third Generation.[10] Nevertheless, the almost complete lack of military experience on the part of Fourth Generation leaders raises questions about the future state of civil-military relations in China.

Shifting to international factors, there are three changes that would seem to discourage major shifts in China's nuclear posture, and three developments that might encourage China to expand its nuclear arsenal. The first factor is China's rise as a regional power. Each year China's influence in Asia grows. Evidence of this includes China's 2002 framework agreement committing it to free trade with the Association of Southeast Asian Nations (ASEAN) in 2010 and China's role in negotiations over North Korea's nuclear weapons program. China's increasing influence is primarily a reflection of its growing role as an economic engine for the region, but also its military power. However, increasing military expenditures also make countries in the region more wary of China. Thus a sudden increase in China's nuclear forces could possibly be detrimental to China's regional influence, as Asian neighbors would react with alarm.

A second change in the international environment favorable to China is the reduction in the US and Russian nuclear arsenals. Due to improved relations with the end of the cold war and arms control agreements such as the Moscow Treaty, US and Russian active nuclear arsenals are slated to be cut by approximately two-thirds by 2012. With this drop in the nuclear stockpiles of its two potential strategic rivals, China faces little pressure to increase its own arsenal. Likewise, the war on terror reduces pressure for further nuclear buildups and has for the most part served to strengthen relations between Beijing and Washington. Due to different priorities, no longer are Washington policymakers as focused on the "China threat." To the extent that terrorism is a threat to Beijing, nuclear weapons will not help, while an expanded arsenal may threaten relations with Washington.

Nevertheless, there are also three developments in the international system that encourage Beijing to further develop its nuclear arsenal. The first is the deterioration in relations with Taiwan. In spite of upwards of $100 billion in Taiwanese money invested on the mainland, China is so far losing the battle for the hearts and minds of Taiwanese; its passage in March 2005 of the anti-secession law has served to further exacerbate tensions. President Chen Shui-bian's victory in the 2004 presidential election and subsequent vow of a new constitution, along with polls showing more and more residents of Taiwan identifying themselves as Taiwanese rather than Chinese, indicate that China will have trouble simply maintaining the status quo. Added to this, while the United States has very publicly discouraged Taiwan from unilaterally moving toward independence, it continues to offer advanced weapons to Taiwan and engages in frequent contacts with Taiwanese military and government officials.

In assessing a potential conflict across the Taiwan Straits, China does not want to use nuclear weapons against Taiwan itself. China would have difficulty justifying the "liberation" of its compatriots on what China claims to be PRC territory through nuclear annihilation. Nevertheless, the limited use of nuclear weapons against opposing forces during a Taiwan confrontation remains an option. Moreover, nuclear weapons would play an important role were the United States to become involved in a cross-straits conflict. In the 1954 Taiwan crisis, the United States threatened China with nuclear attack. In the 1996 crisis, a Chinese official reportedly emphasized China's ability to retaliate with nuclear weapons against the US, telling Chas Freeman that the leaders of the United States "care more about Los Angeles than they do about Taiwan." In 2005, Chinese General Zhu Chenghu also suggested that China might use nuclear weapons against the United States in the event of a conflict over Taiwan.[11] While the possibility of a nuclear exchange may seem implausible to some in light of the imbalance between Chinese and US nuclear forces, there are disturbing questions regarding the role nuclear weapons might play in a confrontation in which the stakes are extremely high. For example, might China threaten to use nuclear weapons against US forces or cities? Would the United States be deterred by such a threat? Could the US be the first to use nuclear weapons? The possibility of such a confrontation may provide motivation for Beijing to field a strategic nuclear force that provides a stronger deterrent against potential US intervention.

A second factor likely to encourage Chinese expansion and modernization of its nuclear program is the US withdrawal from the Anti-Ballistic Missile Treaty and deployment of an anti-ballistic missile system. The problem from the Chinese perspective is that a functioning US ABM system makes China vulnerable to a US first strike. If a US first strike were able to destroy most Chinese strategic missiles capable of reaching the United States, missile defenses could be relied upon to destroy any remnant that China might launch in response. Thus China could be put in an untenable situation. The logical Chinese response will be to build effective decoys or enough additional missiles to overcome an ABM system, possibly including missiles outfitted with multiple independently targetable reentry vehicles (MIRVs).

The third changing factor in the international system is nuclear proliferation. In the last decade, India, Pakistan, and North Korea, all neighbors of China, have developed nuclear weapons. (Russia of course also has nuclear weapons.) While Pakistan and North Korea do not directly threaten China, their acquisition of nuclear weapons (especially North Korea) may pressure other states in the region to follow suit. By contrast, India and China are clear rivals, at least from India's perspective. In 1998, Indian Defense Minister George Fernandez justified India's nuclear tests by pointing to threats from Pakistan and China.[12] China must account for this regional proliferation in its own deployment of medium-range missiles.

Overview of the Book

This introduction has covered China's domestic and external environment. In the second chapter, Christine Cleary provides an overview of the strategic drivers and objective considerations that shape China's nuclear policy. She reviews China's grand strategy, national security interests, and strategic culture in order to determine how these factors inform the assumptions and preferences of the Chinese elite, which in turn shape Chinese nuclear policy. For example, the importance of comprehensive national power to the Chinese elite is discussed, with emphasis on the Communist Party's commitment to economic success, a stable security environment, and regional preeminence. Similarly, key characteristics of Chinese strategic culture, such as primacy of the human element and the preferences for minimalism, strategic defense, and deliberate ambiguity, are identified as having a continuing influence on China's nuclear future.

Cleary also identifies objective factors that seem to have influenced the translation of nuclear strategy into force posture, specifically technology, economics, and domestic politics. While technology and economics are not as great a constraint on Chinese policies as in the past, political considerations will likely prevent major changes in China's nuclear posture. Thus these objective factors seem to suggest that China will gradually modernize its strategic capabilities so as to achieve a "small but modern" nuclear warfighting force. Nonetheless, potential flashpoints, such as Taiwanese independence and US deployment of ballistic missile defenses, have the potential to alter the continuity displayed to date in China's nuclear strategy.

In Chapter 3, Evan Medeiros takes a fresh look at the current content and future direction of China's nuclear doctrine. Chinese beliefs about the roles and missions of nuclear weapons have long been one of the most important but least understood aspects of the evolving mosaic of China's overall nuclear posture. To date, some of the Western writing about Chinese nuclear doctrine is necessarily speculative and relies more on generalizing from capabilities than analyzing Chinese writings about the roles and missions of nuclear weapons. New Chinese writings about nuclear doctrine provide rich detail about who in China thinks about nuclear weapons and deterrence, how they approached this subject in the past, how they think about nuclear weapons now, how these evolving ideas may be influencing ongoing nuclear force modernization, and ultimately how they may affect China's future nuclear posture. A key finding to emerge from these new Chinese source materials is that there is growing intellectual activity about nuclear doctrinal issues within military academic research organizations, as distinct from the nuclear scientific establishment that long dominated this sub-arena of research and policymaking.

This chapter first identifies both the general ideas and the detailed concepts that inform and comprise China's current nuclear doctrine. Second, it specifies the areas of change in Chinese nuclear thinking and highlights possible sources of these shifts. To address these issues, Medeiros argues that China's nuclear doctrine is aimed at sufficiency rather than minimum deterrence. Western analysts should think of Chinese nuclear doctrine as a set of policies that are collectively sufficient, in the Chinese leadership's eyes, to meet their changing national security needs—irrespective of the terms that China uses to characterize its nuclear doctrine. This argument is meant to directly contrast with the dominant claims about China's doctrine as either credible minimum deterrence or limited deterrence, which too starkly frame the current debate.

Phillip Saunders and Jing-dong Yuan examine China's strategic force modernization in Chapter 4. China's strategic modernization programs have sought to address long-standing weaknesses and to build a credible deterrent by improving the survivability of China's nuclear forces. China's Second Artillery Corps is making significant efforts to upgrade the quality of its personnel and to improve the training and readiness of its operational units. The authors expect China to continue efforts to improve the survivability of its nuclear forces, work to defeat US missile defenses by deploying Ballistic Missile Defense (BMD) countermeasures and increasing the size of its arsenal, and likely make modest efforts to enhance nuclear war-fighting capabilities.

In the near term, Saunders and Yuan assess that China will deploy nuclear forces, including new land-based intercontinental ballistic missiles

(ICBMs) and sea-launched ballistic missiles, which are more mobile, survivable, and effective. China's strategic modernization will continue to be plagued by delays and remain somewhat constrained by fissile material stocks and technological limitations, but these limitations will still permit China to develop and deploy a much larger nuclear force. Evolving Sino-US political relations and the potential impact of US ballistic missile defense deployments will have a significant influence on Beijing's decisions about the ultimate size and composition of its future nuclear forces. This provides an opportunity for the United States to use reassurance and strategic dialogue to influence Chinese strategic decisionmaking.

In Chapter 5, Ron Montaperto looks at Beijing's perceptions of United States intentions and capabilities and how these views will influence China's nuclear policies. He notes that Beijing is quite apprehensive about US motives and long-range intentions toward China. Chinese policymakers have decided to work within the existing system of US hegemony, as evidenced by Chinese cooperation in the areas of counterterrorism, Taiwan (to some degree), participation in international and multilateral organizations, and especially nuclear proliferation and arms control.

Nevertheless, Montaperto argues that US nuclear policies are particularly sensitive for China because they threaten China's most fundamental interests, including Taiwan. China's concerns about the survivability of its nuclear force are driving, in part, its current efforts at modernization. In this environment, US decisions on the scope of its missile defense, the mix of offensive and defensive weapons that come as a result of the Nuclear Posture Review, and whether or not these weapons systems are deployed against China will greatly influence the future of the US-China nuclear relationship.

Ting Wai, in Chapter 6, turns to examining China's nuclear strategy in relation to the flashpoint of Taiwan, especially in light of potential US intervention in a military conflict. Observing both mainland China and Taiwan from Hong Kong and extensively utilizing both Chinese and Western sources, Ting is in a unique position to provide analysis on the possible use of nuclear weapons in a Taiwan conflict.

Ting begins with a review of China's missile arsenal, particularly short range ballistic missiles aimed at Taiwan. He then turns to changes in China's strategy, driven by China's own new weapons systems and developments in the United States such as ballistic missile defense and the Nuclear Posture Review. In particular, Ting asserts that there may be compelling reasons for China to abolish its principle of "no-first-use" of nuclear weapons (although in fact this policy may not even now apply to Taiwan). Such a move would require US military planners and political leaders to rethink the consequences if Washington intervenes in a cross-straits crisis by sending its forces to the theater of conflict.

In fact, Ting suggests that nuclear weapons could play a key role in a Taiwan conflict, from US and Chinese efforts at deterrence and counterdeterrence to the use of neutron bombs by Chinese forces against concentrated masses of Taiwan defenders. Thus debate on China's nuclear strategy and Chinese military analysis on the "utility" of nuclear weapons shed a new light on understanding the future of cross-straits conflict. Ting concludes that China will continue to attempt to make use of defense modernization and its nuclear forces to create a militarily overwhelming situation so as to press Taiwan to the negotiation table.

The final chapter by Brad Roberts is not a conclusion for this volume in the traditional sense. However, it is a very fitting closing chapter in that it presents alternative futures for China's nuclear program.[13] Roberts asserts that the future direction of China's nuclear future cannot be determined with certainty. In fact, numerous alternatives have been discussed by Western analysts. Roberts therefore begins by defining a baseline trajectory for the modernization of China's strategic forces, which will bring improved survivability through both qualitative and quantitative improvements. This baseline is defined as restrained modernization aimed at keeping pace with challenges to the viability of China's deterrent posed by improving US defensive and offensive capabilities.

Two departure trajectories are then considered. In one, China is motivated by US efforts at defense transformation, the new triad, and the demonstrated US willingness to use force to seek more rapid and far-reaching improvements in a "sprint" to maximum leverage for a Taiwan crisis. In the other, China seeks to replace Russia as Eurasia's second nuclear power—and not to challenge the US for supremacy. The chapter concludes with an analysis of the complicated mix of incentives and restraints Beijing faces in considering whether to deviate from the baseline nuclear force, including US efforts at "dissuasion."

While it remains difficult to make a definitive assessment as to China's eventual path, the analyses provided in this volume allow for tentative conclusions to be drawn. First, China's priority in the near term will be on building a more survivable force, one less vulnerable to first strike and one that maintains a secure second strike capability. While continuing to cloak its efforts in secrecy and ambiguity, China's nuclear planners want to build a modest force designed to deter and prevent potential nuclear adversaries from coercing Beijing in a crisis. Indeed the buildup is aimed in part at maintaining a balance that keeps Beijing's leadership confident in its ability to not only survive but to win a limited war.

Second, China's perceptions of emerging challenges will shape the structure and pace of its nuclear modernization program. Continuing tensions over Taiwan will continue to influence China's nuclear program. Beijing's policies, plans, and forces will be developed to sow uncertainty about its capability and to send the message that it is willing to inflict unacceptable losses on its potential opponents.

Chinese writings are replete with references to the need to effectively counter the development and deployment of US ballistic missile defenses, long-range conventional precision strike capabilities, and efforts outlined in the Nuclear Posture Review. Potential responses could tie China's nuclear force growth to the deployment of US ballistic missile defenses, moving toward the development of an anti-satellite attack capability, designing and implementing its own BMD system and countermeasures, and substantially building up its theater ballistic missile force well beyond the rate of growth now taking place.

Third, it is important to remember that China's nuclear efforts cannot be viewed solely through a Taiwan or US lens. Beijing's strategic planners must take into account their relations with Russia and India in deciding the pace and manner of nuclear modernization. China is expected to continue to adjust to the current reality of perceived global and regional norms. The result is expected to be modest change in its nuclear programs over a long period of time. Should Beijing undertake a quick and significant buildup, clearly there would likely be major international costs, costs that could seriously undermine its efforts to build cooperation with its neighbors and other international partners.

Fourth, other constraints exist as well. China's economic development remains its top priority. As mentioned earlier, Beijing is determined not to be pulled into the Soviet trap of competing with the US in an arms race; thus nuclear development programs in particular can be expected to grow at a measured pace, albeit in a manner cloaked in secrecy. Additionally, as these chapters show time and time again, China's nuclear development continues to be plagued by delays, technical failures, training deficiencies, and major defense industry–related problems. Collectively, these difficulties can be expected to slow even the best intentions of China's nuclear program planners.

Significant gaps remain in fully understanding the direction China's nuclear programs will take. Many key decisions have yet to be made by the Chinese leadership due to internal political, fiscal, and bureaucratic considerations, while others may be pending the outcome of choices in foreign capitals. By addressing likely and alternative futures, this book gives the reader a framework for analyzing emerging Chinese strategic policy and provides a best estimate of China's nuclear prospects. The risks to international peace and stability are great, should this issue not be discussed, assessed, and influenced. With this volume, it is our hope that we have in some measure contributed to a greater understanding of what China's nuclear future is likely to look like.

Notes

The views expressed in this chapter are those of the authors and do not reflect the official policy or position of the US Air Force, US Army, or any other US government agency.

1. Such threats were made through statements or nuclear deployments in the Korean War and the Taiwan Straits crises of 1954–1956 and 1958. See Richard K. Betts, *Nuclear Blackmail and Nuclear Balance* (Washington, DC: The Brookings Institution, 1987), 31–47, 54–62; John Wilson Lewis and Xue Litai, *China Builds the Bomb* (Stanford: Stanford University Press, 1988), chapter 2; and Melvin Gurtov and Byong-Moo Hwang, *China Under Threat* (Baltimore: Johns Hopkins University Press, 1980), 82.

2. Lewis and Xue, 41, 60–65.

3. David Shambaugh, *Modernizing China's Military: Progress, Problems, and Prospects* (Berkeley: University of California Press, 2003), 278–279. The DF-31, expected to be deployed sometime this decade, will be capable of striking the western portion of the United States.

4. For a discussion of minimum deterrence, and debates about this doctrine, see Robert A. Manning, Ronald Montaperto, and Brad Roberts, *China, Nuclear Weapons, and Arms Control: A Preliminary Assessment* (New York: Council on Foreign Relations, 2000), 30–33. Evan Medeiros, in this volume, argues that China's current doctrine should be labeled "nuclear sufficiency." For a further discussion of the logic behind Beijing's strategic choices, see Avery Goldstein, *Deterrence and Security in the 21st Century* (Stanford: Stanford University Press, 2000), 121–136.

5. One view of a more aggressive Chinese nuclear posture is found in Thomas M. Kane, "Dragon or Dinosaur: Nuclear Weapons in a Modernizing China," *Parameters,* vol. 33, no. 4 (Winter 2003–04): 98–113.

6. "Behind the Mask," *Economist,* March 20–26, 2004: Special Section on A Survey of Business in China, 3.

7. Shambaugh, 223.

8. For an overview of debates over professionalism in the PLA, see June Teufel Dreyer, *China's Political System*, 4th ed. (New York: Pearson Longman, 2004), chapter 9.

9. See Paul J. Bolt and Carl N. Brenner, "Information Warfare Across the Taiwan Strait," *Journal of Contemporary China,* vol. 13, no. 38 (February 2004): 129–150.

10. See Andrew J. Nathan and Bruce Gilley, *China's New Rulers: The Secret Files* (New York: New York Review Books, 2002), chapter 8.

11. Patrick E. Tyler, "As China Threatens Taiwan, It Makes Sure US Listens," *New York Times,* January 24, 1996, A3; Chas Freeman, "Did China Threaten to Bomb Los Angeles?" *Proliferation Brief,* vol. 4, no. 4, March 22, 2001, www.ciaonet.org/pbei/ceip/frc01/; and Joseph Kahn, "Chinese General Threatens Use of A-Bombs if US Intrudes," *New York Times,* July 15, 2005, A8.

12. John F. Burns, "India Defense Chief Calls US Hypocritical," *New York Times,* June 18, 1998, A6.

13. For a discussion of the value of a methodology that utilizes alternative futures in assessing China's policies rather than providing single-outcome predictions, see Josh Kerbel, "Thinking Straight: Cognitive Bias in the US Debate about China," *Studies in Intelligence,* vol. 48, no. 3 (2004): 27–35.

2

Culture, Strategy, and Security

Christine A. Cleary

Since Mao Zedong's decision to invest in a strategic weapons program in the 1950s, the People's Republic of China (PRC) has sought a nuclear weapons capability that would deter threats to the homeland, defend against challenges from continental or sea-based neighbors, and augment international prestige. The pursuit of such a capability—constrained at times by political, economic, and technical considerations—has been slow yet deliberate, resulting in China's minimal but credible retaliatory nuclear strike force. However, a gap between aspirations and operational capability plagues the Chinese nuclear program, necessitating a nuclear strategy cloaked in deliberate ambiguity with a robust emphasis on denial and deception.

China's strategic disposition toward ambiguity, defensiveness, and minimalism interacts with economic and technical constraints and domestic political preferences to shape the PRC's strategic force. China has constructed a small triad of aircraft, land-based missiles, and submarine-launched missiles. China initially relied on Hong-6 and Qiang-5 aircraft as its primary nuclear delivery systems.[1] However, as China's ballistic missile capabilities improved, land-based missiles became the primary nuclear weapons delivery system beginning in 1970, supplemented by a single *Xia* class (Type 092) nuclear-powered ballistic missile submarine, which was operationally deployed with its missiles in 1988. China's strategic force is heavily concentrated in its missiles: it operates approximately 120 ballistic missiles of four types: the DF-3A, DF-4, DF-5/5A, and DF-21A. Each missile carries a single nuclear warhead.[2] Of these missiles, approximately twenty ICBMs are capable of hitting the United States. This number could increase to around thirty by 2005 and may reach up to sixty by 2010.[3]

The objective of this chapter is to present strategic influences—ranging from China's quest for comprehensive national power (CNP) to the more controversial concept of strategic culture—to provide insight into the forces driving China's decisions about its nuclear weapons program. But strategic factors alone cannot account for China's nuclear development. Thus, the chapter also singles out key objective factors—specifically technology, economics, and domestic politics—that seem to have influenced how China translates its nuclear strategy into force posture.[4] This attempt to identify and assess the considerations influencing Beijing's nuclear policy is based mainly on clearly identified strategic priorities of the People's Republic of China, as well as inferences drawn from China's historical experience as a nuclear power.

In looking toward China's nuclear future, one wonders if the forces that drove China to adopt a defensive, minimalist nuclear policy will also motivate Hu Jintao and the Fourth Generation leadership to maintain the continuity in China's strategic force posture. The chapter concludes that Hu will likely maintain a Chinese nuclear strategy with a defensive orientation, while simultaneously continuing with a measured course of strategic modernization, so as to preserve China's flexibility in event of a crisis. Flashpoints such as Taiwan are considered in this discussion as well, since a crisis over the island could portend major changes—including a more accelerated trajectory of force modernization—to China's nuclear forces.

Strategic Considerations

Among the many strategic influences that will help craft China's nuclear future, the most important is the grand strategy of the PRC. Two key elements of Chinese strategy are examined: China's quest for comprehensive national power and Beijing's assessment of the strategic threat environment. These strategic influences deserve careful consideration, since China's quest for CNP determines China's strategic goals, while its assessment of the strategic environment identifies threats to these goals. This two-part dynamic will directly impact how China defends its strategic objectives in general, and how the PRC seeks to modernize its strategic forces in particular. The second part of this section examines strategic culture, a more elusive and controversial analytic concept and, by looking at China's nuclear past, identifies some preferences among the decisionmaking elite that could impact China's nuclear future.

Grand Strategy

According to Khadong Oh Hassig of the Institute for Defense Analyses, China's strategic objectives include protecting China's sovereignty, maintaining China's security, preventing Taiwan's independence, securing a favorable national image, and promoting economic development.[5] These objectives are the ends toward which Beijing's efforts to obtain comprehensive national power, or overall national strength, are directed. In other words, China's grand strategy actively seeks CNP as the means toward achieving China's strategic objectives. Increased CNP will provide China with the optimal allocation of national resources necessary to ensure that its strategic objectives can be met and sustained. As Chinese leaders focus on enhancing national power, they continuously assess the broader strategic threat environment for challenges that may require adjustments to China's grand strategy.

Comprehensive national power. According to a recent Pentagon report, Chinese military strategists define grand strategy as the "overall strategy of a nation or an alliance of nations in which they use 'overall national strength' to achieve national political goals, especially those related to national security and development."[6] "Overall national strength" or "comprehensive national power" according to Li Qingshang, a People's Liberation Army (PLA) colonel, is composed of a country's strength in five major areas—politics, economics, military affairs, science and technology, and foreign affairs.[7]

Michael Swaine and Ashley Tellis further define CNP, arguing that since the end of the Cold War China's grand strategy has sought

> the acquisition of comprehensive national power deriving from a continued reform of the economy without the impediments and distractions of security competition. The traditional objectives that the Chinese state has pursued over the centuries still remain and they *even now* constitute the ends to which all the efforts relating to economic growth and internal transformation are directed. These objectives included assuring domestic order and social well-being; maintaining an adequate defense against threats to the heartland; increasing the level of influence and control over the periphery with an eye to warding off threats that may eventually menace the political regime; and restoring China to regional preeminence while attaining the respect of its peers as a true great power marked by high levels of economic and technological development, political stability, military prowess, and manifest uprightness.[8]

The combination of Li Qingshang's and Swaine and Tellis's interpretations yields three critical strategic objectives with respect to China's grand strategy: (1) internal and external stability and security; (2) continued and successful economic reform; and (3) regional preeminence. All three of these objectives are highly significant; however, the first of the three, internal and external stability and security, is a necessary precondition for the latter objectives.

Strategic threat assessment. Beijing is constantly assessing and hedging against any challenges to China's achievement of CNP. Perceived threats—both internal and external—to the Party's goals of economic success, a stable security environment, and regional preeminence will factor into China's strategic modernization. Domestic stability and a secure international environment are essential to Beijing's pursuit of CNP. Externally, the Sino-US relationship is at times perceived as threatening, while internally, unrest from a variety of factors, including the inequalities produced by economic reforms and secessionist movements, challenges the legitimacy of the Chinese Communist Party (CCP). Similarly, the failure to resolve the Taiwan reunification issue is viewed as an affront to stated PRC goals of territorial integrity, state sovereignty, and economic leadership.

The issue of Taiwanese independence deserves special attention, as it is the flashpoint most likely to alter how the Chinese leadership thinks about nuclear weapons. The issue of Taiwan has become emblematic of China's grand strategy and is a fundamental national security interest. The CCP has staked its reputation on the issues that Taiwan represents: national sovereignty, territorial integrity, and economic leadership. Indeed, Beijing has continuously stressed that Taiwan is of national and vital importance:

> The Chinese government has consistently adhered to the one-China principle and will never give in or compromise on the fundamental issues concerning state sovereignty and territorial integrity. . . . However, if a grave turn of events occurs leading to a separation of Taiwan from China in any name . . . then the Chinese government will have no choice but to adopt all drastic measures possible, including the use of force, to safeguard China's sovereignty and territorial integrity.[9]

Historically, the PRC has demonstrated its inclination to use force in situations perceived as threatening to its national goals or its credibility to defend vital interests. For example, analyses of China's conventional wars, such as the Korean War and the Sino-Indian border war, showed China willing to back up threats with force in order for its pronouncements to be taken seriously.[10] Therefore, it is highly likely that

China will escalate to the use of force should cross-straits tensions become too high.

The PRC will pursue credible military options should such a confrontation arise. China's strategic capability will cast a shadow during escalation; however, it is unclear what role nuclear weapons would play in the operational campaign. Most likely, the PRC will sustain or expand theater advantages, such as dual-capability ballistic missiles, in order to coerce a quick ending to a Taiwanese push for independence. Less likely is the possibility that China will develop or deploy electromagnetic pulse (EMP) weapons to achieve the same effect. Finally, improvements in medium- and long-range capabilities are probable in order to signal Washington that the stakes in Taiwan are too high for US intervention. (See Chapter 6 by Ting Wai in this volume for greater detail on Taiwan scenarios.)

Sino-US relations dominate China's external threat environment. China's strategic perception of the United States is that it is an ideological hegemon, fervently anti-communist, and comprised of a "defense elite [that] worships technology."[11] Beijing is concerned with US ambitions of "absolute security," which includes the pursuit of US missile defenses and a potential US-China-Taiwan conflict.

Thus, the Sino-US strategic relationship will likely dictate how the Fourth Generation leadership pursues its nuclear strategy. Despite being named a "potential competitor" by the US Quadrennial Defense Review, relations between Beijing and Washington are currently amicable. To the best of his ability, Hu Jintao will likely maintain Sino-US relations so as to further his internal goals of domestic stability and economic development. Toward this end, Beijing has played a role in brokering the talks on the North Korean nuclear issue.

For its part, the United States has indicated that it will take a measured approach regarding the Taiwan situation. President Bush's statements on December 9, 2003, to PRC Premier Wen Jiabao claimed that Washington opposes any unilateral decision by Taiwanese President Chen Shui-bian to change the status quo, referring to Chen's 2006 plans to reform the constitution and, potentially, declare independence for the island.[12]

Although Taiwan is the most obvious indication of tensions in the Sino-US relationship, US Ballistic Missile Defense (BMD) remains a thorny issue between the two countries, despite efforts to maintain a stable and cooperative nuclear relationship. The PRC has recently muted its opposition to US plans to deploy BMD; however, elements of the US New Triad, specifically advances in US conventional strike capability, are likely causing China's defense planners concern. Therefore, it is probable that China will continue to modernize its long-range strike systems, most likely expanding ICBM capability in order to penetrate US BMD shields. (See Chapter 5 by Ron Montaperto in this volume for more details on China's approach to the United States.)

China also considers other regional actors in its strategic planning, namely India and Japan. China operates from a position of strategic superiority when planning against India, particularly given the slow rate of Indian missile deployment. However, China will continue to hedge against a potential threat from its nuclear-armed neighbor. Japan is another consideration driving Chinese strategic planning. Beijing is concerned about US-Japanese military cooperation. Similarly, current uncertainty regarding the outcome of events on the Korean Peninsula could prompt Japan to pursue a nuclear capability. If such an event were to occur, China's nuclear force posture would need to be flexible in adapting to this challenge.

The attainment and protection of CNP likely will remain the most important strategic consideration influencing China's nuclear future. In order to ensure the success of its grand strategy, China will strive for internal and external stability, continued and successful economic reform, and regional preeminence. China's strategic capability is most significant in relation to China's interest in external stability. To China, a credible nuclear deterrent provides Beijing political and security benefits, particularly with respect to the issue of Taiwanese independence.

Strategic Culture and Nuclear Weapons

Strategic culture is an elusive analytic concept, which grew out of efforts to understand and predict Soviet nuclear strategy during the Cold War. Jack Snyder, a RAND analyst, was among the first to use the term "strategic culture." He defined it as the "sum total of ideals, conditional emotional responses, and patterns of habitual behavior that members of the national strategic community have acquired through instruction or imitation and share with each other with regard to nuclear strategy."[13] Recent generations of scholars, including Iain Johnston, focus on Chinese strategic culture in terms of the country's strategic preferences and assumptions over time.[14]

The utility of strategic culture as an analytic concept is often challenged. Critics and strategic culture scholars alike have acknowledged that while strategic culture may have an observable effect on state behavior, it may not be unique to a particular state. In addition, strategic culture implies a fixed set of typical beliefs and assumptions shared by members of the state's military and political elite, but does not explain where those beliefs originate, whether they are tied to broader cultural patterns, how they are transmitted from generation to generation, and how or why a state's behavior changes over time.[15] While these criticisms are likely warranted, strategic culture may be able to succeed in analyzing strategic choice, where an ahistorical, neorealist framework or structural framework may not. Johnston argues that strategic culture might explain differences in strategic behavior across different cultures when structural conditions are constant. Thus, "the possibility of different predictions about state behavior underscores the value of exploring the concept of strategic culture, while approaching its analytic value with caution."[16]

Has Chinese strategic culture influenced PRC strategic choice in relation to nuclear policy? Scholars of strategic culture argue that China's deep historical experience shapes its strategic preferences and assumptions, which, in turn, influence how China translates strategy into action. In this case, strategic culture would influence how China devises nuclear strategy, and by extension, how the CCP elite translates that strategy into force posture.

Scholars of strategic culture look to variables such as ancient military thought and warfighting behavior to highlight key trends and characteristics in Chinese strategic behavior, that is, the threat or use of force for political purposes.[17] For example, Andrew Scobell argues that China's strategic culture is dualistic, comprised of two schools of thought: a conflict-averse and defensive-minded school and a realpolitik school, which favors military solutions and is offense oriented. This dualistic strategic culture "disposes Chinese leaders to pursue offensive military operations as a primary alternative in pursuit of national goals, while rationalizing these actions as being purely defensive and last resort."[18] Scobell's depiction of Chinese strategic culture adds interesting contours to an evaluation of China's nuclear evolution. Evidence of both schools of thought can be found in PRC nuclear policy. For example, the defense-mindedness is found in China's no-first-use (NFU) pledge, which states that China will not be the first to use nuclear weapons at any time or under any circumstances. Conversely, China's "active defense" doctrine, which applies to both conventional and strategic forces, can arguably be construed as having a strategically offensive orientation.[19]

It is difficult to select a proper focal point on the wide spectrum of Chinese history in order to identify some strategic preferences and assumptions that may have shaped how the PRC leadership viewed its nuclear capability. However, examining the period from 1946[20] to the present, a few of these preferences become apparent:

- A historically rooted preference to place primacy on the human element in strategy. In relation to the nuclear program, this is most clearly seen in Mao's "man over machine" maxim and the "People's War" doctrine.
- A realpolitik assumption that the possession of a minimal nuclear capability would have significant political and security dividends. To China, joining the nuclear club promised increased international prestige, both in terms of a voice in the communist bloc and as a leader for the non-aligned movement. In addition, the atomic bomb ensured that China could counter US "nuclear blackmail."
- A long-standing preference for strategic defense as the rationale for military actions in pursuit of national interest. This preference is evident in China's NFU policy.
- A preference for strategic ambiguity and deception, which is found in many of the military classics. The Chinese elite have adhered to this preference by refusing to spell out in detail the ultimate objectives of their nuclear program with respect to force mix, targeting doctrine, or optimum force balances between China and the major nuclear powers.[21]
- An assumption that numerical parity with other nuclear powers is not the criteria that determines the credibility of China's deterrent. Rather, the elite have traditionally believed that minimalism would meet the requirements of nuclear sufficiency.[22] In terms of investment, minimalism recommends expenditures on strategic capability remain subordinate to economic growth.

These preferences provide insight into China's nuclear future because while technology, capabilities, and levels of threats will change quickly, strategic culture may impose a historical inertia on Chinese decision-makers that could make them less responsive to specific contingencies.[23]

Primacy of the human element. Mao Zedong originally formulated China's revolutionary struggle in terms of "People's War," stressing the importance of "man over machine." In 1946, he again downplayed the importance of technology and derided the atom bomb as a "paper tiger." Mao's rhetoric is reflective of the historical situation. For example, during the initial nuclear development phase, the social fabric of China was destroyed by class warfare, and Mao searched for a unifying force that would turn the eyes of the Chinese people away from the precarious internal situation. Thus, Mao dubbed US imperialism the enemy and emphasized the significant role that China's human element would play in this struggle.

China's vast population did in fact play a significant role in China's nuclear strategy. A nuclear attack on China's cities would inflict less comparative damage in terms of population percentages than a similar attack on US cities. Assuming that China had a credible, effective second-strike capability, the requirement of attrition, that is, high human cost, found in the People's War doctrine could be achieved. China's human element thus bolstered the country's nascent deterrent, in that a counterattack by Beijing would inflict unacceptable costs on the initiating country. Therefore, China could afford to invest in a minimal nuclear capability and still achieve a credible deterrent threat. George W. Rathjens, an Arms Control and Disarmament Agency official during President Johnson's administration, noted this reality with respect to China's nuclear program, arguing "that a *relatively* small investment in offensive capability can make possible destruction of very great resources." He further observed, "the United States would be far more devastated than China by the destruction of two or three of its largest cities."[24]

The Chinese leadership's derisive attitude toward nuclear weapons and emphasis on the human element may also have been an effort to counteract the effects of fear among its population. For example, Mao acknowledged "the 'unprecedented destructiveness,' not the military decisiveness, of the weapons, but . . . adamantly denied that nuclear threats would cow them."[25] Similarly, the importance of the masses in Chinese nuclear strategy is evident in the leadership's decision to invest heavily in a civilian defense program as opposed to a significant build-up of strategic offensive forces.

In application, the strategic preference for man over machine seems to have delayed any serious thinking about operational aspects of nuclear weapons. As noted, in the People's War doctrine, nuclear weapons did not feature prominently. Mao's few issued statements on the bomb came to be regarded as a complete set of guidelines for the nuclear weapons program. "His maxims and brief instructions provided grist for the mill of all planners and training commands, which dutifully issued their own statements, both secret and open."[26] Mao continued to downplay the role of nuclear weapons and it was not until he was assured of China's technological success in developing modern nuclear bombs and missiles that he recast the revolutionary struggle of People's War into one with a military-technical emphasis that relied on assured nuclear retaliation to ensure deterrence.[27] The primacy of the human element in nuclear strategy and doctrine was a very potent force in the initial stages of the program, but has been muted more recently, due in part to the People's Liberation Army's (PLA) recognition that future wars will be fought under limited, high-tech conditions.[28]

Political and security pay-offs. Mao's China viewed the atom bomb as a symbol of national sovereignty and by extension, as a testament of socialist resolve in the face of US imperialism. Mao was determined to "destroy the nuclear monopoly" of China's adversaries. China's intimate acquaintance with nuclear coercion—in Korea, the Taiwan Straits, and along the Sino-Soviet border—directly impacted Mao's belief that "nuclear weapons in possession of a socialist country are always a means of defense against nuclear blackmail and nuclear war."[29]

Early in PRC history, the Chinese leadership recognized the political utility of nuclear weapons in addition to their security value. Beijing determined that an independent nuclear arsenal would further China's policies and enhance its international standing. Although Mao's formal authorization of the nuclear program likely did not occur until approximately January 1955, some evidence of earlier thinking about a nuclear China can be found.[30] For example, the CCP is said to have been pondering a nuclear weapons capability as early as 1946 when Kang Sheng, head of Communist China's secret service, began systematic recruitment of overseas Chinese nuclear and rocket scientists.[31] In addition to recruiting the technical personnel necessary to initiate a nuclear program, in 1950–1951 the newly founded PRC joined forces with the Soviet Union, and began large-scale uranium mining near Urumuqi in Xinjiang.[32]

China likely sought a nuclear capability in order to increase prestige in the international community and prove its self-reliance. Mao himself characterized the significance of the atom bomb in 1958, when he told his senior colleagues that without atomic and hydrogen bombs, "others don't think what we say carries weight."[33] In addition, it has been argued that China linked the atom bomb to its support for wars of national liberation, especially in Vietnam.[34] Similarly, nuclear capability may have been viewed as a means to enhance China's voice in the communist bloc, particularly with respect to the disposition of the bloc's military power. China's ability to overcome technical hurdles independently and detonate a nuclear bomb raised its prestige. Immediately after its first atomic detonation, China launched a "Nuclear Peace Offensive," which included the NFU pronouncement, a proposal for a global ban on nuclear first use, and recommendations for a multilateral conference to discuss the complete abolition and destruction of nuclear weapons. These efforts served to place China in a positive and prominent position within the international communist movement.[35]

In application, Beijing's realpolitik assumption that nuclear weapons provide political and security benefits has shaped the contours of PRC national security strategy. China's nuclear shadow and rapidly growing economy have moved the country toward its goal of regional preeminence. Likewise, China's strategic capability seemingly has helped to prevent a Taiwanese declaration of independence and could deter US intervention in such a situation.

Strategic defense. Central to China's nuclear culture is the preference for strategic defense. This long-standing tradition dates back to classic military literature. One example is the ancient Chinese thinker Mo Tzu, who devised the concept of "non-offense" (*fei gong*), which advocated responsive rather than provocative actions. This defensive tradition is also manifest in the Great Wall of China.[36]

The preference for strategic defense has penetrated many of China's statements about its nuclear policy. Beijing emphasizes the "defensive" nature of its nuclear policy, citing the NFU principle, which states "China undertakes not to be the first to use nuclear weapons at any time or under any circumstances." Also, China maintains negative security assurances (NSAs), which promise no use or threatened use of nuclear weapons against non-nuclear weapons states or nuclear-free zones at any time or under any circumstances. China has also expressed its disapproval of other countries' "nuclear umbrellas" or the policy of extended deterrence, and to that end has never deployed nuclear weapons on the territory of another country. Finally, China is a signatory to several nuclear weapons free zone (NWFZ) treaties and their protocols.[37]

China's nuclear strategy emphasizes the "retaliatory" nature of the deterrent in order to "defend China against the threat of strategic nuclear attack." This defensive stance remains a constant in Chinese nuclear strategy and was reinforced most recently in the 2002 Defense White Paper.[38] In this document, active defense is defined as a combination of strategic defense with operational and tactical offensive operations during time of war. China maintains that the scale, composition, and development of its nuclear weapons are in line with this doctrine, noting that its strategic missile forces "enormously strengthen our army's real power and nuclear deterrence capability, and are playing an increasingly important role in carrying out our country's active defense strategy."[39]

Thus the ambiguity present in the conventional doctrine extends to nuclear doctrine as well. The conditions under which China would launch a first strike are obscure. Would a nuclear strike aimed at Taiwan violate the NFU pledge, given that China considers Taiwan to be a domestic issue? Similarly, some scholars wonder whether changes in China's strategic capability will begin to change the operational meaning of the NFU principle. They have argued:

> [The] NFU pledge is probably less an altruistic principle, and more a simple reflection of the traditional operational constraints imposed on Chinese doctrine by the country's qualitatively and quantitatively limited nuclear arsenal: China maintains an NFU pledge because it fits with the realities of [China's] nuclear weapons inventory. As its force structure changes, so too might its NFU principle.[40]

Strategic ambiguity and deception. China's nuclear strategy rests on uncertainty and ambiguity as organizing principles. These fundamental components of the Chinese nuclear strategy are largely consistent with the centrality of deception to the Chinese strategic tradition. For example, the Sun Tzu maxim states, "All warfare is based on deception. Hence when able to attack, we must seem unable; when using our forces, we must seem inactive; when we are near, we must make the enemy believe we are far away; when far away, we must make him believe that we are near."[41]

In order to minimize the vulnerability to a preemptive attack on China's nuclear forces, particularly during a time of crisis, Beijing has dispersed its systems and provided minimal information about the specifics of its deployments. In the mid-1980s, improvements in its nuclear forces permitted China to claim greater confidence in its capability to credibly withstand a first strike. However, to this day, the Chinese remain unwilling to spell out in detail the ultimate objectives of their program with respect to force mix, targeting doctrine, or optimum force balances between China and the major nuclear powers.[42] Furthermore, China places significant emphasis on concealing the precise locations and actual numbers of deployed weapons in order to enhance the survivability of its limited retaliatory force.

Minimalism. The strategic choices of the CCP elite with respect to nuclear weapons were shaped by the assumption that numerical parity was not necessary to achieve a credible deterrent.[43] This assumption caused leaders to reason that the ability to hold other nations' cities at risk was enough to ensure "mutual vulnerability" between nuclear powers.

Brad Roberts, a contributor to this volume, has argued, "There is very little sentiment in China for competing in quantitative terms with other nuclear powers. Nuclear minimalism is deeply ingrained and for decades has been seen as meeting the requirements of nuclear sufficiency."[44] Based upon the constraints of the Chinese system, a "sufficient force" would be one that could inflict heavy damage on any prospective enemy's principal population centers, and therefore dissuade any enemy from attacking first. Thus, it was determined that in order to deter the United States, China's ICBMs would have to reach New York and Washington; against the Russians, they would have to hit Moscow.[45]

The aforementioned requirements suggest that China would adhere to a "minimum deterrence" doctrine, which rests on the assumption that a small number of warheads, launched in a counter-value second strike, are sufficient to inflict unacceptable damage on an adversary. Minimum deterrence requires the ability to deliver against an opponent from a handful to several tens of nuclear weapons, a requirement that China's current force posture currently meets.

The Chinese assumption that the Soviet Union collapsed under the weight of an unnecessary arms race likely motivates the PRC adoption of minimalism as a strategic guideline. As a result of this assumption, Chinese leaders have pledged to undertake investment in strategic capabilities judiciously and economically, so as not to undermine longer-term modernization efforts. Thus, China devised a national development strategy that features a long-term commitment to national modernization with an insistence that strategic capability be subordinated to long-term economic growth.[46]

On the surface, the two aforementioned assumptions—that minimalism meets the requirements of nuclear sufficiency and that investment in strategic capabilities should be undertaken moderately—appear to match China's nuclear posture and its national development strategy. Upon further scrutiny, however, objective realities may not be as closely aligned with a preference for minimalism as first appears.

To begin, the terminology surrounding discussions of nuclear doctrine is constructed by the West and might not reflect accurately China's doctrinal development. For example, Iain Johnston describes the ambiguity of the fundamental term "deterrence":

> The Chinese term for deterrence—*wei she*—is ambiguous. It literally means to use awesomeness, or latent power, to terrorize. Often the concept is described by a four character idiom—*yin er bu fa*—meaning to "draw the bow but not shoot." This leaves two somewhat contradictory impressions. One is of massive, undifferentiated, virtually automatic retaliation—an image closer to assured destruction visions of deterrence. The other is the threat of accurately targeted, precise, almost surgical violence—an image closer to warfighting notions of deterrence.[47]

A potential gap in terminology between Western and Chinese concepts of deterrence suggests that perhaps the Western-labeled "minimum deterrence" doctrine does not accurately reflect Chinese realities.

China's comfort level with a posture of minimalism is also questionable. Johnston argues that "a state that accepts minimum deterrence readily accepts qualitative and quantitative inferiority."[48] This inferiority, and the capabilities parallel with it, leaves China inherently vulnerable to a disarming first strike. Furthermore, a minimum deterrence doctrine and comparable force posture preclude China from achieving intrawar deterrence, namely restraining escalatory, potentially nuclear, responses to Chinese military action.[49] Beijing's concerns about US missile defense, in addition to uncertainty regarding US intentions in the region, particularly with respect to Taiwan, suggest that the credibility of China's deterrent may be threatened if it continues to adhere to a minimum deterrence posture. The need to maintain a credible nuclear retaliatory capability in the face of national missile defense would likely push China to speed up its ballistic missile modernization programs, increase deployments of current missiles, or some combination of the two. Should China choose to respond in this way to US missile defense or other challenges, the relative influence of minimalism on strategic choice will likely wane. However, it should be noted that China's deterrent could remain minimal depending on the scope of the modernization efforts. (For more details on developments in Chinese nuclear doctrine and the concept of "minimum deterrence," see Chapter 3 by Evan Medeiros in this volume.)

The national development strategy's claim to subordinate strategic capability to economic growth also raises questions when examined in depth. US scholars are particularly interested in how this claim matches up to actual defense expenditure figures. In March 2002, the Chinese finance minister announced that China was increasing military spending in 2002 by 17.5 percent, or $3 billion, which brings the publicly reported total to $20 billion. The publicly disclosed figures do not include spending for weapons research and for the purchase of foreign weapons.

Actual military spending could total as much as $65 billion, with likely double-digit defense budget growth through 2005, making China the second largest defense spender in the world after the United States, and the largest defense spender in Asia.[50]

It is unclear exactly how much of the increased military spending is directed toward the nuclear program. The Second Artillery Corps, the organization that maintains control over China's conventional and nuclear missile forces, makes up only about 4 percent of the PLA, yet it receives 12 to 15 percent of the defense budget and about 20 percent of the total procurement budget. When the PLA cut one million personnel in the 1980s, the ranks of the Second Artillery Corps actually increased.[51] Figures on the defense budget for the Second Artillery are scarce and those that exist are ambiguous. However, China's increases in overall defense spending call into question the relative weight of minimalism as an influence on the strategic choices of the CCP elite.

Strategic Drivers as China Moves Forward

As the PRC moves forward, the attainment and protection of CNP likely will remain the most important strategic consideration influencing its nuclear future. In order to ensure the success of its grand strategy, China will strive for internal and external stability, continued and successful economic reform, and regional preeminence. China's strategic capability is most significant in relation to China's interest in external stability. To China, a credible nuclear deterrent provides Beijing both political and security benefits, in terms of stability in the region and flexibility in planning.

As China considers its nuclear future, the strategic choices of the CCP elite will likely be influenced to some extent by strategic culture. Historically rooted strategic preferences and assumptions will shape how they think about nuclear policy. Over time, it seems that the Chinese emphasis on the human element in strategy has waned in influence, particularly as the PLA prepares to fight high-tech wars under modern conditions. The long-standing Chinese disposition toward strategic defense, ambiguity, and deception will likely remain fundamental factors shaping nuclear policy. These preferences also serve a timely and important function: China's strategically ambiguous and defensive nuclear strategy cloaks any gap between China's nuclear aspirations and its operational capability. For this reason, it is likely that China's nuclear future will feature some combination of these strategic culture elements. The relative importance of minimalism on strategic choice remains to be seen. Presently, it seems that China may be less comfortable with its minimalist inclinations given the changing strategic environment. However, deeply rooted sentiment regarding the collapse of the Soviet Union due to its arms race with the United States, for example, will probably temper the rate at which China moves away from minimalism.

Strategic drivers will undeniably influence China's nuclear future. However, these factors alone cannot account for China's nuclear direction. Objective factors, which are less resistant to shifts in the strategic environment, must be considered as well and are examined next.

Objective Drivers in Chinese Nuclear Strategy

Currently, economic and technical considerations, which traditionally constrained China's nuclear development, are lessening.[52] China may be approaching a stage in its nuclear evolution where a rapid numeric arms increase is possible; however, political considerations lessen the likelihood that such an arms-race type build-up will occur. The strategic factors influencing China's nuclear modernization have already been discussed. Consider, now, the more objective realities of Chinese strategic modernization: technology, economics, and domestic politics.

Technology and Economics

As a developing state, China lacked both the resources and, initially, the scientific and industrial base, necessary to begin full-scale nuclear weapons production. The development of China's nuclear weapons program was, and arguably still is, bound by economics. During the formative years of the nuclear program, resources were diverted to the atomic bomb, despite the economic chaos that was sweeping the country. The Chinese estimated that

> the expenditures on their nuclear weapons program approximately equaled the cost of building one large modern steel facility. . . . The total cost of the program, from uranium prospecting to a finished bomb, would have been about 12.86 billion yuan in 1981 prices or approximately 10.7 billion yuan in 1957 prices. According to one calculation, this would translate into about US $4.1 billion in 1957 prices.[53]

The cost of the nuclear weapons program was spread over a period of ten years, between 1955 and 1964.[54] The Chinese elite accepted the cost of this investment for a few reasons. First, in the aftermath of the Korean

War, nationalism was at a peak in China, and the linkage of the atom bomb to increased international prestige justified the expense. Second, for China, nuclear weapons were seen as a vehicle for establishing a scientific and industrial base.[55] In fact, the scientific and national importance of the nuclear weapons program insulated it from many of the domestic economic and cultural pressures that could have significantly delayed the program, particularly during the Cultural Revolution and Gang of Four period.[56]

Recent analyses of China's nuclear strategy identify "patterns of rational strategic choice made for China's nuclear posture, though technology limited the realm of the possible for Chinese leaders. Perhaps it could be said that the Chinese made a virtue out of necessity in the construction of their nuclear deterrent, accepting the technological constraints of the system and making rational choices under those constraints."[57] Overall, China seems to have recognized its economic and military limitations, as well as the relationship between the two. Accordingly, China opted to invest in qualitative rather than quantitative improvements in nuclear warheads and missiles, a choice that had direct consequences for China's nuclear strategy and targeting posture. Because its missiles were based on liquid-fuel technology, China's strategic nuclear forces had slow reaction times and were vulnerable to preemptive attack. This necessitated the adoption of various dispersal and concealment measures to enhance survivability.

Marshal Nie Rhongzhen,[58] head of China's overall strategic weapons program after 1958, devised a weapons development strategy consistent with China's technical and economic limitations. His program gave priority to technical research for qualitative improvements over quantitative augmentation.[59] Nie's directives were consistent with Mao's maxim: "Build a few [nuclear weapons], keep the number small, make the quality high."[60] China focused on high-yield nuclear weapons, opting to avoid the costly route of highly accurate delivery systems. The lack of accuracy, in turn, presumably limited China to a counter-value as opposed to a counter-force targeting policy.

In short, technical and economic considerations are salient determinants of China's nuclear strategy, which rests on the possibility that a few undetected Chinese ICBMs, launched in retaliation, are sufficient to deter an adversary from attempting a preemptive nuclear strike against China. As one Chinese academic has noted, it is the adversary's uncertainty regarding Chinese force estimates, rather than the total number of Chinese ICBMs, that is directly relevant to the credibility of the Chinese deterrent in its current form.[61] Foreign uncertainty about the precise size and location of its retaliatory force forms the foundation of China's nuclear strategy and has allowed China to achieve a "stable yet unbalanced" relationship with the other nuclear powers.

Domestic Politics: The Rise of the Fourth Generation

Domestic politics, a continuously shifting factor, shapes the translation of nuclear strategy into force posture as well. Colin S. Gray argues:

> The human dimension of strategy is so basic and obvious that it often escapes notice by scholars. . . . Strategy is "done" by tactics; tactics is "done" by combat forces *inter alia;* and the most important element in combat and support forces is people. To be more precise, the people in question come down to individuals.[62]

In China, the consensus of a few elite directly influences domestic politics and by extension, nuclear strategy. The highly centralized decision-making structure of the CCP often divulges nuclear policy through statements by key figures such as Mao Zedong, Deng Xiaoping, and Jiang Zemin, or through defense white papers. Statements regarding nuclear policy adhere closely to China's strategic guidelines and political ideology, and rarely suggest any significant departures in China's minimal, active defense nuclear strategy. However, each of the CCP's leaders has shaped and impacted the formulation of nuclear strategy in his own way.

Mao's contribution to nuclear strategy has already been discussed at length. In terms of doctrine, Mao's indelible imprint can be seen in the doctrines of People's War and active defense. Mao's individual contribution to nuclear strategy was reflective of his perception of the external threat environment, the internal social and economic turmoil, and China's actual strategic capability.

Deng Xiaoping also influenced the evolution of China's nuclear strategy. In 1985, Deng made a "strategic decision" that China no longer had to prepare to fight an "early, large-scale and nuclear war."[63] The new orientation became one of "peacetime construction." The operational guidelines for the "new" orientation, however, continued to emphasize the development of "key item (*zhong dian*) defense capabilities."[64] The guidelines reinforced nuclear weapons as a critical aspect of overall Chinese security.[65] Similarly, Deng modified PLA doctrine, strategy, and tactics, most notably by devising "People's War Under Modern Conditions," a doctrine that emphasized flexibility and mobile warfare. It is interesting to note that early articulations of this doctrine seem to have coincided with the Chinese development of a second-strike capability in the 1980s, when China first tested an ICBM.

More recently, Jiang Zemin appears to have adapted China's security objectives to the changing strategic environment. His "Five Musts" direct the following:

1. China "must own strategic nuclear weapons of a definite quality and quantity in order to ensure national security."
2. China "must guarantee the safety of strategic nuclear bases against the loss of combat effectiveness from attacks and destruction by hostile countries."
3. China "must ensure that our strategic nuclear weapons are at a high degree of war preparedness."
4. "When an aggressor launches a nuclear attack against us, [China] must be able to launch nuclear counterattack and nuclear re-attack against the aggressor."
5. China "must pay attention to the global situation of strategic balance and stability, and, when there are changes in the situation, adjust . . . strategic nuclear weapon development strategy in a timely manner."[66]

Jiang's statement evidences pragmatic thinking regarding the role of nuclear weapons in maintaining global balance and stability. Although his intention to modernize China's strategic force was obvious, Jiang's statements about nuclear strategy remained ambiguous in terms of their operational meaning.

Since their installation at the 16th Party Congress in November 2002 and the 10th National People's Congress (NPC) in March 2003, the Fourth Generation leadership, led by Party Secretary Hu Jintao and Premier Wen Jiabao, has not indicated that any departures in China's nuclear strategy are on the horizon. Although it may be too soon to tell what the Fourth Generation has in mind regarding nuclear strategy, an examination of Hu Jintao's strategic priorities and the domestic political situation suggest that Hu, like Jiang Zemin, will continue to underscore the importance of limited strategic modernization.

In *China's Leadership in the 21st Century: Rise of the Fourth Generation,* Murray Scot Tanner takes a first cut at Hu's policy views based upon close review of his speeches and writings over the past several years. Tanner claims that Hu views stability as being of overriding importance. Hu is said to have stated that "without a stable environment we [the PRC] can accomplish nothing, and may even lose what we have gained. This is a major principle for running the country, which overrules many minor principles."[67] The emphasis on stability suggests that Beijing's national security strategy will remain focused foremost on internal security, with an eye to emerging threats in the region or significant shifts in the global configuration of power.

Political prudence suggests that Hu take a moderate approach in expanding the size and capabilities of China's strategic forces so as not to provide ammunition to the "China threat" elements in Washington. However, the PRC will continue to modernize its strategic capabilities to achieve a "small but modern"[68] nuclear warfighting force. The quality and, potentially, the quantity of Chinese nuclear forces will improve with or without the deployment of US missile defenses. The criteria for a small but modern force likely includes increased warheads that can target the United States as well as warheads equipped with multiple independently targetable reentry vehicles (MIRVs). In addition, the force would require improved operational capabilities for contingencies in East Asia. Specifically, Beijing will bolster its medium- and short-range strategic forces so as to ensure credible, exploitable options should cross-straits tensions escalate. Moreover, China will proceed with the development and replacement of ICBMs, intermediate- and medium-range ballistic missiles (IRBMs/MRBMs) in addition to submarine-launched ballistic missiles (SLBMs). Finally, improvements in intelligence, surveillance, and reconnaissance (ISR) will remain a critical part of China's strategic modernization.[69] (See also Phillip Saunders and Jing-dong Yuan in this volume for details on China's strategic missile development.)

Finally, political ideology continues to play a significant role in justifying Communist Party decisions. However, since the events in Tiananmen Square in 1989, the CCP seems to have lost its ideological footing, and has since embraced nationalist and unifying rhetoric in order to drive modernization efforts and push market reform.[70] The most obvious manifestations of the emergence of nationalism were the two-day rioting following the NATO bombing of the Chinese embassy in Belgrade in May 1999 and the Chinese reaction to the April 2001 EP-3 incident. Resurgent nationalism is worth noting in regard to nuclear strategy because of its potential to inflame a conflict over Taiwan or demand a tough CCP response to a perturbation in the Sino-US strategic relationship. The CCP under Hu will face pressure to assert Chinese strength in either of these cases, which could warrant a show of force, potentially involving nuclear weapons.

Conclusion

As China looks to the future, the attainment of comprehensive national power likely will remain the overarching goal for the country. In order to ensure the success of its grand strategy, China will strive for internal and external stability, continued and successful economic reform, and regional preeminence. China's nuclear future is most closely linked with how Beijing perceives the strategic threat environment. In order to hedge against any threat to the PRC, it is necessary that that country ensure the credibility of its nuclear deterrent.

China's prospective nuclear policy will be driven by a number of factors. Foremost among these are the strategic influences mentioned above. In addition, China's strategic culture will likely shape the strategic choices of the CCP elite with respect to nuclear weapons. In particular, the long-standing Chinese disposition toward strategic defense, ambiguity, and deception will likely remain fundamental tenets in any alternative nuclear future that arises.

Objective factors, such as economics, technological ability, and domestic politics, will also drive forward China's nuclear policies. On the one hand, the economic and technical constraints that traditionally limited the development of China's nuclear program appear to be lessening. Alternatively, political considerations, particularly China's desire for internal stability and a beneficial international configuration of power in order to pursue economic modernization, suggest that a rapid and significant departure from the status quo is unlikely. This is especially so because such a departure would alarm both the United States and China's neighbors, potentially provoking disproportionate responses such as increased US-allied collaboration on missile defenses.

Hu Jintao will likely maintain a Chinese nuclear strategy with a defensive orientation, while simultaneously continuing a measured course of strategic modernization. A measured, indirect approach to strategic modernization preserves China's flexibility and enhances its long-term development objectives.

However, several uncertainties exist regarding the Fourth Generation's nuclear strategy. The foremost among these is how a crisis involving Taiwan and the United States would influence the CCP's thinking on the utility of nuclear weapons. Regardless of whether the Fourth Generation leadership were to prefer a more diplomatic means of resolving a Taiwan crisis, "the Chinese people are not likely to tolerate any ruling regime they perceive as soft on Western aggression and failing to project a strong China."[71] Thus, Hu may feel pressure from the forces of nationalism to project PRC strength should the Sino-US relationship turn sour. Similarly, continued US deployment of national missile defense or potential US-Japanese collaboration on defenses could provoke a security dilemma within East Asia, in which mistrust between two or more potential adversaries leads each side to take precautionary and defensively motivated measures that can be perceived as offensive threats.[72] Should any of these scenarios occur, we may see a break in the continuity of China's defensive, minimalist nuclear strategy, which would include a more accelerated trajectory of force modernization. (See Chapter 7 by Brad Roberts for a discussion of alternative futures for China's nuclear posture, two of which include substantially accelerated force modernization.)

China's strategic interests interface with more objective realities to produce China's nuclear policies. Understanding these influences is critical to an assessment of the past, present, and future role of PRC nuclear weapons in the global environment. Consideration of these drivers makes possible a more comprehensive evaluation of potential PRC nuclear trajectories and, ultimately, contributes to a better understanding of China's nuclear future.

Notes

1. The Hong-6 (H-6), a long-range bomber, was deployed in 1965. Range estimates for the H-6 vary, but it was within range of US forces in the Pacific, as well as Russian urban areas east of the Urals. The Qiang-5 (Q-5), deployed in 1970, is a Chinese redesign of the Soviet MiG-19. Nearly 1,000 aircraft were built, with 550–600 of the improved Q-5A variant. An unknown number of the Q-5As were modified to carry nuclear weapons. The assumption is that this number is small, with perhaps a regiment of thirty aircraft assigned to the nuclear role. A Q-5 used a loft bombing technique in a Chinese nuclear test in 1972. Though aging, the Q-5 retains good low-level attack capability and speed, assets the H-6 bomber lacks. For more discussion, see the Center for Defense Information's "Nuclear Weapons Database: Chinese Nuclear Delivery Systems" at www.cdi.org/issues/nukef&f/database/chnukes.html#h6.

2. "Chinese Nuclear Forces, 2003," *Bulletin of the Atomic Scientists,* vol. 59, no. 6: 77–80.

3. US Department of Defense, *Annual Report on the Military Power of the People's Republic of China 2003,* July 28, 2003, 31, available at www.defenselink.mil/pubs/20030730chinaex.pdf.

4. With these goals in mind, certain limitations to understanding China's nuclear strategy should be noted. To begin, the central role of opacity in Chinese nuclear strategy, particularly about such issues as command and control, operational doctrine, and targeting, has resulted in a dearth of open sources on these issues. As a result, a great deal of uncertainty exists regarding Chinese nuclear issues, which is exacerbated by differences in terminology and cultural interpretations. However, an examination of Beijing's articulated policies, supplemented by commentaries on

Chinese language materials by Chinese experts and US scholars, yields insight into China's nuclear strategy.

5. Khadong Oh Hassig, "Northeast Asian Strategic Security Environment," Defense Threat Reduction Agency Study, August 22, 2001, available at www.dtra.mi/about/organization/asian.pdf.

6. US Department of Defense, *The Military Power of the PRC, 2003,* 10.

7. Michael Pillsbury, *China Debates the Future Security Environment* (Washington, DC: National Defense University Press, 2000), 211–215.

8. Michael Swaine and Ashley Tellis, *Interpreting China's Grand Strategy: Past, Present, and Future* (Santa Monica, CA: RAND, 2000), 112. Emphasis in the original.

9. "China's National Defense in 2000," Beijing, Information Office of the State Council, People's Republic of China, October 2000, www.china.org.cn/e-white/2000.

10. See, for example, Cheng Feng and Larry Wortzel, "PLA Operational Principles and Limited War: The Sino-Indian War of 1962," in *Chinese Warfighting: The PLA Experience Since 1949,* Mark A. Ryan, David M. Finkelstein, and Michael A. McDevitt, eds. (Armonk, NY: M.E. Sharpe, 2003), 188.

11. Andrew Scobell, *China and Strategic Culture* (Carlisle, PA: Strategic Studies Institute, 2002), 18.

12. "Chen Supports Legal Settlement of Election Disputes," *Hong Kong FPA,* in Foreign Broadcast Information Service (FBIS), April 24, 2004.

13. Jack Snyder, *The Soviet Strategic Culture* (Santa Monica, CA: RAND, 1977), 9.

14. Alastair Iain Johnston noted that certain strategic preferences may not be affected by changes in non-cultural variables such as threat, technology, or organization and thus the possibility of a disjuncture between strategic culture, operational realities, and behavior exists. See Johnston, *Cultural Realism: Strategic Culture and Grand Strategy in Chinese History* (Princeton, NJ: Princeton University Press, 1998), for more discussion.

15. Carolyn Ziemke, *Strategic Personality and the Effectiveness of Nuclear Deterrence,* IDA Document D-2537 (Alexandria, VA: Institute for Defense Analyses, November 2000).

16. Alastair Iain Johnston, "Thinking about Strategic Culture," *International Security,* vol. 19, no. 4 (Spring 1995): 34–35.

17. Ziemke's strategic personality typology traces broad historical and cultural patterns that evolve over the whole course of a nation-state's history. According to Zeimke, strategic personality would evaluate "whether there is something about China's historical experience that predisposes it to defensiveness and deception (and thus accounts for Mao Zedong and Sun Tzu). In addition, it would inquire into the meaning of China's traditional emphasis on deception in terms of its long-term strategic conduct." Ziemke, 6.

18. Scobell, v.

19. According to the government-issued white paper "China's National Defense in 2000," the strategy of active defense means that China pursues a principle featuring defensive operations, self-defense, and gaining mastery by striking only after the enemy has struck. Such defense combines efforts to deter war with preparations to win self-defense wars in time of peace, and strategic defense with operational and tactical offensive operations in time of war.

20. 1946 was chosen as the starting point since it is said that the CCP was pondering a nuclear weapons capability as early as this date. During this year, Kang

Sheng, head of Communist China's secret service, purportedly began systematic recruitment of overseas Chinese nuclear and rocket scientists. See John Wilson Lewis and Xue Litai, *China Builds the Bomb* (Stanford, CA: Stanford University Press, 1988), 35.

21. Jonathan Pollack, "The Future of China's Nuclear Weapons Policy," in *Strategic Views from the Second Tier,* John C. Hopkins and Wiexing Hu, eds. (New Brunswick, NJ: Transaction Publishers, 1995), 164.

22. Brad Roberts, *Tripolar Stability: Relations Among the United States, Russia, and China,* IDA Paper P37-27 (Alexandria, VA: Institute for Defense Analyses, September 2002), 24, available at www.ida.org/IDAnew/Tasks/TripolarStability.pdf.

23. Johnston, "Thinking About Strategic Culture," 34.

24. William Burr and Jeffrey T. Richelson, "A Chinese Puzzle," *Bulletin of the Atomic Scientists,* vol. 53, no. 4 (July/August 1997): 46, available at www.thebulletin.org/issues/1997/ja97ja97richelson.html. Emphasis in original.

25. Mark A. Ryan, "Early Chinese Attitudes Toward Civil Defense Against Nuclear Attack," *Australian Journal of Chinese Affairs,* no. 21 (January 1989): 81–109.

26. Xue Litai, "Evolution of China's Nuclear Strategy," in *Strategic Views from the Second Tier,* John C. Hopkins and Weixing Hu, eds. (New Brunswick, NJ: Transaction Publishers, 1995), 171.

27. Lewis and Xue, 222.

28. It should be noted, however, that while China downsizes its conventional forces, it is investing significantly in recruitment, education, and training of its remaining forces. The PLA's efforts to make its organization more professional stress improvements in the human element in order to ensure that its operators will be able to fight in high-tech conditions. For an interesting discussion of this trend within the PLA Navy, see Bernard Cole, *The Great Wall at Sea: China's Navy Enters the 21st Century* (Annapolis, MD: Naval Institute Press, 2001), 113–137, 179–189.

29. Lewis and Xue, 36.

30. Lewis and Xue claim that by the time Congress had passed the Formosa Resolution on January 29, 1955, the Chinese Politburo had launched the nation's nuclear weapons program, 36–37.

31. Lewis and Xue, 45–46.

32. Ibid.

33. Ibid., 36.

34. Morton Halperin, "Chinese Nuclear Strategy: The Early Post-Detonation Period," *Asian Survey,* vol. 5, no. 6: 271–279.

35. Ibid.

36. Li Jijun, "Traditional Military Thinking and the Defensive Strategy of China," address at the US National War College, *Letort Paper,* no. 1, August 29, 1997.

37. *China's National Statement of Security Assurances* (Beijing: Information Office of the State Council, People's Republic of China, April 5, 1995).

38. "China's National Defense in 2002."

39. Liu and Meng, *Xiandai Jundui Zhihui,* 391, in Alastair Iain Johnston, "China's New 'Old Thinking': The Concept of Limited Deterrence," *International Security,* vol. 20, no. 3 (Winter 1995/96): 9.

40. Bates Gill, James Mulvenon, and Mark Stokes, "The Chinese Second Artillery Corps: Transition to Credible Deterrence," in *The People's Liberation Army as Organization,* James C. Mulvenon and Andrew Yang, eds. (Santa Monica, CA: RAND, 2002), 516.

41. Sun Tzu, *The Art of War,* trans. Lionel Giles, 1, available at http://classics.mit.edu/Tzu/artwar.html.

42. Pollack, 164.

43. Mao's maxim "Small but better" (*shao er jing)* shaped the Chinese strategy, which assumed that a limited but reliable force that could inflict heavy damage on an enemy's population centers would be sufficient to deter an adversary's first strike. See Xue Litai, 172, for more discussion.

44. Roberts, 24.

45. Xue Litai, 172.

46. Xia Liping, "China's Nuclear Policy and Nuclear Disarmament," unpublished research paper, Center for International Strategic Studies, Shanghai Institute for International Studies, Autumn 2002, 2.

47. Johnston, "China's New Old Thinking," 7.

48. Ibid., 18.

49. Ibid.

50. "The Military Power of the PRC, 2003," 41. The CIA *World Factbook* estimates defense expenditures at $55.91 billion for FY 02, which was approximately 4.3 percent of China's GDP. Japan's defense expenditures were $39.52 billion for FY 02, which was approximately 1 percent of its GDP.

51. You Ji, *The Armed Forces of China* (New York: I.B. Tauris Publications, 1999), 85, in the Nuclear Threat Initiative's China Database.

52. Many still contend that China is faced with constraints in its ability to modernize its military and strategic forces as a result of economic factors. See for example, Gill and O'Hanlon, "China's Hollow Military," *National Interest,* no. 56: 55–62.

53. Lewis and Xue, 107–108.

54. Ibid.

55. Xue Litai, 168.

56. Paul Dibb, "China's Strategic Situation and Defense Priorities in the 1980s," *The Australian Journal of Chinese Affairs,* no. 5 (January 1980): 97–115. Xue Litai also suggests that the strategic weapons program was largely successful because it was isolated from the domestic pressures of the Cultural Revolution.

57. Gill, Mulvenon, and Stokes, 511–512.

58. Nie Rhongzhen was vice chairman of the Central Military Commission (CMC) from 1959 on. He became the head of the overall strategic weapons program in 1958. He has often been called "the father" of China's nuclear weapons program. See Lewis and Xue, 247.

59. Lin Chong-Pin, *China's Nuclear Weapons Strategy: Tradition Within Evolution* (Lexington, MA: Lexington Books, 1988), 51.

60. Xue Litai, 171.

61. Li Bin, "The Effects of NMD on Chinese Strategy," *Jane's Intelligence Review,* vol. 13, no. 3 (March 2001), 49–52.

62. Colin Gray, *Modern Strategy* (Oxford: Oxford University Press, 1999), 26.

63. Johnston, "China's New Old Thinking," 9.

64. Lin Chong-Pin, 41.

65. Hongxun Hua asserts that Deng's "strategic transformation" calculated that world war would not occur for a long time and therefore the developmental program for nuclear weapons and strategic missiles was given lower priority than the development of conventional tactical missiles. He claims that in terms of nuclear strategy, China practiced a 'limited development' policy. See Hua Hongxun, "Viewpoint:

China's Strategic Missile Programs: Limited Aims, Not Limited Deterrence," *Nonproliferation Review* (Winter 1998): 63, available at http://cns.miis.edu/pubs/npr/vol05/52/hua52.pdf.

66. "Jiang Zemin Defines Position of China's Strategic Nuclear Weapons," *Tai Yang Bao* (Hong Kong), July 17, 2000, FBIS reference CPP20000717000021.

67. Murray Scot Tanner, "Hu Jintao's Succession," in *China's Leadership in the 21st Century: Rise of the Fourth Generation,* David Finkelstein and Maryanne Kivlehan, eds. (Armonk, NY: M.E. Sharpe, 2003), 58.

68. Paul Godwin discusses the likely composition of a "small but modern" force in "Potential Chinese Responses to US Ballistic Missile Defense," in *China and Missile Defense: Managing US-PRC Strategic Relations,* Alan Romberg and Michael McDevitt, eds. (Washington, DC: Henry L. Stimson Center, 2003).

69. For more in-depth analysis of strategic modernization, see "The Military Power of the People's Republic of China, 2003."

70. Virginia Monken, *China's New Leadership and A Taiwan Confrontation: Implications for Deterrence,* IDA Document D-2869 (Alexandria, VA: Institute for Defense Analyses, August 2003), 8.

71. Ibid., 45.

72. For a discussion of the potential security dilemma in East Asia, see Thomas J. Christensen, "China, the US-Japan Alliance, and the Security Dilemma in East Asia," *International Security,* vol. 23, no. 4 (Spring 1999): 49–80.

3

Evolving Nuclear Doctrine

Evan S. Medeiros

This chapter explores the current content and future direction of China's nuclear doctrine.[1] Chinese beliefs about the roles and missions of nuclear weapons have long been one of the least understood but most important dimensions of the evolving mosaic of China's entire nuclear posture.[2] Many Western analyses of things nuclear in China have been largely focused on incremental improvements in force structure capabilities—new warheads, new missiles, testing series, and related technical upgrades. These are important issues to document and debate, especially as China moves more rapidly toward deployment of mobile, long-range ballistic missiles and improves the sea-based leg of its nuclear force. Yet, there are real limits to an analytical focus on such issues. Monitoring the technical dimensions of China's nuclear modernization provides fragmentary and sometimes misleading cues to the overall goals and intentions of national nuclear weapon programs—in China or any other nation.

Analyzing nuclear doctrine can play an edifying role in understanding and interpreting such improvements in capabilities. Doctrine provides a context for understanding why China may develop, acquire, and utilize new nuclear and missile capabilities. In other words, analyzing doctrine creates an interpretive framework helpful in examining the relative salience and direction of the various aspects of China's nuclear modernization effort. Similarly, doctrine can serve as a tool for assessing the possible future directions of China's nuclear modernization program—an issue of substantial debate among international scholars, analysts, and policymakers in recent years.

The recent availability of new Chinese language source material bearing directly on nuclear doctrine further motivates the assessment of nuclear doctrine in this chapter. To date, some of the Western analysis about Chinese nuclear doctrine is necessarily speculative and relies more on generalizing from China's nuclear capabilities than analyzing Chinese writings about the roles and missions of nuclear weapons.[3] Current Western writings about Chinese nuclear doctrine are, for the most part, underdetermined and undertheorized, largely due to the lack of Chinese materials to date. This small body of literature would uniquely benefit from new sources of Chinese data, specifically addressing doctrinal issues. This chapter, in utilizing new Chinese publications, does not claim to single-handedly resolve current uncertainties about China's nuclear doctrine in one great leap, but rather seeks to move the proverbial ball a bit further down the analytical playing field.

New Chinese writings about nuclear doctrine provide rich details about who in China thinks about nuclear weapons and deterrence, how they approached this subject in the past, how they think about nuclear weapons now, how these evolving ideas may be influencing ongoing nuclear force modernization, and ultimately how they may affect China's future nuclear posture. A key finding to emerge from these new Chinese source materials is that there is growing intellectual activity about nuclear doctrinal issues within military academic research organizations (*junshi xueshu yanjiu jiguan*), as distinct from the nuclear scientific establishment which long dominated this sub-arena of research and policymaking. Military strategists and authors who write about China's overall military doctrine only began in the 1980s to systematically address nuclear doctrine questions. Recent Chinese studies of changes in military doctrine provide new and important insights about nuclear issues. The few articles on doctrine by Chinese nuclear scientists and nuclear arms controllers may increasingly be more the exception than the rule in terms of policy relevance and, when compared to military writings, they offer minimal details about the military's operationalization of doctrine, which is a critical variable in evaluating actual doctrine. Furthermore, although it has long been accepted that China's nuclear bomb builders (i.e., the nuclear scientific community) played the leading role in defining China's nuclear strategy,[4] it is no longer clear their influence still dominates. At a minimum, China's "users" of nuclear weapons appear to be carving out an increasingly important role in defining and operationalizing nuclear doctrine. This trend is also consistent with the accelerating professionalization of the People's Liberation Army (PLA) and its renovation of its entire operational doctrine in the late 1990s as the basis for boosting the PLA's warfighting capabilities.[5]

To shed further light on the dimly lit world of Chinese nuclear doctrine, this chapter has two goals. The first is to identify both the general ideas and the detailed concepts that inform and comprise China's current nuclear doctrine. The second goal is to specify the areas of possible future change in Chinese nuclear thinking and to highlight possible sources of these shifts. In addressing these twin issues, this chapter argues in favor of a flexible conceptualization of Chinese nuclear doctrine that is centered on Chinese-defined notions of "sufficiency and effectiveness." It argues that Western analysts should think of China's nuclear doctrine as a set of Chinese policies that are collectively sufficient and effective, in the Chinese leadership's eyes, to meet their changing nuclear security needs—irrespective of the terms that Chinese strategists use to characterize China's nuclear doctrine.

This argument raises the obvious query: why are the notions of sufficiency and effectiveness useful for analyzing China's current nuclear doctrine? Admittedly, these ideas could apply to every nuclear-armed nation. However, in the context of analyzing Chinese doctrine, this approach adds analytical value insofar as it contrasts with the dominant views of China's doctrine as either credible minimum deterrence or limited deterrence. These two conceptualizations too starkly frame the current debate and do not fully capture the complexity of China's evolving approach to the roles and missions of nuclear weapons. While both of these ideas capture elements of China's current thinking about nuclear weapons, focusing on only one or the other misses key aspects of China's current doctrine.

Furthermore, my use of these terms is meant to capture three aspects of China's current approach to doctrine and nuclear force modernization: (1) China's priority on building a more survivable nuclear force structure for the purpose of credible strategic deterrence and counter-coercion; (2) the variegated nature of the core concepts which this chapter identifies as comprising Chinese nuclear doctrine, combined with the fluid nature of China's current discourse about the relationship between nuclear weapons and its national security interests, which could eventually include using nuclear weapons in limited conflicts for discrete purposes; and (3) the growing external challenges to the credibility of China's current nuclear deterrent capability and its potential responses to these perceived threats. In light of these factors, this chapter maintains that Beijing will do essentially whatever it perceives as necessary to ensure that it possesses in perpetuity a credible capability to prevent nuclear attacks and coercion by other nuclear powers. Thus, in many ways China's doctrine continues to possess, at its core, key axioms of Western conceptions of "minimum deterrence," but in other respects China's responses to new security challenges *may* also countenance using nuclear weapons in ways that do not neatly coincide with minimum deterrence. It is in this sense that notions of "sufficiency and effectiveness" best capture the diverse elements of China's evolving nuclear doctrine.

The first section of this chapter outlines important and seldom addressed methodological challenges relevant to analyses of national nuclear doctrines. These are not meant to be insurmountable obstacles to accurately assessing the Chinese case, but rather they highlight the limitations of a full, final, and complete analysis of Chinese nuclear doctrine. Along these lines, this chapter's arguments are meant as firm—but not static—conclusions, which are subject to variation over time. A second section briefly examines the historical evolution of China's approach to nuclear weapons. This is not a superfluous history lesson. Examining history (especially in light of new source material about past events) similarly provides an additional tool to evaluate the accuracy of previous Western analyses. This section outlines an evolutionary pathway useful for interpreting how China's historical approach to nuclear deterrence influences its present nuclear doctrine. There is a high degree of path dependency in China's thinking about nuclear weapons and deterrence and, therefore, such historical context is important to evaluating current thinking. The third section of the chapter—its main component—outlines the core ideas that inform and comprise current doctrine and also discusses the variables affecting such thinking. The fourth and fifth sections, respectively, address the tensions in China's nuclear doctrine and the perceived challenges to the credibility of the current configuration of China's nuclear posture. A final section explores factors that may either constrain or enable changes in doctrine in the future.

Key Methodological Considerations

Researching, analyzing, and evaluating the nuclear doctrine of China, or any country, is fraught with methodological challenges. Two of these are addressed below. The first set relates to general analyses of nuclear doctrine, and the second set of challenges is specific to China.

First, there are often multiple indicators of the components of a national nuclear doctrine, and they are often inconsistent and contradictory. In many cases, there are at least three types of indicators: theoretical/academic writings about doctrine, official government statements about doctrine (i.e., declaratory policy), and operational planning and exercises by militaries. Further complicating this picture is the existence of both public and internal/classified writings and statements, which raises the possibility of not just three but potentially *five* variables. Thus analyzing these multiple indicators of doctrine provides a confusing and contradictory picture of the policies and procedures a country uses to determine when and how it plans to use nuclear weapons.[6] An example from the history of US nuclear thinking is instructive. When Secretary of Defense Robert McNamara outlined the doctrine of Mutual Assured Destruction (MAD) in the mid-1960s, the inconsistencies between that doctrine and both academic writings and operational planning were glaring, in retrospect.[7] Similar dichotomies between doctrine and war planning have been found in case studies of Soviet nuclear planning during the Cold War.[8] These examples highlight the difficulties in assessing a national nuclear doctrine and the limits inherent in such an analysis.

A second set of methodological challenges stems from the peculiarities of Chinese military thinking. For many decades after China exploded its first nuclear device, China never articulated a coherent nuclear doctrine in public, and new Chinese sources reveal that formal internal research about nuclear strategy did not begin until the mid-1980s. Thus, analysis of Chinese doctrine has always suffered from a dearth of information. China's 2000 White Paper on National Defense was one of the first times that China sought to articulate a doctrine, though the text was merely a collective restatement of past public proclamations about general views on nuclear weapons.[9]

Analyzing Chinese nuclear doctrine is further complicated by the fact that Chinese strategists do not think about doctrine in the same way as many of their foreign counterparts. There is no Chinese term for doctrine; it is not included in major military reference books. Doctrine is a term that is applied only to foreign concepts of warfare.[10] While there is no Chinese term for doctrine, Chinese military academics identify three levels of concepts that guide military operations: strategic-level concepts (*zhanlue*), campaign-level concepts (*zhanyi*), and tactical-level concepts (*zhanshu*). The ideas at all three levels collectively comprise what Western analysts refer to as military doctrine.[11] For the purposes of this chapter and for the ease of the reader, my use of the term "nuclear doctrine" will refer to all the Chinese concepts that collectively identify the roles and missions of nuclear weapons for China.

It is also critical to avoid analyzing Chinese nuclear thinking *solely* through the lens of the US-China nuclear dynamic. While this relationship is a key consideration for Chinese nuclear planners, it is by no means an exclusive one. Focusing on the US-China nuclear dynamic obscures the relevance of the China-Russia and China-India relationships, and produces a skewed understanding of Chinese doctrine and, importantly, its link to force structure modernization. A related methodological caution is to avoid the preoccupation with discerning whether Chinese doctrine is best characterized as a "minimum" or a "limited" deterrent force. Not only is this a false distinction (as Bates Gill, James Mulvenon and Mark Stokes have argued),[12] but a focus on this dichotomy obscures some of the most important contours of Chinese thinking about the conditions under which it would use nuclear weapons. With these two categories of methodological challenges in mind, the next section examines the importance of the historical evolution of Chinese views on nuclear weapons for interpreting current doctrine.

Historical Evolution of Chinese Views on Nuclear Weapons, Nuclear Deterrence, and Nuclear Doctrine

Chinese views on nuclear weapons and nuclear deterrence have long been a preoccupation of Western sinologists and military strategists. Studies by Alice Hsieh, John Lewis, Xue Litai, Chong-pin Lin, Alastair Iain Johnston, and Bates Gill, among others, have detailed the evolving contours of Chinese views of the relative importance of nuclear weapons to Beijing's national security goals. How one conceptualizes this evolution in China's approach to nuclear weapons is a critical element in arguing for a particular position on China's contemporary views on nuclear weapons and nuclear deterrence. In other words, one cannot fully appreciate where China is now and may be going without understanding where it has been.

The evolution of Chinese beliefs about nuclear weapons and nuclear deterrence highlights several considerations directly relevant to its current nuclear doctrine. First, there is a strong degree of path dependence in Chinese views about the relationship between nuclear weapons and national security. As will be addressed later in this chapter, this path dependence is relevant to both the content as well as organizational aspects of China's nuclear doctrine. Second, history highlights the strong (and persistent) Chinese legacies of minimalism, ambiguity, and secrecy in China's approach to its nuclear capabilities and nuclear deterrence. Third, analysis of the past indicates a dynamic interaction among technological capabilities, overall military doctrine, economic resources, and external threat perceptions, all of which collectively shape China's nuclear doctrine and capabilities. Fourth, analysis of newly available

Chinese source materials reveals that China devoted very few resources to researching nuclear doctrine issues formally and systematically. The organizational roots of China's nuclear doctrine are perhaps one of the least explored aspects of this issue. China's research on nuclear doctrine was very under-theorized and under-institutionalized during Mao's era. Detailed and systematic thinking about nuclear doctrine is a post-Mao intellectual enterprise for military and civilian strategists. After about twenty years of research on nuclear doctrine and strategy, this field is only now beginning to reach maturity in China. This historical context also importantly sheds light on current Western debates about how to characterize Chinese doctrine, especially the relevance of the limited deterrence argument.

This study posits four stages in the evolution of Chinese thinking about nuclear weapons and nuclear deterrence. Each period has distinct attributes and characteristics. The first one spans the period from the founding of the People's Republic of China in 1949 to the first successful test of a nuclear device in 1964. The second period from 1964 to 1978 ends with Deng Xiaoping's ascendance to power. A third stage is from 1978 to the end of the Cold War in the early 1990s. A final period stretches from the early 1990s to the present.

1949–1964: Contradictory Impulses

Chinese views about the geopolitical value and military utility of nuclear weapons went through perhaps their most dramatic transformation between 1949 and 1964. Chinese leaders, led by Mao, shifted from a dismissive and disparaging perception of the importance of nuclear weapons to a grudging acceptance of their relevance as both counter-coercion weapons and as symbols of great power status and national technological prowess. This transformation in Chinese views of nuclear weapons was heavily influenced by several factors such as the Communists' recent warfighting experiences in the Chinese Civil War and the Korean War, the dominance of People's War as China's military doctrine, US nuclear threats during the 1954 and 1958 Taiwan Straits crises, and the interplay at that time among Maoist ideology, the Sino-Soviet split, and China's animosity with the United States.

Following the birth of the PRC in 1949, Mao Zedong and other Chinese strategists were initially quite skeptical of the military relevance of nuclear weapons. They stressed—based on their recent experiences in China's Civil War and the Korean War—the importance of "men over machines" in warfare. In the first half of the 1950s, Chinese leaders consistently denigrated the role of technology in warfare and regularly stated that China (unlike the capitalist world) was so large and populous that it could survive a nuclear war and then carry on building worldwide socialism.

Underlying these initial beliefs was a gradual recognition by Mao and other senior military leaders in the 1950s that not only did nuclear weapons play a decisive role in global politics as status symbols, but China also needed to have nuclear weapons to avoid being at the mercy of those who possessed them. International events in the mid-1950s shaped this transformation in Chinese perceptions of the military and geopolitical value of nuclear weapons.[13] As numerous Chinese and Western scholars have already detailed, the US use of nuclear threats against China during the Korean War and during the 1954 and 1958 Taiwan crises demonstrated to Beijing the value of possessing nuclear weapons to prevent coercion.[14] This culminated in Mao's decision in winter 1954–1955 to devote extensive national resources to a very costly nuclear weapon development program.

1964–1978: An Implicit Doctrine Takes Shape

The year 1964 was a seminal one in the evolution of Chinese nuclear doctrine. China's first nuclear test that year catalyzed important changes in the way in which Chinese strategists thought and spoke about nuclear weapons and national security. The most intense ideological layers to China's anti-nuclear propaganda began to fall away. Chinese statements were more explicit about the national security rationales and politico-military value of nuclear weapons. Seldom did these statements describe nuclear weapons as "paper tigers"—even to the Chinese people. China had built a real tiger. Chinese leaders talked about nuclear weapons serving as the "ultimate guarantor" of Chinese national security and claimed that nuclear weapons would forever prevent China from being subject to nuclear threat and "blackmail" by other nuclear powers.[15] Chinese leaders also presented (internally and externally) their nuclear weapons capability as a symbol of major power status and technological progress. These themes persist today. Whereas the United States, UK, France, and Soviet Union relied on an expanding science and technology base to build their strategic weapons, China used its strategic weapons programs as an opportunity to build, organize, and finance a solid national foundation for science and technology research and development.[16]

Despite China's self-lauding of its first test, it lacked an operational nuclear capability. It took several years for China to deploy an effective nuclear strike capability by developing, improving, and expanding its delivery vehicle options. In this sense, China's nuclear capability for the first decade functioned more as a political weapon than a military one. One Chinese scholar refers to China's nuclear doctrine in this period as an "existential deterrent."[17]

Beijing's first nuclear test eventually led to the emergence of a general, implicit, and ambiguous set of beliefs about how to achieve nuclear deterrence, which can only loosely be called a doctrine. Beginning in 1964 and to this very day, China has never articulated publicly a formal nuclear doctrine.[18] In retrospect, China's thinking about nuclear weapons was informed by several general ideas that were mainly an outgrowth of Mao's broader military thought (*junshi sixiang*). This situation was in stark contrast to the highly systematized thinking at that time in the US and Soviet Union about nuclear weapons. The main features of China's implicit doctrine were: the construction of a minimal nuclear force structure to retaliate against enemy targets; maintaining secrecy and ambiguity about China's nuclear capabilities; and the heavy influence of available technology over implicit doctrinal ideas. One of the most interesting and curious features of this time period was the dearth of formal and systematic research within the military, especially the Second Artillery, about nuclear operations.

Mao and nuclear minimalism. One of the most prominent characteristics of China's approach to nuclear modernization in the 1964–1978 period was the emphasis on minimalism, manifest in a small-sized nuclear force structure. Mao and other Chinese strategists, who were all steeped in the long tradition of People's War concepts, stressed that China need only to build enough weapons to hold at risk a small number of enemy targets to obtain deterrence (or at least Chinese leaders believed this was so). For China's political and military leaders, China's nuclear weapons were "one element, but not the decisive element of the PLA's comprehensive deterrence posture."[19]

The salience of this emerging "nuclear minimalism" was evident in Chinese statements and actions. Mao made several statements contextualizing the relative value of nuclear weapons. In one well-known instance, Mao noted that China's nuclear modernization should be guided by the three principles of "*you yidian, shao yidian and hao yidian,*" which translates as "build a few weapons, keep the number small, make the quality high."[20] China also declared its nuclear weapons were for "defensive" use only, that it adhered to a no-first-use (NFU) policy, that it would never use nuclear weapons against non-nuclear weapon states (a negative security assurance), and that it supported total nuclear disarmament.[21] To some degree, China's adoption of an NFU policy and its emphasis on building a minimal nuclear force structure was making a virtue out of a necessity. China lacked the resources and technological capabilities to build a large and sophisticated force. In addition, there is little evidence Mao viewed the advent of the nuclear age as fundamentally changing the nature of warfare among great powers, which was a view prevalent in the Western and Soviet strategic circles at the time.

A lack of systematic thinking about nuclear doctrine. Throughout the 1970s, one of the most consequential—but least examined—aspects of this time period was the paucity of detailed and systematic thinking about nuclear doctrine within China's military—especially the Second Artillery (China's strategic rocket forces). Beginning in 1966 with the initiation of the Cultural Revolution and until its end in the mid-1970s, all of China's military academic institutions were closed. This intellectual hiatus, beginning two years after China entered the nuclear weapons club, left an indelible mark on China's development of a nuclear doctrine. A Chinese study on the history of "military academic research" (*junshi xueshu yanjiu*), published in 1995, explicitly reveals that the Second Artillery conducted very little, if any, work in the 1970s on nuclear doctrine issues. From the founding of the Second Artillery to the early 1970s, "the Second Artillery's military academic research was in an unclear stage (*menglong jieduan*).[22]

In the mid-1970s, the Second Artillery expanded slightly the scope of its military academic work, but this research was still considered to be in its "initial stage." The ascension of Deng back to power after Mao's death catalyzed the entire PLA, including the Second Artillery, to begin exploring nuclear doctrinal and force structure issues for the first time.[23]

As a result of this re-initiation of military academic research in 1978, the Second Artillery held two "operations applications research meetings" that focused on "operational guiding ideology, command systems, the application of principles to operations style, and other important academic issues." The broad and diffuse scope of these meetings offers a clear indication of the lack of systematic thinking in China concerning the requirements of nuclear deterrence. Two seminal documents were produced at this time, prior to 1978. The first is the *Second Artillery Operational Application Principles Provisional Guidelines* (*Dier Paobing Zuozhan Yunyong Zanxing*) and second is the *General Principles of Second Artillery Operations* (*Dier Paobing Zuozhan Gaize*). Despite this initial work, it wasn't until the late 1970s that the Second Artillery military academic research became planned, organized, and regularized. In 1978, China's strategic missile force began considering the requirements of deterrence and its ability to meet them.[24] As one indication of the basic nature of Chinese views about deterrence, throughout the 1970s China continued to publicly state that it opposed a policy of "nuclear deterrence"—a position that ran contrary to its own possession of nuclear weapons.

1978–1991: Moving Beyond Mao

Deng's introduction of "reform and openness" policies, which undermined various elements of the Maoist legacy, and, in particular, Deng's control of the PLA provided an opportunity to strip the bomb of its Maoist political trappings. China's military strategists gingerly began to explore the strategic rationales and concepts underlying China's possession and use of nuclear weapons.[25] The PLA started to develop and articulate (internally) the principles that formed the foundation of a coherent nuclear doctrine. This marked the beginning of systematic thinking, theorizing, institutionalizing, and, eventually, operationalizing a nuclear doctrine for China's strategic forces. For China in the 1980s, these principles called for the possession of a secure second-strike nuclear capability to prevent strategic strikes on the mainland and to deter other nuclear powers from using nuclear weapons to coerce China, which were essentially an extension of Mao's views. A key feature of this time period (which contrasts with subsequent ones) was that China's strategists relied solely on ambiguity and secrecy about the precise size, capabilities, and location of China's nuclear forces to ensure their survivability and, hence, credibility.

Several important changes in China's approach to nuclear weapons began in the late 1970s. First, China's new leaders were much more blatant about the national security rationale for possessing nuclear weapons. In 1983 Deng made several important statements, all of which suggest a basic understanding of deterrence. Deng noted that China's possession of nukes had "forced the superpowers not to use" their weapons against China. He continued that "China only wants to adhere to the principle: we will have what others have, and anyone who wants to destroy us will be subject to retaliation."[26] Deng also confirmed China's adherence to minimalism in its nuclear modernization. In 1983, he stated, "We will continue to develop nuclear weapons in one way or another, but, in any case, on a limited scale."[27]

Second, beginning in the late 1970s, the Second Artillery initiated internal research on issues related to possessing and using nuclear weapons. This research focused on the requirements of nuclear deterrence and the role of various service branches in meeting these general requirements. Freed from the constraints of Mao's influence, systematic work on nuclear doctrine and deterrence had finally begun with the rebirth of military research at the end of the Cultural Revolution.

According to an internal study on Military Academic Research, the Second Artillery's research from 1978 to the end of the 1980s was in the "development stage." In May 1978, the Second Artillery established a Military Studies Office (*Erpao Junshi Xueshu Yanjiu Weiyuanhui*) at the headquarters level (*Silingbu Junshi Xueshu Chu*) that was responsible for research and research management. The Second Artillery also established a Military Academic Research Committee that served as an "academic inquiry and consulting organization." The Second Artillery further held in the late 1970s and early 1980s its second and third "operations applications research meetings." The issues raised at these seminal meetings included the international strategic situation; the use of US and Soviet strategic nuclear forces; Second Artillery operational guiding principles, principles of operations, battlefield construction, and survivability; and Second Artillery operations applications and war preparation construction.

In addition to these meetings, Second Artillery leadership formulated regulations, which in the Chinese military system are critical to the effective operation of any branch of its armed forces.[28] They wrote the *Second Artillery Every Level Headquarters Work Regulations* (*Erpao Geji Silingbu Gongzuo Tiaoli*), *the Missile Troops (Units) Operations Regulations* (*Daodan Budui Zuozhan Tiaoling*), and the *Second Artillery Military Terms* (*Dier Paobing Junyu*). The goal of these regulations was to reform and restructure Second Artillery operations—like much of the PLA's reforms at that time. The formulation of these important regulations as late as the 1980s offers additional evidence of the nascent stage of the capabilities, operations, and thinking of the Second Artillery on nuclear doctrinal issues. Ironically, China had possessed nuclear weapons for close to fifteen years by this point, yet the operations of the Second Artillery had yet to be regularized and formalized.

Second Artillery leaders also initiated research on nuclear campaign theory and produced a seminal document known as *Second Artillery Campaign Theory* (*Dier Paobing Zhanyixue*). This document "became the Second Artillery's campaign training study research materials and underwent testing through campaign exercises, and in the mid-1980's was published and issued to the troops for use."[29] In other words, it may have been China's first functional nuclear doctrine.

In retrospect, 1985 was a seminal year more broadly for PLA research work on nuclear issues as well as military doctrine. That year, Deng brought about a major shift in the mission of the PLA. He officially changed the PLA's orientation from fighting an "all out war, major war, and nuclear war" (*quanmian zhanzheng, da zhanzheng, he zhanzheng*) to fighting limited local conflicts. He also revised China's official assessment of the international security environment from "war and revolution" (*zhanzheng yu geming*) to "peace and development" (*heping yu fazhan*). The significance of this shift cannot be over-emphasized, as it provided a potent political justification for retooling the entire PLA as well as for the reallocation of large amounts of resources from the military to national economic development.[30]

While this strategic decision had many components, it led to a rebirth of research on strategic studies within China's military academic community. As a result, in the latter half of 1985 the Second Artillery began to research "nuclear strategy theory," encouraged by "the popularity of strategy study across the military."[31] In the early 1990s, the Second Artillery's operations theory research further accelerated. In 1990, the Second Artillery held its first "Operations Research Theory Meeting," which sought to link together for the first time nuclear strategy, campaign, and tactics—a critical step in the operationalization of doctrine. The Second Artillery also received permission from the Central Military Commission (CMC) that year to place five issues into the eighth five-year research plan: Second Artillery strategy, campaign, tactics, operational command, and political work.

China debates deterrence. In the 1980s other internal discussions among the broader Chinese community of strategists (not just the PLA) occurred. One key debate centered on whether China would continue to adhere to its public position of "opposing the policy of nuclear deterrence." This discourse provides insights into the ideological constraints on the development and evolution of China's thinking about nuclear weapons. Despite its possession of nuclear weapons, Chinese strategists for decades viewed the concept of "nuclear deterrence" as pejorative and a practice that China should oppose. Due to the Chinese translation of the term "deterrence" as "to intimidate militarily" and using threats to coerce an adversary,[32] Chinese strategists viewed deterrence as a Western term that was inherently aggressive and offensive in nature. It was believed that using such a negative term would harm China's international image as a peace-loving nation and that it was inconsistent with China's views on nuclear weapons. Chinese strategists believed that Beijing only sought nuclear weapons to break the monopoly of the superpowers, not to intimidate others. The outcome of the debate was to allow the internal use of the term but to continue to oppose "nuclear deterrence" in public statements, offering a concrete example of how Maoist ideas about nuclear weapons (and China's traditional international identity) continued to influence Chinese nuclear policies well after Mao's death.[33]

Development and expansion of Chinese expertise on nuclear weapons. The emergence, expansion, and diversification of specialists focused on nuclear arms control research further facilitated and contributed to the institutionalization of internal deliberations about Chinese policies on nuclear weapons and nuclear deterrence.[34] Internal discussions on these topics became more regular and sophisticated throughout the decade. In the early 1980s, China lacked specialists on both nuclear weapons and nuclear arms control issues. China's membership in international arms control forums (the UN and the Geneva-based Conference on Disarmament), as well as its growing relations with countries interested in engaging with China on these issues, sparked the development of this collection of specialists. President Reagan's Strategic Defense Initiative also galvanized and focused the work of this nascent collection of expertise.

The emergence of this community in the 1980s led to an exposure (through various official and unofficial venues) to Western thinking and concepts about nuclear deterrence and nuclear strategies. Exposure to these ideas, and especially Western writings, may have influenced Chinese perceptions of their nuclear doctrine, capabilities, and willingness to assume certain arms control commitments. This "community" was initially quite spread-out among several stove-piped parts of China's bureaucracy, but by the late 1980s it began to congeal. For example, in the late 1980s nuclear scientists and missile engineers began to join the ranks of China's burgeoning arms control community. Their scientific background provided a critical missing element to internal discussions about nuclear doctrine and capabilities, namely the technical skills and experience to assess the impact of arms control commitments on Chinese military capabilities. The development of this community also led to the initiation of internal discussions about nuclear doctrine in the context of discussions about looming global arms control initiatives such as a test ban treaty, a fissile material cutoff treaty, and the ever-present US missile defense programs. Some of these experts, for example, argued in favor of signing the Comprehensive Test Ban Treaty (CTBT) and for China's abandonment of its public opposition to nuclear deterrence.[35]

1991–Present: Moving from a Symbolic to a Credible Nuclear Deterrent

From 1991 to the present has been a highly active period for Chinese thinking and policymaking on nuclear weapon affairs, marked by both internal and public debates in China about nuclear doctrine.[36] In addition, Chinese viewpoints and policies on nuclear weapons and deterrence have become increasingly formalized internally and publicly articulated. This represents important new steps in the evolution of Chinese doctrine. At the same time, China's nuclear capabilities have continued to grow in number and improve in quality over the last decade, while its overall force structure has begun to change in shape and contour.

Internal and external sources of change explain the distinctive development of doctrinal thinking in this time period. Internally, China had completed almost a decade worth of internal writings, researching, and thinking about nuclear strategy and doctrine. By the early 1990s, military and civilian organizations had accumulated the expertise, initiative, and political space to explore and discuss the ultrasensitive issues of nuclear doctrine and force structure. These debates continue today. Externally, the international system and China's foreign relations were rapidly changing shape, and these developments held potentially significant implications for China's future nuclear posture. In other words, the context within which China's nuclear doctrine was being formed changed rapidly, and Chinese strategists were forced to respond. The Soviet Union (the heretofore main focus of Chinese nuclear planning) had collapsed, tensions with the US were rising, and US-China military conflict over Taiwan was emerging once again as a real possibility. The Gulf War demonstrated the relative backwardness of Chinese armaments and the corresponding sophistication of US battle space operations and conventional munitions. These developments led to a reassessment of Chinese thinking about its doctrine and the requirements of deterrence in the 1990s. In particular, Chinese nuclear doctrine, operations, and planning began to reflect the dramatic changes in the international context.

Six major trends characterized this time period. First, the strategic and operational principles underlying Chinese nuclear doctrine came into sharper focus. These were articulated in both internal documents and public statements and are summarized in the next section of this chapter. Second, as China's thinking about nuclear strategy matured, there were also active internal debates about the orientation of China's doctrine; such debates included the well-known one about moving toward possession of a "limited deterrent" as well as the more recent debate about China's continued adherence to its NFU pledge. The quality of these discussions improved compared to the 1980s. Third, internal discussions and debates about nuclear weapons broadened beyond the Second Artillery and the PLA to include civilian analysts from the defense industry and foreign policy community. Chinese debates about arms control issues helped to facilitate this diversification of internal discourse. Fourth, as a result of the previous factors, in the last ten years there has been simply much more open, public discussion and writing about nuclear issues. This draws a stark contrast with the limited and highly secretive internal deliberations in the 1980s. By the end of the 1990s and beginning of this decade, Chinese scholars and officials had become much more willing to address openly issues bearing on nuclear doctrine. There are indications that China may include a new section on nuclear doctrine in a forthcoming defense white paper.

Fifth, China's thinking about its nuclear deterrent appeared to coalesce around the notion that China needed to move toward a credible and visible minimum deterrent that relies on the mobility, invulnerability, and penetrability of its nuclear forces as the foundation for possessing a survivable nuclear force. This contrasts with China's posture in the 1980s, which largely based its survivability on ambiguity and secrecy about numbers and capabilities of nuclear weapons. Many Chinese strategists began to argue openly in the latter part of the 1990s that China needed to move beyond a faith in the "quantitative uncertainty" about China's arsenal for its deterrent to be credible. Force structure modernization in the 1990s reflects in part such concerns.

Sixth, and related to the previous point, Chinese strategists began to conduct sustained and systematic thinking about emerging threats to the credibility of China's nuclear forces, as discussed in further detail by Brad Roberts in this volume. US plans to accelerate its deployment of ballistic missile defenses (BMD), combined with the advent of US long-range conventional strike capabilities, rightly raised significant concerns among Chinese military planners about the continued survivability and retaliatory capabilities of Chinese nuclear forces. This latter capability, in particular, forced Chinese strategists to confront the unsettling proposition that the US could strike China's nuclear forces with conventional munitions, and Beijing would, at least notionally, be hampered in responding due to its NFU pledge. These issues have sparked heated debates in Chinese strategic circles and hold uncertain implications for China's evolving nuclear doctrine.

Current Chinese Nuclear Doctrine: Toward an Understanding of Sufficiency and Effectiveness in China's Approach to Nuclear Weapons

China's nuclear doctrine has two elements: (1) broad ideas and biases which inform Chinese thinking on nuclear questions and (2) specific concepts related to the possession and use of nuclear weapons that define military procurement, planning, and operations. These two components are derived from a close reading of Chinese internal and public writings and discussions with Chinese specialists in the last several years, which have shed considerable light on an issue that has long resided in darkness. As a result, the contours of Chinese policies and debates on these issues have come into much sharper focus.

This chapter argues that China's current nuclear doctrine should be thought of *less* in terms of Western ideas of minimum or limited deterrence and *more* in terms of the concepts of "sufficiency and effectiveness"—regardless of the actual term China uses. While admittedly these latter terms could apply to any nation's nuclear doctrine, this conceptualization is meant to be both comprehensive and edifying, given the narrow parameters of the current US debate about Chinese nuclear doctrine. My approach highlights the dynamic nature of China's current discourse on nuclear weapons as well as the fact that China does not adhere necessarily and definitively to the Western concept of credible minimum deterrence, though that notion plays a central role in current doctrinal thinking. Instead, this chapter maintains that China will use its nuclear weapons and acquire new capabilities in ways that are sufficient to meet its national security needs. The latter requirement may change over time and this could result in modifications to doctrine. For now, China's doctrine has two goals: possessing a secure second-strike capability to deter nuclear strikes on China and preventing other nuclear powers from using nuclear weapons to coerce China in a crisis (i.e., countercoercion).

Focusing on sufficiency and effectiveness captures, for example, instances in which China acquires nuclear capabilities (such as low-yield nuclear devices or multiple-warhead missiles) that do not strictly reflect a minimum-deterrence doctrine, but which address a specific Chinese security concern. As Brad Roberts argues, Chinese strategists in the past (and heavily influenced by Maoist ideas of warfare) viewed "minimalism" in force structure as sufficient to meet China's national security needs.[37] However, in light of the growing sophistication of the PLA's doctrinal thinking combined with China's perception of its changing security circumstances and needs, a minimal force structure may not always be seen as enough—despite the consistent emphasis on minimalism in the past.

Therefore, this chapter argues for a more precise and inclusive characterization of Chinese nuclear doctrine focused on the concept of sufficiency and effectiveness, not credible minimum deterrence. Regardless of how China discusses its doctrine, sufficiency and effectiveness are useful analytic constructs for Westerners to view Chinese nuclear doctrine. The emergence of new threats and new circumstances has prompted Chinese strategists to reconsider the degree to which a consistent emphasis on minimalism (and its classic attributes such as NFU) is enough to meet the expanding demands on China's nuclear arsenal. To be sure, China's traditional stress on minimalism and credible minimum deterrence will continue to strongly influence China's approach to the procurement and deployment of nuclear weapons. But there are other, newer elements to Chinese calculations as well. These include a desire to respond to the emergence of new threats such as missile defenses and long-range, conventional precision-strike weapons—both of which could undermine China's deterrent capability. China also faces the possibility of confronting a nuclear-armed superpower in a regional conflict in which both parties have significant interests at stake. These considerations have injected a certain degree of fluidity and dynamism into current Chinese thinking about doctrine.

This section outlines the case for this new conceptualization of Chinese doctrine by analyzing a bevy of Chinese source materials. It initially puts forward general ideas and beliefs that inform Chinese policies regarding the role of nuclear weapons and the functioning of nuclear deterrence. A second part identifies specific strategic- and campaign-level concepts that form the backbone of Chinese nuclear doctrine. A third section highlights Chinese concerns about the continued credibility of their current nuclear forces and raises related issues about the future evolution of Chinese doctrine.

Core Elements of Current Nuclear Doctrine

In the past ten years, Chinese nuclear analysts have engaged in perhaps the most systematic internal discourse about nuclear strategy, doctrine, and campaign planning since the founding of the People's Republic in 1949. Drawing on an extensive exploitation of new Chinese source materials, there are several ideas and concepts that guide Chinese thinking about the roles and missions of nuclear weapons. This segment first offers a few general ideas that are evident in and permeate Chinese discussions about the roles and missions of nuclear weapons. These ideas suggest that China continues to view nuclear weapons as mainly a deterrent against strategic attack and coercion and thus not for damage limitation purposes. A second segment of this section identifies four specific Chinese doctrinal concepts that shape actual procurement, planning, and operations.

Chinese strategists view nuclear deterrence as principally a "psychological battle" between China and other nuclear-armed countries. Chinese strategists view nuclear deterrence as a psychological contest to counter the use or threatened use of nuclear weapons against China by displaying in various ways its resolve to counterattack. It is difficult to overstate the importance that the psychological dimensions of nuclear deterrence play in Chinese nuclear planning and operations. During peacetime and wartime, China postures its nuclear capabilities to shape external perceptions of China's willingness to retaliate and to avoid coercion. Perception management is a pervasive theme in Chinese writings about the use of its nuclear forces—especially during crises with nuclear adversaries.[38]

In this context, and in contrast to US and Soviet experience during the Cold War, relative numbers of nuclear weapons are not central to Chinese military planners. As long as they can effectively threaten to carry out unacceptable damage on an adversary, then deterrence is obtained—in China's eyes. Another key aspect of this "battle of wills" for China is fostering uncertainty about its nuclear capabilities. Chinese military thinkers consistently stress the centrality of using deception to foster ambiguity about China's nuclear capabilities. Some strategists refer to a dedicated government strategy to obscure China's capabilities in order to bolster China's deterrent.

Furthermore, the Maoist tradition of nuclear minimalism and building only a modest nuclear force structure continues to influence (not dominate) current doctrinal thinking. However, current Chinese arguments in support of minimalism differ from past ones. They do not appear to be based on an appeal to Maoist principles of warfare (such as People's War), but rather on newer strategic beliefs about the political and military value of nuclear weapons in a complex international security environment, balanced against the costs of a large-scale nuclear expansion effort. In discussing the limits on the size of China's nuclear forces, China's National Defense University's Gu Dexin, along with Niu Yongjun, argue that China's "limited" and modest development of nuclear weapons is not "an expedient calculation, but is a type of national policy (*guoce*)." They argue that this balancing of national economic development goals with nuclear force development dates back to Mao and Deng and is a "unique characteristic of China's nuclear strategic thinking."[39]

A related belief informing support for a modest force is the explicit rejection of falling into the "Soviet trap" of participating in a debilitating arms race with the US; most Chinese strategists believe arms racing contributed to the demise of the Soviet Union and seek to avoid a similar outcome. According to Gu Dexin's study published by China's National Defense University, "Even though nuclear forces are an important part and an important branch of the armed forces, they cannot be the foundation and nucleus of national defense forces. As a result, a nuclear race with the superpowers is both impossible and unnecessary."[40]

A final, key idea informing China's doctrine is a belief among many Chinese strategists about the unique and special nature of nuclear weapons as military tools. This notion, in particular, heavily influences Chinese beliefs about how credible nuclear deterrence is obtained, and specifically about Chinese standards for "unacceptable damage." A senior engineer in the Second Artillery argued in a 2001 article that nuclear weapons possess "supernormal power" and thus only a few are necessary to deter others. For him, the operational value that Chinese strategists place on nuclear weapons (and the intermediate conclusion that China only needs a limited number of them) is largely grounded on the assumption that the United States is so highly casualty-averse that the risk of even one successful missile strike on a large US city is enough to deter the United States.[41] Interviews with Chinese nuclear strategists have affirmed this view and some have even been more explicit. They have argued, for example, that few in China accept McNamara's standard of "assured destruction," which was first outlined in the 1960s. Rather, they argue that China's ability to threaten a few of the adversary's cities with a small number of nuclear weapons would be sufficient to ensure deterrence, a notion which some Chinese call "assured retaliation."[42]

Four Key Concepts In Chinese Nuclear Doctrine

Chinese general beliefs about nuclear weapons are expressed in four key concepts, at the strategic and campaign levels, that form the backbone of Chinese nuclear doctrine.[43] Each one of these four elucidates different aspects of China's current approach to the roles and missions of nuclear weapons.

1. Strategic Level:
   - *Houfa Zhiren* (gaining mastery by striking after the enemy has struck)
2. Campaign Level[44]
   - *Yanmi Fanghu* (close defense or self-protection)
   - *Zhongdian Fanji* (key-point counterstrikes)
   - *Fan Heweishe* (counter nuclear deterrence/counter intimidation)

Striking after the enemy has struck (houfa zhiren). One of the most important principles in Chinese nuclear thinking is "gaining mastery by striking after the enemy has struck," or *houfa zhiren.* This concept is a hallmark of Chinese nuclear doctrinal thinking and dates back to the original 1987 version of *Science of Military Strategy.* It is a strategic-level concept that broadly informs all the PLA's policymaking related to nuclear weapons. *Houfa zhiren* is a conceptual expression of China's consistent emphasis on building a secure second-strike (or as the Chinese say, counterstrike) capability, as well as China's no-first-use commitment.

China's articulation of this principle is meant to codify that China's nuclear forces are for deterrence *based on a survivable second-strike capability*—and not necessarily for warfighting or damage limitation. A bevy of Chinese military books (including instructional and teaching materials for young officers) argue that China's nuclear weapons serve two purposes: nuclear deterrence (*he weishe*) and nuclear counterstrike/nuclear retaliation (*he fanji/he baofu*). These dual ideas are repeatedly raised in both internal and open writings. The frequent use of these twin ideas, even in internal military writings, suggests a wide degree of formal acceptance—not merely propaganda. In these books, there is seldom a direct discussion of nuclear warfighting contingencies in which nuclear weapons are used for more than deterrence or retaliation purposes. Indeed, the nuclear counterstrike campaign (*he baofu zhanyi*) is the only nuclear contingency that the PLA leadership has identified for the Second Artillery. Xue Xinglin's *Campaign Theory Study Guide* defines nuclear counterstrike campaigns:

> Second Artillery nuclear counterstrike campaigns refer to Second Artillery nuclear campaigns carrying out several guided missile nuclear strike combat operations in order to achieve specified strategic campaign objectives in accordance with the unified plan and highly centralized command. They include two types of operational methods, independent nuclear counterstrike campaigns and participation in joint nuclear counterstrike campaigns. Since Second Artillery nuclear forces are the backbone of our country's nuclear forces, joint nuclear counterstrike campaigns are usually based on Second Artillery nuclear forces as well as naval nuclear submarine force nuclear forces and air force bomber forces nuclear forces participating in triad (*san wei yi ti*) nuclear counterstrike combat operations.
>
> Nuclear counterstrike campaigns, according to the division of nuclear forces participating in the campaign, have independent nuclear counterstrike campaigns and joint nuclear counterstrike campaigns; according to the divisions of the scale of the campaign, there are large-scale nuclear counterstrike campaigns and small-scale nuclear counterstrike campaigns.[45]

China's emphasis on the concept of *houfa zhiren* raises obvious questions about the relevance and credibility of China's commitment to NFU, especially in light of US experiences with similar Soviet pledges in the Cold War. Is NFU a real constraint on Chinese nuclear operations or an empty assurance? There are multiple indications that Chinese policymakers and nuclear planners currently treat NFU as a real constraint on their planning and operations. First, as argued in the previous section, the discussion in internal and military circulation books of "nuclear counterstrike campaigns" is consistent with adherence to this NFU commitment; these military publications do not discuss first-strike campaigns as a possibility—a direct contrast with Soviet doctrine during the Cold War. Even members of China's Second Artillery have reaffirmed and argued in favor of maintaining China's NFU.[46] Some specifically note the importance of continued adherence to the NFU pledge for China's international image. The consistent and overwhelming emphasis in PLA writings on improving the survivability of China's nuclear capabilities serves as an additional indication of the expectation among the military that China's political leaders take their NFU pledge seriously.

Second, authoritative PLA writings about Second Artillery nuclear operations further suggest an acceptance of NFU as a national policy. These writings frequently note that the Second Artillery will be operating in a nuclear environment in which China has already been attacked. For example, the text of *The Science of Military Campaigns* (*Zhanyixue*) affirms this view. It says the Second Artillery would carry out its strategic nuclear campaign only after the enemy had struck China with nuclear weapons. The text says that a nuclear retaliation campaign would take place in a "grim nuclear environment" (*yanku de he huanjing*). Also, since the Second Artillery would be the "key point target" (*zhongdian mubiao*) of the enemy's first strike, the Second Artillery must be prepared to operate under "exceedingly harsh nuclear conditions" (*jiqi yanku de he tiaojian*). The Second Artillery would suffer heavy damage as the result of a nuclear attack. *The Science of Military Campaigns* estimates that the casualties among Second Artillery personnel would be significant, that weapons, equipment, roads, and bridges would be destroyed, and that China's command, control, and communications system (*zhihui tongxin xitong*) would be degraded.[47] In addition, an article in the Second Artillery's engineering journal on improving survivability began with the premise that China would launch a nuclear strike after being attacked by an adversary.[48]

One of the most interesting indicators of China's commitment to NFU is in the Chinese discussion of using demonstration strikes—with conventionally armed nuclear missiles—during a crisis to signal China's resolve. In such instances, China's ultimate goal is to deter an adversary from initiating nuclear conflict. In one article on Second Artillery operations, the author discusses the use of demonstration actions to enhance the credibility of Second Artillery deterrence and notes that: "When the enemy does not use nuclear weapons first, the 'demonstration attack' by the Second Artillery is done with conventionally armed missiles. The target of the attack should be fairly concealed, and the accuracy of the attack should be high in order to show maximally our power, achieving the effect of killing one as a warning to a hundred."[49]

To be sure, the continuing relevance and wisdom of China's NFU pledge is being debated internally. Opponents to NFU have sprung up within the PLA in recent years.[50] At least four arguments are levied against NFU. First, because China's nuclear forces are already vulnerable to a first strike, NFU makes them even more so. Second, some maintain that NFU limits China's ability to deter non-nuclear WMD threats, long-range, conventional precision strikes on Chinese nuclear weapon facilities, or conventional strikes with WMD-like effects. A third argument is that as China modernizes its nuclear capabilities, it could bolster the military effectiveness of that deterrent and reduce the negative political implications of a large missile build-up by declaring publicly a doctrine of minimum deterrence while also abandoning NFU. Last, NFU may complicate China's efforts (from a command and control perspective) to launch a second-strike because China's nuclear forces are forced (under NFU) to rely so heavily on dispersal and concealment to survive. As a result of these concerns, in recent years PLA strategists have debated modifying or conditionalizing China's NFU commitment. The political leadership apparently rejected their efforts. Some officials and scholars have hinted that in a real nuclear crisis China's NFU would not be a major constraint, though anecdotal accounts on this point are mixed.[51] (For a discussion of NFU in the event of a Taiwan crisis, see Ting Wai in this volume.)

Close defense/self-protection (yanmi fanghu). Close defense has been one of the core concepts behind China's possession of nuclear weapons for decades. One source indicates that its adoption dates back to the early 1980s when this idea was used as one of two strategic guiding principles for the Second Artillery.[52] The principle of close defense is meant to capture the PLA's top priority on ensuring the survivability of Chinese nuclear forces in order to launch a counterattack. This emphasis on surviving a first strike is likely one of the reasons that *yanmi fanghu* has been articulated by the Second Artillery from the earliest days of its nuclear campaign planning. Xue Xinglin's detailed study on military campaigns offers an unusually explicit description of the principle of close defense/self-protection:

> "Close defense" is the Second Artillery's basic way of increasing survivability and guaranteeing nuclear counterstrike strength and is a prerequisite for carrying out a nuclear counterstrike campaign. What close defense emphasizes is comprehensive and continuous campaign defense, and rigorous and active defense measures. Not only is it necessary to adopt every measure, to decrease the damage caused by enemy nuclear strikes, but it is also necessary to counter enemy conventional weaponry well, especially preparations against high-tech precision guided munitions strikes.
>
> Not only is it necessary to perform well the preparatory work to prevent sudden enemy strikes early on in the war, but it is also necessary to perform well the organization and implementation work of preventing sudden enemy strikes in the middle and later periods of war. It is also necessary to strengthen and establish defense organization, adopt effective measures in operational engineering, defensive systems, force deployment, base deployment, concealment and camouflage, and other aspects, and to make efforts to increase battlefield survivability.[53]

Key-point counterstrikes/nuclear targeting (zhongdian fanji). A third principle in Chinese nuclear doctrine is key-point counterstrikes or *zhongdian fanji*.[54] This concept has been one of the long-time cornerstone ideas informing Second Artillery operations for the last two decades. The origin of this term's usage in a nuclear weapons context dates back to Deng Xiaoping's reference to "key point strikes" in a 1983 comment.[55] Since Deng's usage, this phrase became central to Chinese nuclear orthodoxy—regardless of its originally broad meaning and application to conventional military strike operations.[56]

The essential idea behind "key-point counterstrikes" is that the Second Artillery, in targeting an adversary's "key points," will bolster the credibility of China's nuclear deterrent and, thus, prevent nuclear attack. A second aspect of this term may be even more important to understanding the unique aspects of China's current nuclear doctrine. Chinese writings also strongly suggest that China would notionally use key-point counterstrikes in a conflict to hinder an adversary's war-making ability and foster such a strong psychological blow that the adversary terminates nuclear operations. In this sense, a central element of key-point nuclear counterstrikes is to bring about de-escalation and termination of nuclear war. Xue Xinglin's study defines key-point counterstrikes as

> concentrated nuclear firepower striking enemy vital targets creating significant damage and causing psychological shocks to the enemy in order to achieve the greatest nuclear counterstrike results. Key-point counterstrikes are the concrete application of concentrated forces carrying out the concept of annihilation warfare in nuclear counterstrike campaigns. Second Artillery nuclear counterstrike campaigns are carried under the conditions of sudden enemy attacks. In order to change an overall inferior situation into a locally advantageous position and to change the passiveness of the early period of the war into proactiveness as the war progresses, then it is necessary to make use of force flexibly and with key points, to be good at grasping beneficial opportunities, and to concentrate nuclear firepower to carry out strikes against important enemy targets at the appropriate time.[57]

Unlike the other core concepts in Chinese nuclear doctrine, writings about the target sets for key-point counterstrikes indicate that Chinese thinking does not neatly coincide with Western notions of minimum deterrence. Xue Xinglin's 2001 study on military campaign theory identifies a mix of hard and soft civilian and military targets for nuclear counterattack operations. These include the enemy's political and economic centers (especially major population centers); the enemy's oil, electricity, steel, and other major industrial targets; the enemy's railroad hubs, mobilization stations, and other transportation centers; the enemy's primary military targets including airfields, naval bases, as well as long-range air and naval operational capabilities; and "when necessary and according to the battlefield situation and campaign requirements," enemy's heavy forces and strategic (campaign) reserve staging areas.[58] This set of targets could be consistent with either warfighting plans or de-escalation and war-termination goals; otherwise why would China target so many military-related facilities?

Other texts shed further light on this question. According to the 2001 *Science of Military Campaigns,* the objectives of a retaliatory nuclear strike are to paralyze the enemy command system (*tanhuan . . . zhihui xitong*), cripple enemy war potential (*xueruo . . . zhanzheng qianli*), frustrate the enemy's strategic intentions (*cuobai . . . zhanlue yitu*), shake the enemy's determination (*dongyao . . . zhangzheng yizhi*), and contain the escalation of the nuclear exchange (*ezhi hezhanzheng shengji*).[59]

This extensive discussion of striking military targets in nuclear operations raises two possibilities for evaluating China's nuclear doctrine. First, Chinese military planners consider limited nuclear warfighting as part of their effort to deter nuclear attack in the first instance and eventually to respond to an attack on China if deterrence fails. In this sense, military planners are willing to engage in low-level nuclear conflict in the belief that nuclear escalation can be controlled. This interpretation, however, is assessed as not likely as it is inconsistent with other aspects of China's nuclear doctrine (addressed above) as well as China's nuclear force structure. China lacks the capability to conduct precision nuclear strikes on specific military targets or to engage in prolonged nuclear warfare.

A second, more plausible explanation is that Chinese nuclear planners seek to use a nuclear retaliatory strike for de-escalation and possibly even war-termination purposes. As indicated by their writings noted above, China would use a nuclear counterstrike to cripple an adversary's capabilities and to foster the maximum psychological effect in one massive counterattack in order to bring about a halt to further nuclear exchanges—or possibly even the entire military conflict. This interpretation is far more consistent with other elements of Chinese doctrine as well as broader Chinese beliefs about the value of nuclear weapons. To be sure, such a de-escalation strategy has its own shortcomings. It is not clear China possesses the necessary operational capabilities to carry it out effectively and, even if it did, it is not clear such an approach would work. China could simply invite another wave of nuclear attacks in which its modest nuclear force could be entirely eliminated—depending on the adversary's capabilities.[60]

Interestingly, Chinese writings about striking military targets in nuclear strike operations have persisted for over a decade, dating back to the late 1980s. This suggests a degree of consistency over time in Chinese thinking about nuclear targeting—and views on the possibility of de-escalation. A 1987 book on strategic studies discussed target sets beyond counter-value sites including strikes on "strategic targets," "weakening the enemy's war potential," and targeting an adversary's "strategic assault forces."[61] While these general terms were never specified, they strongly suggest targeting of military facilities. A military circulation study published in 1989 was even more explicit about striking military sites. It specifically referred to striking enemy missile bases, bomber bases, and SLBM bases. The volume also noted that "striking key points is even more important for middle-level nuclear powers" (such as China), though no additional clarification was provided. These early writings suggest, perhaps, confusion at that time among Chinese military strategists about the targeting requirements of a credible second-strike deterrent capability. Chinese strategists may have thought that targeting such facilities would enhance strategic deterrence rather than undermine that capability. Or they could reflect a consistent Chinese belief that the best use of nuclear counterstrikes is to retard an enemy's war potential and to try to catalyze de-escalation.

Counter nuclear deterrence and nuclear signaling (fan heweishe). A fourth principle informing Chinese nuclear doctrine is counter nuclear deterrence or *fan heweishe.*[62] This is a distinctly Chinese term insofar as an analogous one does not exist in the Western strategic nuclear lexicon. This term's origin in Chinese strategic thought derives from the pejorative meaning associated with the term "deterrence" (*weishe*). To many Chinese strategists for years until the 1990s, the Western concept of deterrence was akin to using a large threat (or *wei* [might or power]) to intimidate and coerce an adversary. Thus, deterrence is a specific policy choice that requires "countering."

Chinese texts discuss counter deterrence as a military operation used to demonstrate China's determination and will to use nuclear weapons, usually in response to an adversary's efforts to coerce China with nuclear threats. In this sense, Chinese views of the role and function of counter deterrence are roughly equivalent to one of the central pillars of Western nuclear deterrence theory: for a deterrent force to be credible, a nation needs to possess not only a capability to inflict unacceptable damage but must also communicate the resolve to use it. For China, counter-deterrence operations seem to be efforts to communicate its willingness to respond to nuclear threats and/or attacks. In this sense, counter deterrence for China is a form of signaling of resolve. According to *Science of Military Campaigns:*

> We conduct [counter deterrence combat] to counter enemy nuclear deterrence and to contain and foil some of the enemy's important strategic intentions or risky operations and to support national political and diplomatic struggle. We should pay attention to the following when conducting counter-nuclear deterrence combat: number one, we should closely combine anti-nuclear deterrence operation with political and diplomatic struggle. Counter-nuclear deterrence operation is actually a contest of psychological will. . . . Number two, we should fully prepare for nuclear retaliation. In counter-nuclear deterrence combat, the campaign commander of the Second Artillery has to firmly establish the principle of "being ready to fight while deterring." We should have the troops fully prepared for nuclear retaliation. Comprehensive and firm combat readiness is itself an important means and firm backing to show a strong resolve and will.[63]

In discussing counter deterrence, neither *Science of Military Campaigns* nor *Science of Military Strategy* explains what types of signals China might send (i.e., peacetime and wartime) or how it might communicate them (i.e., open or secretive.) For example, in a crisis, would Chinese leaders withdraw or conditionalize their NFU commitment as a signal to the United States or others? To date, there is only one openly known incident, in Fall 1969, when China may have placed the Second Artillery on alert status, and then likely sent a nuclear "signal" to the Soviet Union by testing two nuclear weapons only six days apart—a shorter interval than in any other point in China's testing history.[64]

Chinese views on the timing of its nuclear counterstrikes sheds further light on the content of nuclear doctrine. In past decades, Mao said that after a first strike on the mainland China might wait weeks, or even months, before launching a nuclear counterstrike. Modern Chinese strategic thinkers have moved decidedly away from Mao's musings on this critical issue. Chinese views on retaliation have converged on the belief that the Second Artillery must respond immediately (or at least as quickly as possible) to a first strike on China.

The timing of retaliatory strikes is raised in both *Science of Military Campaigns* and *Science of Military Strategy.*[65] Seldom have these ideas been addressed previously in Chinese writings. Passages in *Science of Military Campaigns* suggest that Chinese strategists currently believe it necessary to retaliate rapidly or even immediately after a first strike is launched. The Second Artillery, according to *Science of Military Campaigns,* must "respond rapidly" (*kuaisu fanying*) because modern wars are characterized by "suddenness" (*turanxing*) and "intensity" (*canlie-*

xing). This is especially so in a nuclear conflict. The book noted, "rapid response has already become one of the fundamental requirements for modern campaign operation"; "in case nuclear deterrence fails," the Second Artillery must "immediately carry out the nuclear counterattack in accordance with the nuclear retaliation order of the supreme command."[66] *Science of Military Strategy* also includes general, non-China-specific arguments about the timing of retaliatory strikes.

The detailed nature of these writings about timing further indicates that Chinese military planners continue to think more systematically about steps to improve the survivability and credibility of China's nuclear posture. The public emphasis on rapid retaliation may be part of China's effort to signal its determination to retaliate, and thus to deter an adversary's first strike. In a conflict, both a first strike on China as well as a Chinese second strike on an adversary would likely be disastrous for the mainland given the modest size of its arsenal. Therefore, preventing an initial strike in the first place should be China's paramount goal of deterrence, and the emphasis on rapid retaliation may be an effort to buttress this capability.

Interestingly, none of these writings indicate an explicit Chinese preference for either launch-on-warning (LOW) or launch-under-attack (LUA) policies. It is not clear if this is a deliberate uncertainty or not. Each one of these policies would present China with unique challenges. An effective LOW posture would require an extensive and advanced early warning network. LUA would require the PLA to possess a large and hardened command, control, and communication infrastructure. If China desired either one of these policies, it is not clear it possesses the operational capabilities to implement them. In addition, there is no discussion in these writings of the trade-offs between LUA postures and the increased chances of accidental and unauthorized missile launches. The consistent Chinese emphasis, especially in public documents, on the centralized control of the release of nuclear weapons suggests that an LUA posture would, at a minimum, require a modification of China's existing policies on nuclear command and control.

Tensions in China's Current Nuclear Doctrine

One of the inevitable conclusions of the preceding analysis is that there are several internal ambiguities and tensions in Chinese writings on nuclear weapons and deterrence. The ways in which Chinese strategists address these ambiguities and tensions will serve as important indicators of the overall direction of Chinese nuclear doctrine in the future.

Two of these are addressed below.

The most glaring ambiguity in China's doctrine is the conditions under which NFU applies. As argued above, Chinese leaders and military planners appear to treat NFU as a constraint, but it is not clear when and how it applies to actual combat situations. Chinese writings on NFU are expressed via the core operational concept of *houfa zhiren* or "gaining mastery by counter-attacking." Yet, it is not clear what is allowed under *houfa zhiren;* what counts as sufficient provocation for a counterstrike to be initiated? Some military writings about *houfa zhiren*—in conventional warfare—suggest it could entail striking *before the enemy has actually attacked.* For example, the 2001 version of *Science of Military Strategy* states, "Second strike upholds the principle of not firing the first shot, but by no means is equivalent to abandoning the advantage of first opportunity (*xianji*) in campaigns or tactics." Thus, preemption in some circumstances can be consistent with *houfa zhiren.* To be sure, this section of text was not specifically discussing nuclear operations and was focused on conventional warfare. It nonetheless raises questions about the scope of China's NFU.

A related issue of direct relevance is the extent to which NFU applies to circumstances in which an adversary uses advanced, long-range precision conventional weapons to strike strategic military targets including nuclear forces, nuclear infrastructure, chemical and biological weapon facilities, conventional forces, war-supporting industries, or military command and control facilities. Would China consider a conventional attack on one or a combination of those facilities to be equivalent to a nuclear first strike and respond with nuclear weapons? Similarly, how would China respond to a conventional attack that produced an effect similar to the use of weapons of mass destruction, for example, if an adversary used conventional weapons to destroy the Three Gorges dam? There are some indications that the Chinese are beginning to consider these ideas but no indication of their linkage to China's NFU pledge.[67]

Second, an explicit tension in Chinese writings on nuclear doctrine is the relationship between maintaining secrecy about capabilities (a long-accepted aspect of China's approach to deterrence) while at the same time revealing China's will and determination to use nuclear weapons in a crisis. Chinese texts increasingly discuss the importance of signaling China's determination to retaliate by using the concept of counter deterrence. It is not clear how China balances the consistent emphasis on promoting secrecy and ambiguity about its nuclear capabilities against the importance of successfully signaling the readiness and determination to retaliate. On the one hand, by revealing its capabilities or "displaying form," the Chinese potentially limit the tools available for signaling and create opportunities for an adversary to develop countermeasures to its capabilities. On the other hand, not revealing capabilities creates the conditions under which misperceptions can form and miscalculations can occur. The manner in which China balances these competing demands will reveal much about China's confidence in its evolving capabilities and its approach to deterrence.

New Challenges Emerge

Perhaps the greatest tension in Chinese nuclear doctrine is whether and/or how China will react to the growing number of perceived challenges to the relative strength of China's nuclear capabilities. In the late 1990s, Chinese strategists became increasingly focused on the emergence of threats to China's nuclear capabilities, which initiated a questioning within the military about the continued credibility of its deterrent. Chinese strategists began considering whether China's nuclear modernization would have to move in new directions and acquire new capabilities to address these developments. Some of these concerns also hold implications for China's overall nuclear doctrine, perhaps leading to modifications in some aspects of doctrinal thinking. This could occur, for example, through a reinterpretation of the concepts addressed above.

Chinese strategists highlight several looming threats. First and foremost, beginning in the late 1990s, the United States' accelerated pursuit of nationwide and theater missile defense capabilities raised immediate concerns among Chinese military planners and policymakers. Most view US BMD plans as partially, if not wholly, directed at China in an effort to deny Beijing a nuclear deterrent and possibly the ability to deter the US from coercing China with nuclear weapons—especially during a Taiwan conflict. A related Chinese concern is that deployment of a BMD system would lead the US to be more aggressive and arrogant in international relations due to its self-perceived invulnerability to coercion and threats from others.[68]

Second, Chinese military strategists worry about the implications of the United States' 2002 Nuclear Posture Review (NPR), which redefined the US triad to include strategic strike (conventional and nuclear), strategic defenses (active and passive), and a "dynamic" nuclear production infrastructure. Of particular concern to China is the growing US emphasis on long-range conventional precision strike weapons to achieve "strategic effects." Chinese military planners fear the US could use such conventional weapons to destroy Chinese nuclear facilities—but not be subject to nuclear retaliation because of China's NFU pledge. A related concern stemming from the NPR is the belief that in the latter 1990s China assumed a larger role in US nuclear war planning. Chinese strategists point to leaked portions of the NPR that reportedly discuss the potential use of nuclear weapons against China in a Taiwan conflict.[69] Chinese scholars also regularly argue that the United States put China back into its nuclear strategic war plan (the Single Integrated Operations Plan) in the late 1990s. The Bush administration's emphasis on preemptive strikes as a defining element of its national security strategy added to these already acute worries.[70] (For more on Chinese views of US policies, see Chapter 5 by Ron Montaperto in this volume.)

Third, Chinese scholars have expressed concern about recent changes in Russian nuclear doctrine and Russia's long-term response to US efforts to achieve decisive superiority in military capabilities. Some Chinese are concerned that within a decade Russia's increased emphasis on nuclear weapons (particularly tactical nuclear weapons) to compensate for its weak conventional capabilities, combined with a Russian willingness to countenance nuclear warfare in limited conflicts, could threaten China if political relations become acrimonious.[71] A fourth concern is the emergence of an active Indian nuclear weapons program. India's nuclear tests in 1998 set off alarm bells throughout the PLA. After the tests, Indian officials justified them by pointing to the threat posed by China. While Sino-Indian diplomatic relations have improved since 1998 and the "China threat" line has been dropped (at least publicly), the formalization and growth of India's nuclear arsenal since 1998 (especially the articulation of a public nuclear doctrine) has not gone unnoticed by Chinese strategists. As a result, India has likely assumed a greater role in Chinese nuclear planning. To be sure, this is also likely a function of the PLA's very minimal attention to India's nuclear capabilities prior to the 1998 tests.

A final area of concern for Chinese strategists is the perceived failure of international arms control and nonproliferation efforts in the late 1990s. Chinese expectations in the mid-1990s about the growing importance and restraining effect of arms control and nonproliferation accords are now viewed as misperceptions. Some Chinese strategists expected global arms control agreements (such as the Comprehensive Nuclear Test Ban Treaty) to reduce eventually the role of nuclear weapons in world politics, though few hold that belief anymore. Several developments contributed to this view. The US Senate's rejection of the CTBT, the US withdrawal from the ABM Treaty, the nuclear tests in South Asia, and the belief the United States is developing "mini-nukes," among other issues, collectively led to this pessimism among Chinese diplomats, scholars, and military officers. These concerns now manifest themselves in Chinese assessments of the international security environment, which forecast continued nuclear proliferation, the emergence of both regional and nationwide missile defense systems, and the possibility of vertical proliferation focused on qualitative improvement in nuclear weapons among major nuclear powers—especially the United States.[72] These changing perceptions of the international nuclear environment play a central role in debates in many circles (especially within the PLA) about China's future nuclear capabilities and doctrine.

Conclusions

Understanding nuclear doctrine is critical to analyzing the uncertain and evolving portrait of China's comprehensive nuclear modernization effort. Doctrine, a heretofore underexamined aspect of this nuclear upgrade campaign, sheds light on the linkages between Chinese national security goals and the mechanical dimensions of the nuclear modernization enterprise. Doctrinal thinking about the requirements of strategic deterrence has become far more widespread, sophisticated, and institutionalized in the last decade—especially in the professional military community. Doctrine appears to be playing an increasingly important role in guiding modernization. Thus, the doctrinal horse now appears to be firmly in front of the force structure cart, in stark contrast to the first few decades of China's nuclear weapons program.

The availability of new Chinese sources combined with a greater willingness in China to discuss nuclear strategy questions has opened the door to exploring an issue that long resided in darkness and confusion—both within China as well as outside. Indeed, Beijing's increased willingness to talk and write about nuclear doctrine is part and parcel of the broader "internationalization" of China. Although it has been over two decades since China adopted Deng's "reform and openness" policies, accelerating interaction with transnational communities of experts is beginning to influence positively Beijing's willingness to discuss such sensitive topics.

Access to new research materials serves many purposes: they confirm past beliefs, dispel others, and reveal the multifaceted and textured nature of Chinese thinking about the roles and missions of nuclear weapons. The most immediate conclusion to be drawn from the above analysis is that current doctrine may indeed be evolving, in response to more and higher quality internal deliberations as well as external stimuli. It is a moving target and should be assessed from that vantage point. There are several core ideas and biases that permeate strategic thinking and will likely continue to inform both force structure modernization and operational nuclear planning. Achieving a credible deterrent in perpetuity by taking various measures to improve survivability will be the main preoccupation of Chinese leaders, military planners, and defense scientists alike in the coming years.

Yet, some elements of these core doctrinal concepts are malleable and potentially subject to change. Future modification or abandonment of China's no-first-use pledge is perhaps the most obvious possibility. In addition, Chinese efforts to reinterpret or broaden certain key concepts (such as "key-point counterstrikes" or "counter nuclear deterrence") could move the military farther down the nuclear doctrinal continuum toward a set of policies which consider using nuclear weapons in limited conflicts for discrete purposes, such as escalation control and/or damage limitation strikes. A Taiwan contingency is the most obvious reference point for this. While most Chinese analysts often reject such notions, some military writings about doctrine seem to countenance them as measures of last resort.

There are few signs of significant changes in thinking to date, both in terms of doctrinal writings or force structure modernization. However, Chinese perceptions of the international strategic environment have changed in recent years, affected in particular by US missile defense plans, proliferation trends in Asia, and shifting US nuclear posture. The changing nature of the "international situation" and China's "strategic requirements" could lead China—as its capabilities improve—to reconsider whether its possession of such a modest nuclear force and doctrinal orientation is sufficient to meet its national security demands. In this sense, the term "sufficiency and effectiveness" best captures the multilayered and dynamic nature of China's current approach to nuclear doctrine.

The barriers to major doctrinal changes are not insignificant, save a major and dramatic shift for the worse in China's security situation. There are military, economic, and political impediments to such moves. The predominant military thought of Mao and Deng, which is still highly revered as orthodoxy in the PLA, has long emphasized the value of possessing only a modest-sized nuclear arsenal focused on ensuring survivability; this orthodoxy further emphasizes that nuclear weapons are only a *part* of China's overall national military deterrent, not its core. Such a strategic orthodoxy is not easily overcome in a Party-led army like the PLA.

Economically, China's top leaders have multiple priorities in addition to PLA modernization, such as ensuring domestic stability and repairing the myriad social dislocations caused by rapid but decidedly uneven growth. Similarly, PLA leaders have a long list of military priorities, of which nuclear modernization is only one. PLA modernization is heavily focused on preparing for a conventional military contingency over Taiwan. Thus, among the PLA leadership there is an economic disincentive to overturn long-held beliefs about the modest role of nuclear weapons in warfare.

Politically, it is not clear that China's Fourth Generation political leaders would support a radical change in Chinese doctrine to a more activist nuclear posture. Their calculations are not just based on resource constraints. Such a step would represent a radical break with past Chinese leadership approaches to nuclear weapons—a risky move for a new slate of leaders. In addition, such a move is also inconsistent with China's current foreign policy and "international position," to use the Chinese parlance. China's new leaders are trying to promote an image of China as "a responsible major power" (*fuzeren de daguo*) engaged in a "peaceful rise" (*heping jueqi*). A new, more offensively oriented nuclear doctrine may not be welcome by China's leaders, as it could be costly for China's broader foreign policy goals and its international image.

This chapter concludes by offering possible indicators of future changes in China's nuclear doctrine. These include Chinese efforts to conditionalize or abandon the NFU pledge, redefinition of core doctrinal concepts, discussions of more focused nuclear targeting for damage limitation purposes, development of MIRV warheads, or explicit adoption of launch doctrines such as LUA or LOW. Additional possible indicators include the nature of China's responses to US missile defense plans and debates about force structure modernization priorities such as the relative importance of land-based versus sea-based ballistic missile capabilities. While some of the indicators are already appearing, it is not yet clear how they fit into the overall mosaic of Chinese doctrine. An issue that would benefit from continued research is China's views on nuclear signaling, especially wartime signaling. This topic, in particular, will significantly improve the prospects for crisis stability in US-China relations. It is also potentially an issue open to discussion with Chinese officials and scholars. Collectively, all of these variables demand continued attention by the international community of China watchers and nuclear mavens alike. Chinese nuclear doctrine is the subject of sustained debate within the PLA and the broader Chinese community of nuclear and international security strategists. It may change in shape, color, and contour in the coming years, and these developments hold direct implications for US national security and Asian stability.

Notes

1. Nuclear doctrine in this chapter is defined as (1) the concepts and ideas which define the roles and missions of nuclear weapons for the Chinese military and (2) the policies used to achieve the former, including those specifically related to targeting, timing, and basing of nuclear weapons and associated delivery systems—missiles, bombers, and sea-based platforms. This conception of "nuclear doctrine" is applied to the Chinese context in the second section of the chapter.

2. The term "nuclear posture" is defined in this chapter as a comprehensive and collective term to include nuclear doctrine, nuclear force structure capabilities and deployment, and employment practices and policies.

3. Obvious exceptions to this are Alastair Iain Johnston, "China's New 'Old Thinking': The Concept of Limited Deterrence," *International Security,* vol. 20, no. 3 (Winter 1995/96): 5–42; Alastair Iain Johnston, "Prospects for Chinese Nuclear Force Modernization: Limited Deterrence versus Multilateral Arms Control," *China Quarterly,* no. 146 (June 1996): 548–576. Also see Michael Chase and Evan S. Medeiros, "China's Evolving Nuclear Calculus: Modernization and the Doctrinal Debate," in *A Revolution in Doctrinal Affairs,* David Finkelstein and James Mulvenon, eds. (Santa Monica, CA: The RAND Corporation, forthcoming).

4. This is the view depicted in the seminal study on China's nuclear bomb program, John Wilson Lewis and Xue Litai, *China Builds the Bomb* (Stanford, CA: Stanford University Press, 1988). Also see Xue Litai, "The Evolution of China's Nuclear Strategy," in *Strategic Views from the Second Tier,* John C. Hopkins and Weixing Hu, eds. (New Brunswick, NJ: Transaction Publishers, 1995), 167–192.

5. On this point see David Finkelstein and James Mulvenon, eds., *A Revolution in Doctrinal Affairs* (Santa Monica, CA: The RAND Corporation, forthcoming); Testimony of David Finkelstein, *Hearing On Military Modernization and the Cross-Strait Balance,* before the US-China Economic and Security Review Commission, February 6, 2004.

6. These issues are addressed in Desmond Ball, "US Strategic Forces: How Would They Be Used?" *International Security,* vol. 7, no. 3 (Winter 1982–1983): 31–60. In this article, Ball specifically addresses the issue of the discontinuity between declaratory and operational nuclear policy.

7. Lawrence Freedman, *The Evolution of Nuclear Strategy* (New York: St Martin's Press, 1981), 245–249; Lawrence Freedman, "The First Two Generations of Nuclear Strategists," in *Makers of Modern Strategy,* Peter Paret, ed. (Princeton, NJ: Princeton University Press, 1986), 735–778.

8. John Battilega, "Soviet Views of Nuclear Warfare: The Post–Cold War Interviews," unpublished manuscript (Denver: Science Applications International Corporation, n.d.).

9. *China's National Defense in 2000* (Beijing: State Council Information Office, October 2000), www.china.org.cn/e-white/2000/index.htm.

10. David Shambaugh, *Modernizing China's Military: Progress, Problems and*

Prospects (Berkeley: University of California Press, 2003), 56–60.

11. This hierarchy can be found in Chen Haoling, *Junshi Kexue Wenxian Xinxi Jiansuo Zhinan* (*Research Guide for Military Science Documents and Information*) (Beijing: Junshi Kexue Chubanshe, 2000); also Shambaugh, 58–59.

12. Bates Gill, James C. Mulvenon, and Mark Stokes, "The Chinese Second Artillery Corps: Transition to Credible Deterrence," in *The People's Liberation Army as Organization,* James C. Mulvenon and Andrew N.D. Yang, eds. (Santa Monica, CA: RAND, 2002), 510–586.

13. This is detailed in Lewis and Xue, *China Builds the Bomb,* and Xue, "The Evolution of China's Nuclear Strategy."

14. According to John Gittings, the United States threatened China seven times with the use of force, though not all of them were nuclear threats. Two were during the Korean War in February and May 1953; three were made by John Foster Dulles to deter Chinese intervention in Indochina on September 2, 1953, December 29, 1952, and March 29, 1954; and the last two were made by Dulles (March 8, 1955) and Eisenhower (September 1958) in the context of the Quemoy and Matsu crises. The latter two were nuclear threats. John Gittings, *The World and China* (Oxford: Oxford University Press, 1967), 203.

15. These are documented in Lewis and Xue, *China Builds the Bomb,* 11 and 72.

16. Evan Feigenbaum, *China's Techno-Warriors* (Stanford, CA: Stanford University Press, 2003).

17. Li Bin, "The Impact of US NMD on Chinese Nuclear Modernization," *Pugwash Online,* April 2001, www.pugwash.org/reports/rc/rc8e.htm.

18. This point is also made in Xue Litai and in Johnston "Chinese Nuclear Force Modernization."

19. Xue Litai, 171.

20. Mao Zedong as quoted in Xue Litai, 171.

21. China's official statement following its first test can be found in Lewis and Xue, 241.

22. "Dier Paobing Junshi Xueshu," (Second Artillery Military Studies), in *Junshixue Yanjiu Huigu yu Zhanwang* (*Military Academic Research Review and Prospects*) (Beijing: Academy of Military Sciences Press, 1995), 358–371. (Hereafter this book is referred to as JXYHZ.)

23. JXYHZ, 361.

24. Ibid.

25. This argument is made in James Mulvenon, "Chinese and Mutually Assured Destruction: Is China Getting MAD?" in *Getting MAD: Nuclear Mutual Assured Destruction, Its Origins and Practice,* Henry D. Sokolski, ed. (Carlisle, PA: Strategic Studies Institute, US Army War College, November 2004), 239–260.

26. Li Fumin and Li Dunsong, "A Brief Account of the Growth and Development of Our Country's Strategic Missile Troops," *Junshi Shilin* (*Military History*), no. 5 (1988): 51.

27. Shi Yan, "Creation and Development of China Second Artillery Corps," *Junshi Shilin,* no. 6 (1989): 48.

28. These types of regulations are critical because they provide the institutional foundation for implementing the various concepts and principles that senior leaders have promoted.

29. JXYHZ, 366.

30. David M. Finkelstein, *China Reconsiders Its National Security* (Alexandria, VA: Center for Naval Analyses, December 2000), 8–9.

31. This fascinating 1980s debate is detailed in JXYHZ, 361–362.

32. This definition is from John DeFrancis, *ABC Chinese-English Comprehen-*

sive Dictionary (Honolulu: University of Hawaii Press, April 2003).

33. JXYHZ, 361–362.

34. Evan S. Medeiros, "A Cultural Evolution: The Development of China's Arms Control and Nonproliferation Community," in *Integrating a Rising Power into Global Nonproliferation Regimes: US-China Negotiations and Interactions on Nonproliferation, 1980–2001*, unpublished doctoral dissertation, 2002.

35. These arguments are detailed in Medeiros, "A Cultural Evolution," based on extensive interviews with Chinese arms control experts.

36. 1991 was chosen as a cutoff date largely because the gradual shifts in Chinese thinking about nuclear weapons generally coincide with the major changes in international politics that began in 1991 with the collapse of the Soviet Union.

37. Brad Roberts, *China-US Nuclear Relations: What Relationship Best Serves US Interests?* (Alexandria, VA: Institute for Defense Analyses, August 2001).

38. See Zhao Xijun, ed., *Shezhan* (*Deterrence Warfare*) (Beijing: Guofang Daxue Chubanshe, May 2003), 180–193.

39. Gu Dexin and Niu Yongjun, *Heyouling De Zhengdong—Ershishiji Hewenti Huihu Yu Sikao* (*Rumblings of the Nuclear Specter: Looking Back at and Considering the Nuclear Problem in the 20th Century*) (Beijing: Guofang Daxue Chubanshe, 1999), 274–288.

40. Ibid., 282.

41. Wu Kai, "Dui He Liliang De Sikao," (Military Experts Discuss Nuclear Capability), *Bingqi Zhishi* (*Ordnance Knowledge*), April 2001. This article is an interview with Zheng Zhiren.

42. Interviews with Chinese analysts involved in nuclear weapons policy, Beijing, China, 2003 and 2004.

43. This section draws heavily on the following sources: Xue Xinglin, ed., *Zhanyi Lilun Xuexi Zhinan* (*Campaign Theory Study Guide*) (Beijing: Guofang Daxue Chubanshe, 2001); Wang Hongqing and Zhang Xingye, eds., *Zhanyixue* (*The Science of Military Campaigns*) (Beijing: Guofang Daxue Chubanshe, May 2000); Wang Wenrong, ed., *Zhanluexue* (*The Science of Military Strategy*) (Beijing: Guofang Daxue Chubanshe, 1999); Yao Youzhi and Peng Guangqian, eds., *Zhanluexue* (Beijing: Junshi Kexue Chubanshe, 2001); *Zhanyixue Yanjiu* (*Research on the Science of Military Campaigns*) (Beijing: Guofang Daxue Chubanshe, 1997), 278–286; Gu Dexin and Niu Yongjun, 274–288; Hu Guangzheng, ed., *Zhongwai Junshi Zuzhi Tizhi Bijiao Jiaocheng* (*Teaching Materials on a Comparison of Chinese and Foreign Military Organizational Systems*) (Beijing: Junshi Kexue Chubanshe, 1999), 223–250.

44. One source refers to these first two concepts as "the guiding ideology (*zhidao sixiang*)" for Second Artillery counterstrike campaigns. See Xue Xinglin, 386–387.

45. Ibid.

46. Wu Kai, 2.

47. *Zhanyixue*, 370.

48. Alastair Iain Johnston, "Some Thoughts on Chinese Nuclear Deterrence," paper prepared for a conference on Chinese military doctrine, The CNA Corporation, February 2, 2000.

49. Yang Ruxue, "The Second Artillery's Application of Deterrence in Hi-Tech War," unpublished manuscript; also see Zhao Xijun, 180–193. This latter source includes a specific discussion of "missile deterrence methods" (*daodan weishe fangfa*), which encompasses non-nuclear strikes using nuclear-capable missiles to deter an adversary.

50. Interviews with Chinese military officials, government analysts, and university-based scholars, Beijing, China, 2002–2004. Also see Johnston, "Some Thoughts on Chinese Nuclear Deterrence."

51. Johnston, "Some Thoughts on Chinese Nuclear Deterrence," 5–6.

52. Yao Yunzhu, "Differences Between Western and Chinese Deterrence Theories" (unpublished manuscript) as noted in Johnston, "Some Thoughts on Chinese Nuclear Deterrence."

53. Xue Xinglin, 386–387.

54. This is a PLA-wide principle that applies to all sorts of conventional operations as well. See Taylor Fravel, "The Evolution of China's Military Strategy: Comparing the 1987 and 1999 Editions of *Zhanlue Xue*," paper presented at RAND-CNA meeting on "The Revolution in Doctrinal Affairs," December 2002.

55. In November 1983, in discussions with foreign guests, Deng Xiaoping said: "If you want to destroy us, you yourselves will suffer key-point retaliation." Gu Dexin and Niu Yongjun.

56. It is important to note that when discussing conventional military operations, Chinese military texts refer to key-point strikes or *zhongdian daji*, but in discussing nuclear matters they specifically use the slightly different terminology of key-point counterstrikes or *zhongdian fanji.*

57. Xue Xinglin, 385–386.

58. Ibid.

59. *Zhanyixue,* 369.

60. To be sure, a third possibility is that Chinese nuclear planners understand neither the basic principles of nuclear deterrence nor the limits of their own nuclear capabilities.

61. Yao Youzhi and Peng Guangqian, *Zhanluexue;* Johnston, "Some Thoughts on Chinese Nuclear Deterrence."

62. Another way to translate this term is counter nuclear intimidation, as it captures the counter-coercion element of this distinctly Chinese concept. The author is grateful to Lonnie Henley for highlighting this alternative translation of this term.

63. *Science of Military Campaigns,* 372.

64. Scott Sagan et al., "The Madman Nuclear Alert: Secrecy, Signaling, and Safety in October 1969," *International Security,* vol. 27, no. 4 (2003): 150–183.

65. This discussion draws from Michael Chase and Evan S. Medeiros, "China's Evolving Nuclear Calculus: Modernization and the Doctrinal Debate."

66. All of these quotations are drawn from *Science of Military Campaigns,* 370–371.

67. Wu Peng and Si Shilei, "Study of Consequences of Attacks on Nuclear and Chemical Facilities," *Guofang,* September 15, 2002, 19–20, as translated in FBIS. Taiwanese officials stated in June 2004 that they possess the capability to conduct such strikes. See Jacky Hsu and Shi Jiangtao, "Taipei Says its Forces Could Hit the Three Gorges Dam, But Do Not Plan To," *South China Morning Post,* June 10, 2004.

68. There are numerous Western and Chinese reports about China's views regarding US national and theater ballistic missile defense programs. See Kori Urayama, "China Debates Missile Defense," *Survival,* Summer 2004, 123–142; Li Bin, Zhou Baogen, and Liu Zhiwei, "China Will Have to Respond," *Bulletin of the Atomic Scientists,* vol. 57, no. 6 (November/December 2001): 25–28; Paul Godwin and Evan S. Medeiros, "China, America, and Missile Defense: Conflicting National Interests," *Current History,* vol. 99, no. 638 (September 2000), 285–289; and Brad Roberts, *China and Ballistic Missile Defense: 1955 to 2002 and Beyond* (Alexandria, VA: Institute for Defense Analyses, September 2003).

69. Conversations with Chinese diplomats and military officers, March and October 2003; "Spokesman Answers a Question on US News Report that China has Become a Target of US Nuclear Weapons," Chinese Foreign Ministry website, March 11, 2002; Zhu Ming, "Be Prepared To Use Nuclear Weapons—Logic of 'Absolute

Security,'" *Jiefang Ribao,* March 12, 2002, as translated in FBIS; Zhou Jianguo, "Nuclear Strategy of Bush Administration Moving Gradually From Deterrence to Actual Combat," *Jiefangjun Bào,* March 18, 2002; Li Bin: "Are US Nuclear Weapons Aimed at China?" *Shijie Zhishi,* April 1, 2002, 16–17, as translated in FBIS.

70. Wu Rui and Li Bin, "The Impact of US Nuclear Policies on China—A Political Perspective," paper presented at the Conference on Northeast Asian Security: A Mixture of Traditional and Untraditional Security, jointly organized by Renmin University, China; London School of Economics and Political Science, UK; University of Durham, UK; and Free University, Brussels, Belgium, April 2–3, 2004, in Beijing, China, http://learn.tsinghua.edu.cn/homepage/2000990313/4042.htm.

71. On changes in Russian doctrine see Nikolai Sokov, "Russian Ministry of Defense's New Policy Paper: The Nuclear Angle," Monterey, CA: Center for Nonproliferation Studies, http://cns.miis.edu; Chinese concerns about these developments are based on interviews in March and October 2003, Beijing, China.

72. These views are prevalent among Chinese strategists. See JXYHZ, 364–371; Wu Kai; Li Bin, "Saving Arms Control," *Beijing Review,* April 18, 2002; and Wei Qiyong, Qin Zhijin, and Liu Erxun, "Analysis of Changing Emphasis in US Military Strategy," *Daodan yu Hangtian Yunzai Jishu* (*Missile and Aerospace Delivery Technology*), August 10, 2002.

4

Strategic Force Modernization

Phillip C. Saunders and Jing-dong Yuan

Ever since China deployed its first intercontinental ballistic missiles (ICBMs) in 1981, strategic modernization has been an important goal for the People's Republic of China (PRC). China's first ICBMs were crude missiles with significant operational limitations compared to the fourth generation ICBMs that the United States and the Soviet Union were developing and deploying in the 1980s. Although China's initial ICBMs had an important symbolic value and supported China's nuclear doctrine of minimum deterrence, Chinese weapons designers and strategists urged leaders to support efforts to develop a new generation of nuclear warheads and ballistic missiles that would incorporate technological improvements. The Chinese leadership's overall policy priorities, resource constraints, and technological impediments resulted in relatively slow progress in Chinese strategic modernization programs over the last two decades. However, recent assessments of Chinese current and potential strategic capabilities by western intelligence agencies and academic experts have generated renewed debate on the future trajectory of Chinese nuclear forces.

Three sets of considerations are driving renewed international interest in Chinese strategic modernization.[1] The first is the potential impact of China's strategic modernization on global arms control and nonproliferation efforts. The post–Cold War era has seen increased emphasis on the threat posed by the proliferation of nuclear, chemical, and biological weapons of mass destruction and their delivery systems. China's strategic modernization efforts might directly or indirectly stimulate proliferation in other countries and might also damage prospects for significant global arms control agreements. For example, India cited the threat from Chinese nuclear weapons as a justification for its 1998 nuclear tests.[2] China is building up its nuclear arsenal while the other declared nuclear weapons states are all reducing the number of their deployed nuclear weapons, including the recent nuclear arms reduction agreement between the United States and Russia limiting their respective strategic arsenals to a ceiling of 2,200 each by 2012.[3]

A second consideration is the potential impact of improved Chinese nuclear and missile capabilities on US security interests and on regional security in Asia. One dimension focuses on the implications for the US ability to fulfill its alliance commitments and to intervene in regional conflicts in the Asia-Pacific region. This concern is most salient over China's possible use of military threats or force against Taiwan. A second dimension concerns the longer-term implications of China's rising power for Sino-US relations. Interactions between US efforts to deploy ballistic missile defenses (BMD) and China's strategic modernization could generate an action-reaction spiral that leads to a strategic arms race. Even if this outcome is avoided, increased strategic mistrust and suspicion in the strategic realm could easily spill over into the broader bilateral relationship in a variety of negative and potentially destabilizing ways.[4]

A third factor is uncertainty about China's future strategic intentions as it grows more powerful. Does China's strategic modernization primarily reflect a desire to achieve a stable deterrent relationship with other great powers? Is it an indication that China is increasingly concerned about the implications of US BMD for the effectiveness of its limited nuclear retaliatory capabilities? Or does it reflect the determination of China's leaders to have the strategic forces necessary to support their ambition to recover lost territories and dominate the East Asian region? Rising nationalism, a new generation of political leaders, and uncertainty about China's future economic and political stability all create concerns about how China's growing strategic capabilities might be used in the future.

This chapter analyzes ongoing Chinese strategic force modernization in terms of delivery system modernization, efforts to improve education and training, future directions, and major resource and technological constraints. Any assessment must also take account of evolving Sino-US political relations and the potential impact of US ballistic missile defense deployments. Developments in these areas will greatly influence Beijing's decisions on the size and composition of its future strategic force and on its arms control and nonproliferation commitments. China's strategic force modernization in turn will affect the security calculus of Russia, India, and Japan. The direct and indirect impact of Chinese decisions about strategic force structure could have a ripple effect that challenges stability in both East Asia and South Asia.

China's Strategic Force Modernization

China's initial quest for a nuclear capability was motivated by recognition of the political value of nuclear weapons and by Mao Zedong's determination to remove China's vulnerability to nuclear blackmail.[5] Following its first nuclear test in 1964, Beijing announced that it would adhere to a policy of no-first-use (NFU) of nuclear weapons and called for worldwide nuclear disarmament.[6] Alone among the original five nuclear weapon states, China adopted a minimal deterrent strategy relying on a small number of nuclear weapons to deliver punitive, countervalue responses to an adversary's first strike. China's choice of minimal deterrence was influenced both by political factors and by technological constraints on its nuclear arsenal and delivery systems. China initially relied on Hong-6 (B-6 BADGER) and Qiang-5 (A-5 FANTAN) aircraft as its nuclear delivery systems. However, as China's ballistic missile capabilities improved, land-based missiles became the primary nuclear weapons delivery system beginning in the 1970s, supplemented by a single *Xia* class (Type 092) nuclear-powered ballistic missile submarine operationally deployed with its missiles in 1988.[7]

China's land-based strategic and tactical ballistic missiles are operated by the PLA's Strategic Missile Force (SMF, or *zhanlue daodan budui*), also known as the Second Artillery Corps (*di'er paobing*). The Strategic Missile Force was formally established in July 1966, although surface-to-surface missile troops (*diduidi daodan budui*) have existed since December 1957. The first SMF Commander was Xiang Shouzhi and the first Political Commissar was Li Tianhuan, both survivors of the Long March.[8] Composed of 100,000 officers, noncommissioned officers, and regular conscripts, the Second Artillery Corps is the smallest of the various services and branches in the PLA's order of battle. In 1984, the Central Military Commission (CMC) conducted a major restructuring of the PLA and assigned strategic alert (*zhanlue zhiban*) responsibilities to the SMF, placing Second Artillery Corps missile units on alert to respond to a nuclear attack. The SMF was reorganized to reduce the number of engineering units while enhancing and expanding the overall combat capabilities of launch units and relevant support units.[9] In addition to its strategic nuclear mission, the Second Artillery Corps also operates China's conventionally armed short-range ballistic missile (SRBM) forces. The current Commander and Political Commissar are, respectively, Jing Zhiyuan and Sui Mingtai.[10]

The Second Artillery Corps is organized around a central headquarters (*lingdao jiguan* or *zongbu*) in Xishan (northwest of Beijing), and six army-level bases (*junji jidi;* see Appendix 1 for a breakout). In all, the Second Artillery has six organizational levels: (1) headquarters; (2) army-level missile bases; (3) missile brigades (*daodanlü*); (4) launch battalions (*fasheying*); (5) launch companies (*fashelian*); and (6) launch platoons (*fashepai*). The top three levels are each broken out into four subordinate departments: headquarters department (*silingbu*), political department (*zhengzhibu*), logistics department (*houqinbu*), and the technical equipment department (*jishu zhuangbeibu*). Levels 5 and 6 are sometimes also referred to as launch units (*fashe fendui*). For nuclear forces, launch battalions are the basic firepower units (*jiben huoli danwei*), while conventional missile forces use launch platoons as the basic firepower units.[11]

A widely cited source estimates that China's current nuclear forces consist of more than 400 warheads, including about 280 strategic warheads and about 120 tactical warheads (see Table 4.1).[12] China's strategic arsenal is deployed on a triad that includes about 130 land-based missiles, 130 strategic bombers, and one ballistic missile submarine equipped with twelve submarine-launched ballistic missiles (SLBMs). China's "East Wind" (*dongfeng*) series of land-based strategic missiles ranges from the 1800-km DF-21A (CSS-5) to the 13,000-km+ DF-5A (CSS-4) ICBM, which is capable of striking targets throughout the continental United States. China's tactical nuclear weapons may include artillery shells, atomic demolition munitions, and short-range missiles. Although this estimate provides a useful starting point, it is unclear whether China's aging strategic bomber force still has a nuclear mission and open-source evidence on the existence of Chinese tactical nuclear weapons is scanty.[13]

Land-Based Ballistic Missiles

Land-based ballistic missiles are the mainstay of China's strategic nuclear deterrent. Chinese missiles suffer from several weaknesses compared to equivalent US and Russian strategic missile forces. China's ICBM force is composed of low-accuracy missiles equipped with high-yield warheads. These missiles are based in silos and caves that are vulnerable to nuclear attack. Most current missiles use liquid fuel propellant

Table 4.1 Estimate of Current Chinese Nuclear Forces

Delivery system	NATO designation	Number	Year deployed	Range (km)	Warhead x yield (Mt/kt)	Number of warheads
Strategic Weapons						
Land-based Missiles						
DF-3A	CSS-2	40	1971	2,900	1 x 3.3 Megaton (Mt)	40
DF-4	CSS-3	12	1980	5,500	1 x 3.3 Mt	12
DF-5A	CSS-4	20 (18–26)	1981	13,000	1 x 4–5 Mt	20 (18–26)
DF-21A	CSS-5	48	1985–1986	1,800	1 x 200–300 kiloton (kt)	48
SLBMs						
JL-1	CSS-N-3	12	1988	>1,000	1 x 200–300 kt	12
Aircraft						
Hong-6	B-6 BADGER	100	1965	3,100	1–3 x bomb	100
Qiang-5	A-5 FANTAN	30	1970	400	1 x bomb	30
Tactical Weapons						120
Artillery						
Atomic						
Demolition						
Munitions						
SRBMs						
DF-15 (M-9)	CSS-6	300–350		200–600	10–20 kt	
DF-11 (M-11)	CSS-7	100		200–300	(most/all have conventional warheads)	
Total						400

Source: Adapted from Robert S. Norris and Hans M. Kristensen, "Nuclear Notebook: Chinese Nuclear Forces, 2003," *Bulletin of the Atomic Scientists,* vol. 59, no. 6 (November/December 2003): 77–80.

and must be fueled and have their warheads attached before they can be launched. As a consequence, China's ICBM force has a relatively low level of readiness and cannot support a launch-on-warning or launch-under-attack doctrine. Moreover, the lack of ground- and space-based early warning systems means that China might not have reliable warning of an attack on its nuclear arsenal. As a result, China's current strategic missiles have a relatively low ability to survive an adversary's disarming first strike. China has attempted to compensate for this vulnerability by building false silos and concealing the precise number of ICBMs in its inventory to reduce an adversary's confidence that a first strike could destroy all of China's ICBMs.[14] Chinese leaders have lived with a relatively vulnerable nuclear force for decades, but China's strategic modernization efforts are aimed at creating a force less vulnerable to a nuclear first strike.

China has begun deploying a new generation of solid-fueled mobile missiles as part of efforts to upgrade the capabilities of its land-based strategic missile force (see Table 4.2). The DF-21A is the first of these missiles, which may incorporate advanced technologies such as Global Positioning System (GPS) or radar-based terminal guidance systems for improved accuracy.[15] China was expected to retire its older liquid-fueled missiles as more advanced missiles became available, but appears to be retaining older missiles in its active forces for now. China has also been replacing DF-5 missiles deployed in the 1980s with longer-range DF-5A variants that could potentially be fitted with multiple warheads. China's medium- and intermediate-range missile forces include:

- DF-3A (CSS-2) liquid-fueled medium-range ballistic missiles, which were expected to be replaced by newer generation DF-21A missiles.[16] (China sold 20–30 older DF-3s to Saudi Arabia in 1988, which are reportedly now nearing the end of their service life.) However, the 2003 Department of Defense report on PRC military power indicates that DF-21A missiles are *supplementing* the DF-3A rather than *replacing* the older system, which was initially deployed in 1971.[17] This suggests that China is placing a higher priority on maintaining its existing nuclear force posture even as it deploys a newer generation of more capable missiles. Increasing maintenance costs as DF-3A missiles age, inherent operational limitations of liquid fueled missiles, and the rationale for consolidating training and maintenance suggest that DF-3A missiles will eventually be retired.

Table 4.2 China's Current and Projected Strategic Missile Forces

Chinese designation	NATO designation	Initial operational capability	Fuel/ Basing	Range (Km)	Warhead yield/type
DF-3/3A	CSS-2	1971	Liquid/ Transportable	2,800	1–3 mt
DF-4	CSS-3	1980	Liquid/cave	4,750	2 mt
DF-5/5A	CSS-4	1981	Liquid/silo	13,000	3-5 mt MRV[b]
DF-21/21A	CSS-5	1986	Solid/TEL	1,800	200–300 kt
JL-1	CSS-N-3	1988	Liquid/SLBM	>1,000	250 kt
DF-31[a]	CSS-X-9	Tested in 1999, 2000, and 2001	Solid/TEL	8,000	unknown
DF-31A[a]	none	Under development	Solid/TEL	12,000	unknown
JL-2 (based on DF-31)	CSS-NX-5	Under development; Tested	Solid/SLBM	8,000[a]	unknown

Source: Adapted from Robert S. Norris and Hans M. Kristensen, "Nuclear Notebook: Chinese Nuclear Forces, 2003," *Bulletin of the Atomic Scientists,* vol. 59, no. 6 (November/December 2003): 77–80.

Notes: a. The Cox Commission report gives a 7,500-mile (12,000 km) range for the JL-2 missile. See House Report 105-851, *Report of the Select Committee on US National Security and Military/Commercial Concerns with the People's Republic of China,* 187, www.access.gpo.gov/congress/house/hr105851/VI-09-Chap4.pdf. However the source cited for this estimate, the Department of Defense's 1998 report *Ballistic and Cruise Missile Threat,* actually gives an estimate of "4,500 miles +" (8,000 km +) for the JL-2. For an updated version of the National Air Intelligence Center's report *Ballistic and Cruise Missile Threat,* see www.acq.osd.mil/mda/mdalink/bcmt/slbm_4.htm.

b. Suspected but unconfirmed.

- DF-4 (CSS-3) missiles that were deployed beginning in 1980. These missiles may still have some useful service life left, but will likely be retired once a sufficient number of newer-generation DF-31 missiles become available. If Chinese military leaders feel a strong sense of threat, they may retain the DF-4 force indefinitely.
- DF-5 and DF-5A (CSS-4 and CSS-4 mod 2) ICBMs, which are the only operational Chinese missiles capable of reaching all of the continental United States. China has been replacing older DF-5 missiles deployed in the 1980s with longer-range DF-5A variants, a process expected to be completed by mid-decade.[18] The new DF-5A missiles will remain highly vulnerable to a first strike,

but will serve as a hedge against delays in developing and deploying next generation ICBMs. China could keep the DF-5A in its force indefinitely if it feels the need to maximize the number of warheads the Second Artillery can deliver. Because liquid-fueled DF-5A missiles have more thrust than China's next generation of solid-fueled ICBMs, they may eventually be fitted with multiple warheads (if China chooses to deploy this capability).[19]

- The DF-21A (CSS-5), a solid-fueled, mobile missile, which represents the first of a new generation of Chinese strategic missiles. China is developing a variant of the DF-21A armed with a conventional warhead, and has reportedly been making efforts to improve the DF-21A's accuracy via upgraded guidance systems. One Japanese source claims a DF-21A was flight-tested with multiple warheads in December 2002, but if this test occurred it most likely consisted of a single warhead missile with several decoy warheads.[20]

China's next generation ICBMs, the DF-31 and DF-41, have been under development since the mid-1980s, but the development process has been plagued with delays. The road-mobile DF-31 and DF-41 missiles were originally intended to replace China's current generation DF-4 and DF-5A missiles, which are based in caves and silos. Although the DF-31 remains on track for deployment later this decade, the DF-41 program appears to have been cancelled. China is developing a longer-range variant of the DF-31, known as the DF-31A, which will be capable of reaching the east coast of the United States. China's ICBM modernization programs include:

- The DF-31 (CSS-X-9), an 8,000-km ICBM with an estimated circular error probable (CEP) of 1,000–2,000 feet. A three-stage, solid propellant, road-mobile ICBM mounted on a transporter-erector-launcher (TEL), the DF-31 has been flight-tested several times since 1999. Several tests have reportedly been successful; there are reports of at least one failure.[21] The DF-31 can target the western part of the United States, but cannot reach the east coast. The US Department of Defense originally expected the DF-31 to begin deployment "before mid-decade," likely in 2004 or 2005.[22] The 2005 Department of Defense (DOD) report on Chinese military power suggests the DF-31 will reach initial operational capability (IOC) in 2005–2006.[23] Chinese ballistic missile programs have frequently encountered delays during the development process.[24]

- The DF-41, a 12,000-km ICBM, that was being developed to replace China's aging DF-5A ICBMs. Several reports indicate that the DF-41 program has been cancelled,[25] and the system is not mentioned in the Pentagon's recent reports on China's military power. Unlike the DF-31, which was prominently displayed in the PRC's 50th Anniversary Parade in 1999, the DF-41 has never been seen in public. The DF-41 program may have been cancelled due to limitations in China's ability to miniaturize nuclear warheads. China is now developing the DF-31A, a longer-range variant of the DF-31, which is expected to supplement or replace the DF-5A.[26]

Nuclear-Powered Ballistic Missile Submarines (SSBNs)

China currently has only one SSBN, the Xia-class submarine (Type 092). Commissioned in 1981, the Xia carries 12 *Julang-1* (Great Wave) SLBMs and became operational in 1988. Each Julang-1 is armed with a single nuclear warhead and has a range of 2,150 km. The Xia SSBN has been plagued with technical problems and has rarely left port. The Xia began a five-year-long overhaul in 1995 and was reportedly sighted at sea in December 2000 PLAN exercises.[27] Although many analysts have questioned whether the Xia submarine is still operational, the fact that it has been overhauled and reequipped with JL-1 SLBMs suggests that China intends to keep the submarine operationally deployed for some time to come.[28]

Development of a new SSBN, the Type 094, began in the late 1980s and has continued for years without deployment.[29] The Type 094 SSBN is being built by the Nuclear Submarine Research Institute of the Chinese Naval Vessels Academy and the Nuclear Submarine Shipyard at Liaoning Province's Huludao Island. The new submarine is expected to incorporate significant improvements over the Xia in areas such as quieting and sensor systems, sonar, and propulsion. The first Type 094 is expected to be operational by the end of the decade.[30] The first prototype submarine has reportedly already been built. China may make additional refinements or improvements in the Type 094 design before beginning serial production. Reports have suggested that China may eventually build four to six Type 094 submarines. Each Type 094 will carry 16 Julang-2 (JL-2) missiles, a modified version of the DF-31.[31] However, the Type 094 project, like other Chinese submarine programs, has repeatedly encountered serious technological problems.[32] Technical and operational factors will likely create continuing difficulties for

Chinese efforts to redress the deficiencies in the submarine leg of its strategic triad.

Strategic Bombers

China possesses about 100 Hong-6 (B-6/BADGER) and 30 Qiang-5 (A-5/FANTAN) bombers believed to be dedicated to nuclear weapons delivery. The Hong-6 has a range of 3,100 km and can carry one to three nuclear bombs, while the Qiang-5 has a limited range of only 400 km and carries a single bomb. These aging bombers do not constitute a credible retaliatory force against adversaries equipped with modern air defenses. The People's Liberation Army Air Force's (PLAAF's) strategic bomber force is the weakest leg of the Chinese triad and has encountered various difficulties over the years, including maintenance problems and limited pilot flight training time common to other parts of China's air force.[33] Since the early 1990s, China has purchased advanced Russian fighters (including Su-27s and Su-30s) and deployed an indigenous fighter-bomber (the FB-7). However, there is no evidence to indicate that any of these aircraft will carry nuclear warheads. Despite repeated reports of possible Russian sales of bombers,[34] China does not appear to be making efforts to upgrade the air leg of its strategic triad. China's 2002 Defense White Paper refers to the nuclear missions of the Second Artillery Corps and the Navy's SSBN force, but makes no mention of a nuclear role for the Air Force.[35]

China's current strategic nuclear arsenal supports its doctrine of minimum deterrence, but lacks the accuracy, survivability, and C3I (command, control, communications, and intelligence) systems necessary for fighting in a nuclear environment. Moreover, there are significant deficiencies in China's nuclear triad compared to US and Russian strategic forces that call the survivability of China's nuclear deterrent into question, especially against an adversary with missile defenses. In the past, China has relied on decoy silos and uncertainty about the precise size of its ICBM force to deter potential attackers. The modernization programs discussed above will eventually produce a much more survivable Chinese nuclear deterrent.

Second Artillery Corps Education and Training Activities

In addition to modernizing its nuclear delivery systems, the Second Artillery Corps is making significant efforts to upgrade the quality of its personnel and to improve the training and readiness of its operational units.[36] Like other parts of the PLA, there is an increasing emphasis on formal academic credentials for Second Artillery Corps officers and technical cadres. The SMF has at least three academies that train command officers, staff, technical personnel, and non-commissioned officers. These include:

- The Second Artillery Corps Command Academy (*er pao zhihui xueyuan*) in Wuhan. This academy provides intermediate training for officers and advanced technical personnel.
- The Second Artillery Corps Engineering Academy (*er pao gongcheng xueyuan*) in Xi'an, a comprehensive university offering basic command and technical training for prospective SMF officers.
- The Second Artillery Corps Qingzhou Non-Commissioned Officers Academy (*di'er paobing qingzhou shiguan xuexiao*). This academy trains NCOs for the SMF.[37]

Two other PLA academies also train some Second Artillery Corps officers and technicians. These facilities are:

- The Langfang Army Missile Academy (*langfang lujun daodan xueyuan*) in Hebei Province. This academy trains command officers and technical personnel. Subjects include tactical missiles, missile launch engineering, and antitank missile command and control.
- The Missile Academy in the Air Force Engineering University (*kongjun gongcheng daxue daodan xueyuan*) in Xi'an. This academy focuses on surface-to-air missile defense and guidance radar engineering. About 2,300 cadets study computer engineering, electrical engineering, missile engineering, missile control and testing, and other subjects in six departments.[38]

Given the specialized nature and demands of the nuclear mission, the Second Artillery Corps has stringent requirements for personnel in terms of technical knowledge and skills and a greater need to retain its trained personnel. The retention problem is a PLA-wide issue, as the mandatory length of conscription service is reduced and as opportunities for employment in other sectors of the economy become more attractive relative to military service. The SMF has adopted several methods to deal with the changing situation. One is to develop and strengthen existing military academies charged with training command

and technical officers and NCOs for the SMF. As the above list indicates, at least five such academies are in place devoted to turning out officers and NCOs on a regular basis. According to *Jiefangjun Bao* (*PLA Daily*) reports, these academies have over the years introduced, modified, and improved courses covering various subject matter related to technical characteristics of ballistic missiles, missile engineering, command automation, missile firepower, air defense, launch engineering, and other relevant topics.[39]

A second method is to recruit qualified officer candidates from civilian university campuses. These candidates tend to have a wider range of background training including social sciences, natural sciences, and applied sciences. The SMF has also signed special agreements with civilian universities to train students for the SMF. Students at these universities receive full-tuition scholarships and are committed to serving in the SMF after graduation.[40] A third approach is to train qualified NCOs in order to retain their skills and encourage long-term service in the military. This may help compensate for reductions in the length of conscription service to two years. One SMF base has established a so-called talent inventory where over one thousand NCOs with special skills and comprehensive technical knowledge are listed. A system of selecting and rewarding skilled personnel has also been established at this base.[41] Some Second Artillery postdoctoral research personnel receive special allowances from the central government to help retain their skills for military use.[42] Another report indicates the Second Artillery Corps has some 160 professionals with doctorates or postdoctoral education. In addition to "better living and working conditions," these professionals receive one-time subsidies of 50,000 yuan (about US$6,000) to join the Second Artillery.[43]

The Second Artillery Corps has also devoted considerable effort to improving the quality of its training, including emphasis on real and simulated exercises. In recent years, SMF training has focused on rapid reaction, camouflage, mobility, electronic warfare, and precision attacks in order to improve combat capabilities under real wartime situations. For instance, training units are no longer allowed to select weather conditions, marching routes, and terrain situations. Instead, exercises are conducted in difficult circumstances, with tighter schedules and shorter reaction times. One launch company claimed to have mastered seventeen new methods of operating strategic missiles, enabling the unit to conduct all-weather and all-directional launches.[44] More realistic training probably contributes to improved combat effectiveness, but it is difficult to draw firm conclusions about Second Artillery capabilities from the available information.

Mobile launch capabilities and night movement have been another focus of SMF training exercises. Mobile launches have been a weak link in the SMF's warfighting ability. Enhancing survivability requires launch units to operate under mobile conditions and in night cover to avoid detection. This demands the ability to establish and maintain reliable communications, combat coordination, damage control, equipment repair, and rapid launch.[45] Combined training exercises are being introduced to improve coordination between command, technical, and logistics units, with the goal of integrating previously separate training activities.[46] Logistics support has been another area targeted for training improvements. Joint exercises involving various rear service, armament, and other logistics units in surveying, meteorological measurements, and intelligence gathering have been conducted at one SMF base to improve overall levels of coordination. Logistics units and launch units have also sought to develop closer coordination during launch exercises. For example, ordnance warehouses are now required to shorten the time for delivery of missile supplies under adverse weather conditions.[47] The SMF has also reportedly improved its surveying and mapping capabilities with the assistance of theater-specific, all-weather, highly accurate mobile equipment. This has enhanced operational capability by reducing reaction times and improving accuracy in hitting targets.[48]

Some SMF exercises increasingly use simulations of real-war situations in order to improve command and training systems, survivability, and counterattack capability. The entire process from preparing for missile launch to hitting targets can be simulated, as can the ability to monitor progress, assess the quality of the exercise, and raise the level of difficulty. It is interesting to note that in one exercise, the "red army" waited in underground facilities for several days before launching nuclear counterattacks.[49] The SMF's academies have played an important role in developing simulation equipment/systems to help troops to improve efficiency in training and handling complicated missile systems. The Second Artillery Corps Engineering Academy has developed a "simulation and training system for a certain missile model."[50] The PLA's Langfang Army Missile Academy has developed surface-to-surface campaign tactical missile simulation training programs suitable for training commanders at the missile brigade, launch battalion, and launch vehicle levels.[51]

The reports summarized above indicate that the Second Artillery Corps is making significant efforts to improve the quality and realism of training, with an emphasis on mobility, rapid reaction, and the ability to operate at night and in adverse weather conditions. These areas are critical to the ability of China's strategic nuclear forces to survive an adversary's first strike before launching retaliatory attacks. The reports suggest that logistics support, mechanization, and the frequency of combined exercises are improving, but from a fairly low baseline. The trends indicate that SMF training is moving in the right direction, but there still are unanswered questions with respect to quality of officer and NCO training and the overall effectiveness of SMF units.

Future Directions for Chinese Strategic Forces

The previous sections have described China's current nuclear forces, reviewed the strategic delivery systems currently in development, and examined efforts to improve the quality of Second Artillery Corps personnel and the operational training of strategic missile units. China's future strategic capabilities will ultimately depend on the size of its deployed nuclear arsenal and the ability of the Second Artillery Corps to use nuclear weapons and support systems to perform its missions of strategic deterrence and (if necessary) nuclear counterattack. This section examines how China's strategic capabilities and nuclear force structure are likely to evolve over the next ten to fifteen years. We expect that China will continue long-standing efforts to improve the survivability of its nuclear forces, work to defeat US missile defenses by deploying BMD countermeasures and increasing the size of its arsenal, and likely make modest efforts to enhance nuclear warfighting capabilities.

Improving Survivability

The central thrust of China's strategic modernization involves efforts to improve the survivability of China's nuclear forces via greater mobility, shortened launch preparation time, better command and control, and protection or concealment of hardened silos. China's strategic missile modernization is essentially following the same technological trajectory as the American and Soviet missile forces, albeit at a slower pace and in lesser numbers. This mode of modernization has been under way at a measured pace for two decades and will continue regardless of changes in the external environment. The delivery systems that will make up China's future nuclear forces are described above. A credible minimum deterrent in an environment *without* ballistic missile defenses would probably involve an expansion of the total number of Chinese ICBMs and SLBMs of intercontinental range, perhaps to a total of fifty to sixty warheads. This assessment is based on the assumption that China would want significant numbers of both land-based and sea-based missiles in order to diversify its delivery systems and guard against possible technological improvements in tracking mobile missiles or in antisubmarine warfare that could reduce the survivability of its nuclear forces. Some of this quantitative expansion is dictated by the fact that the addition of just two Type 094 SSBNs would add thirty-two warheads to China's arsenal.[52]

Since China first deployed ICBMs in the early 1980s, it has sought to maintain the credibility of its deterrent through quantitative ambiguity rather than by possession of a large nuclear arsenal.[53] When China first began to deploy its ICBMs, fake silos were built to improve the chances of China's fixed ICBM launch sites surviving an attack. China is now moving into a new stage where the credibility of its strategic nuclear deterrent will depend on the survivability, mobility, and effectiveness of its missile forces.[54] More mobile (and hence more survivable) nuclear forces reduce an adversary's confidence that a first strike could destroy most or all of China's missiles, thus enhancing the credibility of China's nuclear deterrent. A former deputy commander of the Second Artillery Corps highlighted survivability, accuracy, penetration capability, and quicker reaction times as areas where improvements in the Chinese strategic missile force were necessary.[55]

The current modernization program will replace liquid-fueled missiles based in caves and silos with solid-fueled, road-mobile missiles, resulting in significant increases in survivability, accuracy, and reduced launch preparation time (from 2–3 hours to 5–10 minutes). The DF-31 and the DF-31A missiles will form the core of the future Chinese land-based strategic missiles force. DF-31 missiles will likely enter service in 2005–2006, replacing older liquid-fueled DF-4 missiles.[56] The current assessment is that the DF-31 will be a single-warhead missile, although it may be equipped with decoy warheads and other countermeasures to penetrate US missile defenses.[57] The pace of DF-31 deployment will likely depend on whether additional development and production problems arise and on the Chinese leadership's perception of the urgency of reinforcing the credibility of its nuclear deterrent. The number of DF-31s that China deploys will depend partly on Chinese assessments of the effectiveness of US missile defenses in the face of Chinese BMD countermeasures. The status of the Type 094 SSBN program, China's ability to keep older DF-4 and DF-5A ICBMs operational, and any delays in development of the longer-range DF-31A ICBM will also influence the total number of DF-31 missiles. The DF-31A is expected to achieve IOC in 2007–2009.[58]

The second leg of China's efforts to build a more survivable nuclear force rests on the Julang-2 (JL-2), a second-generation SLBM that will be deployed on an indigenously produced second-generation Type 094 submarine. A solid-fueled missile based on the DF-31, the JL-2 is expected to have a maximum range of 8,000 km. Two successful tests of the rocket engine for the missile were conducted in 1983 and 1995, respectively.[59] The Pentagon expects the Type 094 SSBN to become operational by the end of the decade.[60] A recent press report claims that the first Type 094 submarine was launched in July 2004 and that the JL-2 missile suffered a flight test failure in 2004.[61] China's Xia SSBN required seven years between its initial launch (1981) and its first successful firing of a JL-1 missile (1988).[62] Advances in the Chinese missile and submarine programs since the 1980s will probably reduce the lag between initial launch and full operational capability, suggesting the Type 094 might be operational within four or five years. If the JL-2 missile and the Type 094 submarine perform as expected, the submarine leg of China's triad would become effective for the first time. Operational deployment of capable SSBNs would help preserve a Chinese second strike capability in the event of a nuclear first strike, thus significantly improving the survivability of China's nuclear deterrent. However once China's second generation SSBNs begin conducting operational patrols, the US Navy is likely to attempt to track them using US nuclear attack submarines, just as it routinely did with Soviet SSBNs. This may raise concerns about the survivability of Chinese SSBNs in the event of a conflict with the United States and will certainly increase the potential for collisions or accidents.

Although the modernization programs described above will give China a more survivable nuclear deterrent, they will also create new concerns about accidental or unauthorized launches. China's strategic nuclear forces are under the direct command of the Central Military Commission.[63] Little is known about the precise details of China's nuclear command and control system. China is not believed to use PAL (permissive-action-link) devices, which are a technical means of preventing accidental or unauthorized launches of nuclear weapons. However, a set of launch authorization procedures does exist, and the current separation of warheads and missiles reduces the chance of unauthorized launches.[64] China's new mobile ICBMs and SLBMs will have warheads mated with their missiles, reducing the effectiveness of physical security in preventing unauthorized launches. These missiles will push operational launch authority to lower levels, require a more sophisticated command and control system, and likely rely more heavily on technical means to prevent unauthorized launches.

Defeating Missile Defenses

Despite assertions by some US officials that US missile defense deployments will not affect China's strategic modernization efforts, the size, perceived effectiveness, and potential expandability of US missile defenses are likely to have a direct impact on the pace and scope of China's strategic modernization.[65] Deployment of even a thin ballistic missile defense system that protects the US homeland would threaten China's current strategic nuclear deterrent. Beijing worries that its limited number of ICBMs would not be able to penetrate a US national missile defense system after absorbing a US first strike. Chinese leaders are determined not to accept vulnerability to US nuclear blackmail as a permanent condition. China will most likely respond to US BMD deployments by increasing force levels and deploying new technologies as necessary to maintain a credible nuclear deterrent.[66] In addition to efforts to improve survivability, this will likely involve a significant increase in the number of new Chinese ICBMs aimed at US targets, retention of older strategic missile systems, deployment of countermeasures to penetrate or defeat US missile defenses, and the possible deployment of multiple warheads on China's DF-5A ICBM.

The rationale behind a strong Chinese reaction to US missile defenses and hence a larger strategic nuclear force is explained by Li Bin, a prominent Chinese nuclear strategist:

> Chinese nuclear deterrence depends directly on American perceptions about the Chinese nuclear retaliatory capability. . . . Without the backup of NMD [National Missle Defense], the Americans would always worry about a Chinese retaliation with the few Chinese nuclear weapons that might survive a US first nuclear strike against China. The deployment of an NMD system would provide the American public with an illusion that the several surviving retaliatory Chinese ICBMs would be intercepted by the NMD system—since it is both designed and said to be able to defeat attacks by small numbers of missiles. If the Americans tended to believe that a first nuclear strike plus an NMD system would be able to disarm the Chinese nuclear retaliatory capability, the US could become incautious in risking nuclear exchanges with China in a crisis.[67]

Chinese concerns over US missile defenses are driven by both assessments of Washington's strategic intentions toward Beijing and the extent to which the credibility and effectiveness of China's small-size nuclear retaliatory capabilities would be undermined by US missile defense deployments. Beijing is convinced that the ultimate goal of US missile defense policy is a drive for absolute security for the United States, which implies vulnerability for everyone else. Chinese security analysts cite four possible motivations for US missile defense plans. The most extreme suggests that the real intention of US missile defenses is to secure the control of outer space. A second view is that missile defense deployment might not actually neutralize Chinese nuclear retaliatory capabilities, but might weaken US perceptions of Chinese capabilities and their psychological impact on US behavior. This might encourage the United States to adopt more aggressive policies that do not take China's interests into account. A third view holds that missile defense reflects the political influence of the US defense industrial complex, which stands to gain major benefits through defense contracts. A fourth view is that US missile defense is a conspiracy intended to involve China in a prolonged arms race to bleed the country into economic bankruptcy, just as it did to the former Soviet Union. These analyses of US strategic intentions are coupled with suspicions that US plans to deploy missile defenses in Asia are intended to improve US political and military ties with Taiwan and might therefore encourage Taiwan independence. Some Chinese analysts also worry that the deployment of missile defenses might provide a shield for Japanese rearmament.[68] (For more on Chinese views of US intentions, see Chapter 5 by Ron Montaperto in this volume.)

While debates continue within the US strategic community on new approaches to arms control and nonproliferation and on the implications of missile defenses for US nuclear policy, the Bush administration has made up its mind to pursue deployment of missile defenses in combination with unilateral deep cuts in the US strategic nuclear arsenal.[69] Chinese analysts believe the United States already has the largest conventional and nuclear arsenals in the world, and view missile defense as aimed at sustaining the US unipolar position and maintaining military superiority at the expense of the security of other countries.[70]

Chinese analysts have been worried about the potential impact of US missile defenses since the mid-1980s, when the Reagan administration began the Strategic Defense Initiative.[71] For several years, Chinese analysts have been discussing the responses Beijing should adopt in the face of US BMD deployment.[72] In addition to the ongoing efforts to improve the survivability of Chinese nuclear forces described above, Chinese responses could consist of three categories of programs: an expansion of the size of China's current ballistic missile force, technical countermeasures to penetrate and defeat US BMD systems, and the possible use of asymmetrical measures such as development of anti-satellite (ASAT) weapons to attack key components of the US system.[73]

China will almost certainly expand its nuclear forces significantly as the United States begins to deploy ballistic missile defenses. US planners assume that four interceptors would be needed for each incoming ballistic missile, but Chinese experts assume a two-to-one ratio of interceptors to targets.[74] If the United States had deployed the 100-interceptor NMD system originally proposed by the Clinton administration, China would probably have wanted at least fifty warheads to survive a US first strike in order to maintain confidence that some of its surviving missiles could penetrate US defenses. This would likely require a total force of 100–200 missiles (or a smaller number of missiles equipped with a multiple-warhead capability). Although the actual effectiveness of a US BMD system would be unknown to both sides, China is likely to assume the system is highly effective and to size its forces accordingly. The result could be a disjuncture between American and Chinese views of what constitutes a reasonable Chinese response to BMD deployment.

Estimates of Chinese responses are complicated by the fact that the precise BMD architecture the United States will ultimately deploy is still undetermined. A US intelligence estimate on foreign responses to US NMD deployment (based on the Clinton-era NMD system) reportedly concluded that China would expand its nuclear arsenal to a quantity large enough to overwhelm a limited US NMD system, perhaps deploying as many as two hundred warheads.[75] A subsequent US intelligence estimate suggested that China would likely increase the total number of nuclear warheads on ICBMs to 75–100 by 2015.[76] Although the initial US BMD system scheduled to be deployed in fall 2004 will have very limited capabilities against Chinese missiles, the United States is currently pursuing a wide range of systems and technologies, including boost-phase, mid-course, and terminal defense systems. The Missile Defense Agency is also considering future advanced concepts that might include space-based weapons. As a result, Chinese strategic planners confront considerable uncertainty about the ultimate size and effectiveness of future US missile defenses. More advanced US BMD architectures would result in correspondingly larger increases in China's ICBM force.[77]

A second area of emphasis will consist of technical efforts to penetrate or defeat US ballistic missile defenses. Although it is impossible to assess the state of Chinese efforts to develop BMD countermeasures fully using open sources, published writings and conversations with Chinese strategic analysts clearly indicate that Chinese researchers are pursuing a wide range of approaches.[78] One Chinese analyst cited a range of potential technical countermeasures, including the use of decoys, chaff, stealth technologies to reduce the radar and infrared signatures of incoming warheads, and maneuvering warheads that would be more difficult to intercept. These technical countermeasures could be supplemented by efforts to increase the number and improve the survivability of Chinese ICBMs.[79] Chinese engineers have built technical models of potential US BMD systems to assess the likely effectiveness of BMD countermeasures.[80] China has reportedly tested at least some BMD countermeasures, but these capabilities have not yet been deployed on operational missiles.[81] Many Chinese statements about potential BMD countermeasures have come in the context of China's campaign to oppose US deployment of missile defenses, and may represent efforts to influence US policy rather than accurate assessments of China's current research program. Nevertheless, it is clear that Chinese scientists understand the major technical approaches to defeating ballistic missile defenses and are examining a range of technologies for potential development and deployment.[82] We expect China's next generation DF-31 and DF-31A ICBMs to incorporate BMD countermeasures; older missiles such as the DF-5A and the DF-21A may also eventually be retrofitted with countermeasures. China's degree of confidence that its ICBMs equipped with BMD countermeasures will penetrate current and future US ballistic missile defenses will almost certainly affect Chinese assessments of how large an ICBM force is necessary for a credible nuclear deterrent. However, uncertainties about the size and effectiveness of future US missile defenses and about the effectiveness of future Chinese BMD countermeasures make it difficult to gauge the relative weight China will place on increased force survivability, increased numbers of ICBMs, and BMD countermeasures.

China might also try to respond to US BMD deployment through asymmetric means, such as development of an ASAT system that could attack space-based components of a US BMD system. Even though little direct evidence exists about specific Chinese ASAT weapons programs, Chinese scientists have conducted a variety of ASAT-relevant research and there is a strong strategic logic for the development of ASAT weapons.[83] US missile defense systems would depend heavily on satellite sensors, so a Chinese ASAT capability could be useful in disabling US satellites, thereby paralyzing US missile defenses. Chinese experts have suggested that direct space-launched attacks from satellites armed with nuclear warheads and ASAT weapons could be useful responses to US BMD deployments.[84] The United States increasingly relies on satellites when firing precision-guided munitions. These weapons formerly used laser target designators, but now depend on global positioning satellites to find their targets.[85] China may also face hostile US action against its own space assets in the future. PLA analysts are certainly aware of US preparations for future space warfare against China. Such scenarios have acquired greater salience after reports of a January 2001 space war game held at the US Air Force's Space Warfare Center in Colorado, in which China was clearly the designated opponent.[86] While Chinese advocates of ASAT weapons development cite their potential value in countering US missile defenses, ASAT weapons would appear to be an expensive and technologically uncertain means of increasing the credibility of China's nuclear deterrent. ASAT weapons are therefore unlikely to play a central role in China's response to BMD deployments.

Enhancing Nuclear Warfighting Capabilities?

Alastair Iain Johnston has described a debate among Chinese strategists about whether China should adopt a doctrine of limited deterrence (rather than minimal deterrence) that includes a nuclear *warfighting* capability in addition to a *retaliatory* capability.[87] Advocates of limited deterrence argue that the PLA must possess the capability to fight on an escalating rung of *both* conventional and nuclear war in theater and strategic contexts. A limited deterrence doctrine would reject the assumptions underpinning mutually assured destruction in favor of the belief that nuclear escalation could be controlled. Escalation dominance usually requires either superior nuclear capabilities or a greater willingness to accept damage from a nuclear exchange in order to deter an adversary from escalating to a higher level of destruction. Such a posture would require a significant expansion and restructuring of China's nuclear forces, including development of the following capabilities:

- Greater number of strategic missiles with a wide range of launching modes (airborne, ICBMs, SLBMs, and cruise missiles)
- Greater accuracy, mobility, and survivability
- Better C4I systems for early warning and command and control
- Missile defense systems and civil defense capabilities
- Anti-satellite (ASAT) weapons to destroy enemy space assets to paralyze its overall warfighting capabilities

- Launch-on-warning (LOW) posture contrary to China's declared NFU policy[88]

China's current strategic modernization efforts will eventually produce some of the weapons systems needed to support limited deterrence, including more accurate mobile missiles and submarines capable of launching long-range SLBMs. However, wholesale adoption of a limited deterrence doctrine would require much larger Chinese nuclear forces in order to target US nuclear forces and attempt to achieve escalation dominance. China would need to move well beyond its current modernization program to develop new capabilities such as advanced early warning satellites and radars, more effective and flexible C3I systems, anti-satellite weapons, and ballistic missile defenses of its own. China's industrial and technological infrastructure is currently incapable of meeting most of these requirements, but several decades of research and development and a massive commitment of additional resources might eventually permit a shift to a full-scale limited deterrence doctrine. Given competing domestic priorities and the likely international costs, however, China's leaders are unlikely to support such a shift.

While Chinese leaders are unlikely to support a limited deterrence doctrine, they may fund some investments in strategic capabilities that would improve China's ability to fight a limited nuclear conflict with the United States over Taiwan. These might include improvements in China's strategic command and control systems, deployment of DF-21 missiles with BMD countermeasures that could target US bases in Asia, and efforts to improve China's strategic intelligence and early warning capabilities. While China is unlikely to achieve escalation dominance over US nuclear forces, these investments might enhance the credibility of Chinese threats to use nuclear weapons against US bases or allies, thereby improving China's political bargaining position in a crisis over Taiwan. (See Chapter 3 by Evan Medeiros in this volume for more discussion of China's doctrine.)

Constraints on China's Strategic Modernization

The pace and scope of China's strategic modernization have been, and will continue to be, affected by a host of internal and external factors. Internal factors include available financial resources, technological capability, the weight of the military in strategic policymaking, the balance between economic development and military modernization, strategic perceptions, and nuclear doctrine. External factors include deployments of ballistic missile defenses, China's arms control commitments, major-power relationships, China's dependence on foreign trade, investment, and economic assistance, international strategic trends, decisions by other major nuclear weapon states, and the state of the global arms control regime.[89]

Several of these factors are likely to constrain China's strategic modernization efforts over the next ten to fifteen years. Hard constraints, which will limit strategic modernization regardless of the wishes of China's leaders, include China's fissile material stocks and limitations on the technology available for use in missiles, nuclear weapons, and strategic support systems. Soft constraints, which rest on leadership calculations about the costs and benefits of strategic modernization, include questions about the relative priority of strategic modernization and the damage a nuclear buildup might cause to China's international image and relations with other countries.

One potential hard constraint is the availability of weapons-grade fissile material (e.g., highly enriched uranium and plutonium) to produce additional nuclear weapons. China reportedly stopped enriching uranium for nuclear weapons in 1987 and ceased production of plutonium for weapons in 1991. Estimates of the size of China's stock of weapons-grade fissile material vary from 4 to 24 tons.[90] China's existing stock of weapons-grade fissile material may be sufficient for 500 to 2,000 additional nuclear warheads.[91] This suggests that limited fissile material stocks are not likely to be the binding constraint on Chinese strategic modernization.

A second potential hard constraint may be China's inability to produce solid-fuel, mobile ICBMs equipped with multiple warheads. This requires mastering three difficult technologies: constructing high-thrust solid fuel motors, deploying multiple payloads from a single missile, and miniaturizing nuclear weapons to fit on lightweight reentry vehicles. China has deployed solid-fuel mobile missiles (DF-21A) and conducted successful tests of longer-range, solid-fuel missiles (DF-31). However, open sources provide insufficient information to determine the thrust produced by the solid-fuel rocket motors that will be used in the DF-31 and DF-31A, making it hard to assess the total payload these missiles will be able to carry. In 1981, China launched three satellites from a single rocket platform. Analysts suggest this was an indication that China was pursuing a multiple warhead capability,[92] although this assertion has been disputed.[93] China has subsequently launched small multiple satellites from one rocket as part of its commercial space launch program.[94] Delivering multiple payloads from a single missile is probably not a binding constraint on China's ability to deploy multiple warheads. Between 1992 and 1996, China conducted nine nuclear tests, many with small yields, as part of efforts to develop miniaturized nuclear warheads for its next generation missiles.[95] Information obtained from open sources and nuclear espionage informed and probably accelerated these efforts. The US intelligence community concluded in 1999 that China has had the technical capability to develop multiple warheads for the DF-5A missile for many years, but has not chosen to deploy this capability.[96] A tentative conclusion is that China may currently be unable to master the relevant technologies to the degree necessary to produce next-generation solid-fuel, mobile ICBMs equipped with multiple warheads. China could potentially compensate for this technological constraint by deploying increased numbers of single-warhead mobile missiles or by deploying multiple-warheads on its vulnerable DF-5A liquid-fueled missile. The first option is more expensive; the second option would have reduced survivability compared to a mobile missile with multiple warheads.

The relative success of China's technological efforts to develop and deploy effective BMD countermeasures constitutes a third potential hard constraint on strategic modernization. This constraint is speculative, given that it requires assessments of the future capabilities of US missile defense systems, the effectiveness of Chinese efforts to develop and deploy BMD countermeasures, and the ability of the United States to modify its missile defenses to defeat deployed Chinese countermeasures. There is insufficient information available to make reliable judgments on these future capabilities. However, there is a strong strategic logic for China to cooperate with Russia in developing countermeasures to defeat US missile defenses. Such cooperation could significantly enhance China's ability to deploy effective countermeasures. If technological constraints limit the effectiveness of Chinese BMD countermeasures, China is likely to deploy increased numbers of ICBMs as a substitute.

In addition to these potential hard constraints, two soft constraints are likely to limit China's future strategic capabilities. The first is the willingness of China's civilian leaders to invest additional resources into China's strategic modernization. Because this is a question of leadership priorities rather than the availability of resources, it represents a soft constraint.[97] China's leaders have historically placed a high political value on China's possession of nuclear weapons. Nuclear capability not only gave China political prestige for breaking the developed countries' nuclear monopoly, but also provided protection from nuclear blackmail by the superpowers. China's leaders view their nuclear deterrent as an important constraint on US power and a means of forcing the United States to take China's core interests into account. They are likely to invest whatever resources are necessary to maintain a credible nuclear deterrent as the United States deploys ballistic missile defenses. However, Chinese leaders have also historically viewed excessive investment in nuclear forces as a waste of resources, a lesson reinforced by their analysis of the causes of the collapse of the Soviet Union. Given competing priorities, the leadership's determination to avoid a costly arms race with the United States, and perceptions of the limited returns from excessive investments in nuclear weapons, China's leaders are likely to limit funding for strategic modernization efforts to the amounts necessary for building a credible and survivable nuclear deterrent. This constraint is likely to frustrate the ambitions of those who believe China should develop a robust nuclear warfighting capability.

A second soft constraint lies in the damage a major Chinese nuclear buildup might do to China's international image. Chinese leaders have responded to concerns about a future China threat by emphasizing China's benign strategic intentions and promoting the concept of China's "peaceful rise." This has included efforts to improve relations with China's neighbors and with other great powers, including the United States. A major Chinese nuclear buildup at the time when the other major nuclear powers are reducing their nuclear arsenals could damage China's international image and raise strategic tensions at both the regional and global levels. This would harm China's economic development efforts and could encourage neighbors such as Japan to develop nuclear weapons of their own. These concerns make Chinese leaders unlikely to approve a large expansion of China's nuclear capability unless their assessment of the international strategic environment changes dramatically. One potential driver for such a shift would be if Chinese leaders conclude that a powerful, unconstrained United States was likely to use unilateral and military means to pursue its strategic interests while disregarding the core interests of other great powers such as China. Although Chinese analysts have expressed serious concerns about Bush administration policy statements such as the Nuclear Posture Review and the 2002 National Security Strategy and actions such as the invasion of Iraq, the trend toward a more assertive US strategic role is unlikely to lead to a breakdown in Sino-US relations. Indeed, the messy aftermath of the US invasion of Iraq suggests that the United States is moving away from unilateral military intervention.[98]

Conclusion

China's strategic modernization efforts over the last twenty years have sought to address long-standing weaknesses and to build a credible minimal deterrent by improving the survivability of China's nuclear forces. Absent widespread deployments of ballistic missile defenses, China's current modernization program will produce nuclear forces that will support a more credible nuclear deterrent by 2010–2015. This force would consist of mobile land-based DF-31 and DF-31A ICBMs, JL-2 SLBMs based on Type 094 nuclear submarines, and older liquid-fueled DF-5A missiles. Such a credible, minimal deterrent force would likely involve an expansion of the total number of Chinese ICBMs and intercontinental SLBMs, perhaps to 50–60 warheads.

Based on available sources (see Appendix 2 for a discussion of the limitations of open-source analysis), the authors are confident that the key future Chinese strategic delivery systems have been identified and that the motivations and broad outlines of China's likely responses to US BMD deployments are accurately presented. The judgment that technical constraints have prevented China from developing multiple warheads for its next generation DF-31 and DF-31A missiles is speculative, but consistent with unclassified US government assessments. Little independent information is available on the deployment timelines for new Chinese weapons systems; we have relied primarily on unclassified US government assessments. Finally, we believe the ultimate size of China's strategic nuclear forces will be shaped by the Chinese leadership's calculations of costs and benefits, the state of US-China relations, and Chinese assessments about the size and effectiveness of US missile defenses in the face of Chinese BMD countermeasures. Our conclusions reflect uncertain judgments about these factors.

US decisions about ballistic missile defenses and about the role of nuclear weapons in US strategy will influence the pace of Chinese strategic modernization and shape Chinese decisions about force structure. Chinese leaders are determined not to accept long-term vulnerability to US nuclear blackmail and will fund the force improvements necessary to build and maintain a credible nuclear deterrent. In addition to ongoing efforts to improve survivability of nuclear forces, this will involve a significant increase in the number of new Chinese ICBMs that can reach US targets, retention of older strategic missile systems, deployments of countermeasures to penetrate or defeat US missile defenses, and the possible deployment of multiple warheads on China's DF-5A ICBMs. Technological limitations will likely prevent China from deploying multiple warheads on its next-generation mobile ICBMs, but will not prevent China from using BMD countermeasures and larger numbers of ICBMs to achieve a credible nuclear deterrent. China's degree of confidence that its ICBMs and SLBMs equipped with BMD countermeasures can penetrate current and future US ballistic missile defenses will affect assessments of how large a force is necessary. Uncertainties about the size and effectiveness of future US missile defenses and about the effectiveness of future Chinese BMD countermeasures make it difficult to gauge the relative weight China will place on increased force survivability, increased numbers of ICBMs, and BMD countermeasures. However the resulting Chinese force will be significantly larger than it would be absent US deployment of missile defenses.

Technology and resource constraints have shaped and often limited China's strategic modernization efforts, but political and strategic factors have played an equally important role. Perceived nuclear threats from the United States played a major role in China's initial decision to develop nuclear weapons.[99] Concerns in the early 1980s about the potential impact of the Strategic Defense Initiative prompted Chinese efforts to develop the new strategic weapons systems that will be deployed later this decade. US decisions about its own nuclear forces, nuclear doctrine, and political relationship with China will influence the decisions Chinese leaders make about the size and composition of China's future strategic forces. US decisions and actions also influence the overall health of the global arms control and nonproliferation regime, another factor in Chinese decision-making. The United States needs to recognize this strategic interaction and take China's likely reactions into account when deciding the role that nuclear weapons should play in US strategy.

The United States could use strategic dialogue to influence China's strategic modernization efforts by clarifying the parameters of its planned BMD architecture and discussing China's responses. Strategic dialogue is important because differing US and Chinese assessments of the likely effectiveness of US missile defenses mean that many Americans will view China's response as excessive, even if China feels it is being restrained. The goal should be to minimize damage to bilateral relations through mutual strategic reassurance.[100] If the United States accepts a modest increase in Chinese strategic forces as a rational response to BMD deployment, the negative impact on relations would be reduced. The United States might offer assurances about the ultimate scope of its BMD system; China might offer greater transparency about its modernization plans (possibly including force structure levels keyed to specific US missile defense architectures). Addressing Chinese concerns without allowing Beijing to dictate US policy could help avert misperceptions and potentially moderate the size of China's nuclear buildup. However, this approach would require the United States to accept the inevitability of a nuclear deterrent relationship with China, a controversial position in the United States. Moreover, any serious strategic dialogue requires reciprocity. Greater transparency on China's part about its views on nuclear deterrence and its planned nuclear force structure would go a long way toward dispelling US and regional concerns.

The Bush administration has taken important steps to improve dialogue by engaging in more regular security consultation with the Chinese government. These efforts include resumption of bilateral Defense Consultation Talks and discussions about strategic security, arms control, and nonproliferation at the undersecretary-of-state/vice-foreign-minister level, and establishing a new "global dialogue" at the deputy-secretary-of-state level that will address a range of political, economic, and security issues.[101] The two countries are now actively cooperating in fighting terrorism and on efforts to create a Korean Peninsula free of nuclear weapons. This enhanced security cooperation will not necessarily make it easier to resolve difficult and contentious issues such as Taiwan, but it does create a better atmosphere for frank strategic discussions. Given the negative impact a significant expansion of China's nuclear force would have on regional security dynamics and global arms control efforts, the United States should do what it can to reassure China about its strategic intentions and to persuade China to restrain the size of its future nuclear forces.

Appendix 1: PLA Strategic Missile Forces Bases and Order of Battle[a]

80301 Unit (Base 51)

HQ: Shenyang, Liaoning Province
Brigade Bases:

- Tonghua, Jilin (818 Brigade)
- Dengshahe, Liaoning (810 Brigade)
- Jinchang (816 Brigade)
- Hancheng (806 Brigade)[b]
- One unidentified mobile brigade

Missile Types:

- DF-3A/CSS-2 (Tonghua, Dengshahe)
- DF-21/CSS-5 (Tonghua)

The 80301 unit covers the Korean Peninsula, Japan (including Okinawa), and the Russian Far East.

80302 Unit (Base 52)

HQ: Huangshan, Anhui Province[c]
Brigade Bases:

- Leping, Jiangxi (815 Brigade)
- Lianxiwang, Hubei (807 Brigade)
- Qimen, Jiangxi (811 Brigade)
- Yingtan, Jiangxi (817 Brigade)
- 818 Brigade???[d]
- 819 Brigade???[d]
- 820 Brigade???[d]

Missile Types:

- DF-3A/CSS-2 (Lianxiwang)
- DF-15/CSS-6 (Leping)

This unit has primary responsibility for missile bombardment of Taiwan in case of war. The 815 Brigade, based in Leping, was involved in the March 1996 missile exercises off the coast of Taiwan. In the event of conflict, the brigade would disperse to prearranged launching points in Fujian Province.

80303 Unit (Base 53)

HQ: Kunming, Yunnan Province
Brigade Bases:

- Chuxiong, Yunnan (808 Brigade)
- Jianshui, Yunnan (802 Brigade)

Missile Types:

- DF-3A/CSS-2 (Jianshui, Kunming)
- DF-21/CSS-5 (Chuxiong)

The 80303 unit covers India and Southeast Asia.

80304 Unit (Base 54)

HQ: Luoyang, Henan Province
Brigade Bases:

- Luoning, Henan (801 Brigade)
- Sundian, Henan (804 Brigade)
- Yiyang, Henan (813 Brigade)

Missile Types:

- DF-5A/CSS-4 (Luoning, Xuanhua[e])
- DF-4/CSS-3 (Sundian[f])

The 80304 unit is China's primary deterrence force, equipped with DF-5A ICBMs that can strike targets in the United States, Russia, and Europe.

80305 Unit (Base 55)

HQ: Huaihua, Hunan Province
Brigade Bases:

- Tongdao, Hunan (805 Brigade)
- Jingzhou, Hunan (803 Brigade)
- Huitong, Hunan (814 Brigade)

Missile Types:

- DF-4/CSS-3 (Tongdao)
- DF-3A

The 80305 Unit is equipped with DF-4 ballistic missiles that can strike Guam.

80306 Unit (Base 56)

HQ: Xining, Qinghai Province
Brigade Bases:

- Datong, Qinghai (809 Brigade)
- Delingha, Qinghai (812 Brigade)
- Wulan, Qinghai (812 Brigade)

Missile Types:

- DF-3A/CSS-2 (Datong)
- DF-4/CSS-3 (Delingha, Da Qaidam)

The 80306 unit is equipped with DF-4 IRBMs that can strike targets in India and Russia.

Possible Additional Bases, Facilities, and Operating Areas

- Yidu, Shandong (DF-3A/CSS-2)
- Qingdao/Jianggezhuan Submarine Base (Home port of the Type 092 Xia class SSBN; JL-1 SLBM)
- Wuzhai Missile and Space Test Center, Shanxi (DF-31)
- Nanping (DF-15/CSS-6 firing positions for the 815th Brigade in Fujian Province)
- Yong'an, Xianyou (DF-11/CSS-7 firing positions for the 815th Brigade in Fujian Province)
- Tai-Hang (DF-31): Suspected site of "Great Wall Project" of tunnels for hiding mobile ICBM/IRBMs, according to Globalsecurity.org

---

Notes: a. Information is drawn primarily from Gill et al., "China's Strategic Rocket Forces: Transition to Credible Deterrence." Other sources include Federation of American Scientists, "Chinese Missile Facilities," www.fas.org/nuke/guide/china/facility/missile.htm; William M. Arkin, Robert S. Norris, and Joshua Handler, *Taking Stock: Worldwide Nuclear Deployments 1998* (Washington, DC: Natural Resources Defense Council Nuclear Program, 1998); Allen and Kivelehan; Lewis and Hua; Kenneth Allen, "PLA Second Artillery Organizational Structure," *Chinese Military Update,* vol. 1, no. 7 (January 2004): 1–5; Mark Stokes, "Chinese Ballistic Missile Forces in the Age of Global Missile Defense"; Mark Stokes, *China's Strategic Modernization: Implications for the United States* (Carlisle, PA: Strategic Studies Institute, US Army War College, 1999); and Center for Nonproliferation Studies, "Second Artillery Corps (SAC)," 2003, www.nti.org/db/china/sac.htm. The authors thank Shi-chin Lin for research assistance.

b. Gill lists this brigade as located in Shaanxi Province in northwest China. The authors doubt this attribution, since Hancheng is too far away from the base headquarters.

c. Allen and Kivlehan suggest that there are seven brigades at this base; most other sources list four to five brigades. The discrepancy is due to the assumption by Allen and Kivlehan that the growing number of PRC DF-15 missiles requires additional brigades, which would likely be assigned to Base 52.

d. Suspected but unconfirmed.

e. This location would be in Hebei province to the north.

f. According to the Federation of American Scientists, Sundian is one of five locations at which a total of between 10 and 20 DF-4s were deployed as of early

1998. Sundian is reportedly headquarters for one of three DF-4 launch brigades subordinate to the Second Artillery Corps 80304 Unit. www.fas.org/nuke/guide/china/facility/sundian.htm.

Appendix 2: A Note on Sources

There are important limitations in analyzing China's strategic modernization using open sources. Because the credibility of China's nuclear deterrent rests partly on ambiguity about the size of the force, China makes considerable efforts to control information about the precise capabilities and exact numbers of its nuclear weapons and delivery systems. Chinese strategic analysts frequently rely on Western estimates in their analyses because of the unavailability of official information from their own government. China's series of white papers on national defense gives some useful basic information about the capabilities, doctrine, missions, and organization of China's strategic forces, while events such as the 1999 parade to commemorate the 50th anniversary of the founding of the People's Republic of China have provided glimpses of new strategic weapons such as the DF-31 missile. Careful mining of the Chinese press and magazines devoted to military issues can produce useful nuggets of information, although the most detailed and spectacular reports usually come from Hong Kong newspapers that are unreliable. Analysis of Chinese scientific and technical publications often provides insights into ongoing research with strategic applications. Nevertheless, the lack of detailed, reliable open-source information on the numbers and capabilities of Chinese strategic weapons systems is a significant limitation.

The availability of unclassified reports from the US government (and, to a lesser degree, from the Taiwan government) helps fill these gaps. In particular, a close reading of the annual reports on the military power of the People's Republic of China produced by the US Department of Defense and of the National Intelligence Council's unclassified estimate on "Foreign Missile Development and the Ballistic Missile Threat Through 2015" provides much useful information on the status of China's strategic modernization programs. The allegations of Chinese nuclear espionage that were the focus of the Cox Committee's investigation also produced details about US estimates of China's nuclear weapons capability, although some of the conclusions of the report must be treated with caution.

Conversely, Chinese analysts have been able to write more freely about China's concerns about US ballistic missile defense programs and the implications for China's nuclear deterrent. Analysis of these writings and conference presentations provides valuable insights into Chinese strategic concerns, including China's interest in developing BMD countermeasures. The opportunity to talk with Chinese government officials, military officers, strategic analysts, and engineers at official and unofficial conferences can also provide useful insights. Additionally, Chinese scientific and technical publications provide a partial window into Chinese efforts to develop BMD countermeasures. This information is insufficient to assess the state of China's progress in actually developing or deploying countermeasures, but is good enough to illuminate the main outlines of the research effort.

Notes

Research for this chapter was funded by the Defense Threat Reduction Agency. The views expressed are those of the authors and do not reflect the official policy or position of the National Defense University, the Defense Threat Reduction Agency, the Department of Defense, or the US government.

1. The initial debate in the 1960s focused on how China's acquisition of nuclear weapons might destabilize the Asia-Pacific region. Many of the dire predictions proved to be unfounded. For an example, see Morton H. Halperin, *China and the Bomb* (New York: Praeger, 1965). For a review of US intelligence estimates and government deliberations about the impact of a Chinese nuclear weapons capability, see William Burr and Jeffrey T. Richelson, "Whether to 'Strangle the Baby in the Cradle': The United States and the Chinese Nuclear Program, 1960–64," *International Security,* vol. 25, no. 3 (Winter 2000/01): 54–99. For declassified intelligence estimates, see *Tracking the Dragon: National Intelligence Estimates on China During the Era of Mao, 1948–1976* (Washington, DC: National Intelligence Council, October 2004).

2. Jaswant Singh, "Against Nuclear Apartheid," *Foreign Affairs*, vol. 77, no. 5 (September/October 1998): 41–52.

3. "Treaty Between the United States of America and the Russian Federation on Strategic Offensive Reductions," *Arms Control Today,* vol. 32, no. 5 (June 2002): 9–11, www.armscontrol.org/act/2002_06/docjune02.asp.

4. For a summary of these concerns, see Evan S. Medeiros and Phillip C. Saunders, *Building a Global Strategic Framework for the 21st Century: Report from the Fourth US-China Conference on Arms Control, Disarmament and Nonproliferation* (Monterey, CA: Center for Nonproliferation Studies, 2002), www.cns.miis.edu/cns/projects/eanp/research/uschina4/4thconf.pdf.

5. John Wilson Lewis and Xue Litai, *China Builds the Bomb* (Stanford: Stanford University Press, 1988); Zhang Shu Guang, *Deterrence and Strategic Culture: Chinese-American Confrontation, 1949–1958* (Ithaca, NY: Cornell University Press, 1992). On US nuclear threats to China, see Gordon H. Chang, "To the Nuclear Brink: Eisenhower, Dulles, and the Quemoy-Matsu Crisis," in *Nuclear Diplomacy and Crisis Management,* Sean M. Lynne-Jones, Steven E. Miller, and Stephen Van Evera, eds. (Cambridge, MA: MIT Press, 1990), 200–227.

6. However, Alastair Iain Johnston suggests that some Chinese military writings interpret NFU loosely to allow room for launch-on-warning or launch-under-early-attack policies. Johnston, "China's New 'Old Thinking': The Concept of Limited Deterrence," *International Security,* vol. 20, no. 3 (Winter 1995/96): 5–42.

7. See John Wilson Lewis and Xue Litai, "Strategic Weapons and Chinese Power: The Formative Years," *China Quarterly*, no. 112 (December 1987): 541–554. The Type 092 submarine joined the PLA Navy in 1983, but its JL-1 missiles were not successfully tested from the submarine until September 27, 1988. We use 1988 as the operational date for the Type 092 submarine throughout this paper. See John Wilson Lewis and Xue Litai, *China's Strategic Seapower: The Politics of Force Modernization in the Nuclear Age* (Stanford: Stanford University Press, 1994), 119–120, 202–205.

8. Kenneth Allen and Maryanne Kivlehan, "Implementing PLA Second Artillery Doctrinal Reforms," in *China's Revolution in Doctrinal Affairs: Emerging Trends in the Operations Art of the Chinese People's Liberation Army,* James Mulvenon and David M. Finkelstein, eds. (Alexandria, VA: CNA Corporation, 2005, 149–204); Bates Gill, James Mulvenon, and Mark Stokes, "China's Strategic Rocket Forces: Transition to Credible Deterrence," in *The People's Liberation Army as Organization,* Reference Volume v1.0, James C. Mulvenon and Andrew N.D. Yang, eds. (Arlington, VA: RAND, 2002), 517–530; You Ji, *The Armed Forces of China* (New York: I.B. Tauris Publishers, 1999), chapter 4.

9. Hu Guangzheng, ed., *Zhongwai Junshi Zuzhi Tizhi Bijiao Jiaocheng* (*Comparison of Chinese and Foreign Military Organizations and Systems*) (Beijing: Military Science Press, 1999), 223–226.

10. "Jing Zhiyuan Promoted to Commander of PLA Second Artillery Corps," *Taipei Chung-Kuo Shih-Pao,* January 17, 2003, FBIS CPP20030117000028.

11. Kenneth Allen, "PLA Second Artillery Organizational Structure," *Chinese Military Update,* vol. 1, no. 7 (January 2004): 1.

12. Robert Norris and Hans M. Kristensen, "NRDC Nuclear Notebook: Chinese Nuclear Forces, 2003," *Bulletin of the Atomic Scientists,* vol. 59, no. 6 (November/December 2003): 77–80, www.thebulletin.org/issues/nukenotes/nd03nukenote.html. For other estimates see "China," in Joseph Cirincione with Jon B. Wolfsthal and Miriam Rajkumar, *Deadly Arsenals: Tracking Weapons of Mass Destruction* (Washington, DC: Carnegie Endowment for International Peace, 2002), 141–163; *The Military Balance 2002–2003* (London: Oxford University Press for the International Institute of Strategic Studies, 2002), 145; and Hans M. Kristensen and Joshua Handler, "Appendix 10A. World Nuclear Forces," in *SIPRI Yearbook 2002: Non-Proliferation, Arms Control, Disarmament* (Oxford: Oxford University Press for the Stockholm International Peace Research Institute, 2002), 552–557.

13. Evidence about whether China currently possesses tactical nuclear weapons is ambiguous. For a detailed assessment of various open-source estimates, see Charles D. Ferguson, Evan S. Medeiros, and Phillip C. Saunders, "Chinese Tactical Nuclear Weapons," in *Tactical Nuclear Weapons: Emergent Threats in an Evolving Security Environment,* Brian Alexander and Alistair Millar, eds. (London: Brassey's, 2003).

14. John Wilson Lewis and Hua Di, "China's Ballistic Missile Programs: Technologies, Strategies, Goals," *International Security,* vol. 17, no. 2 (Fall 1992): 25.

15. Seymour Johnson, "China Seeks Technology for Next-Generation Missiles," *Jane's Missiles and Rockets,* vol. 3, no. 5 (May 1999); and Kang Jianbin et al., "GPS in Ballistic Missile Guidance Instrument Error Separation," *Daodan yu Hangtian Yunzai Jishu* (*Ballistic Missiles and Space Launch Technology*), February 2002, 41–45, FBIS CPP20020722000254.

16. US Department of Defense, *Annual Report on the Military Power of the People's Republic of China 2002,* July 12, 2002, 27, www.defenselink.mil/news/Jul2002/d20020712china.pdf.

17. US Department of Defense, *Annual Report on the Military Power of the People's Republic of China 2003,* July 28, 2003, 31, www.defenselink.mil/pubs/20030730chinaex.pdf.

18. US Department of Defense (2003), 31.

19. US Department of Defense (2002), 28; *The Military Balance* (2003–2004), "Table 3. Operational Offensive Nuclear Delivery Systems," 221.

20. Hiroyuki Sugiyama, "China Successfully Tests Multi-Warhead Missiles," *Yomiuri Shimbun,* February 8, 2003, FBIS JPP20030207000154.

21. Robert Norris and William Arkin, "NRDC Nuclear Notebook: Chinese Nuclear Forces, 2001," *Bulletin of the Atomic Scientists,* vol. 57, no. 5 (September/October 2001): 71–72; Howard Diamond, "Chinese Strategic Plans Move Forward With Missile Test," *Arms Control Today,* vol. 29, no. 5 (July/August 1999): 27, www.armscontrol.org/act/1999_07-08/chija99.asp; and, "DF-31," *Global Security.org,* www.globalsecurity.org/wmd/world/china/df-31.htm.

22. US Department of Defense (2002), 27.

23. US Department of Defense, *The Military Power of the People's Republic of China 2005,* July 2005, www.defenselink.mil/news/Jul2005/d20050719china.pdf.

24. Lewis and Hua, 5–40.

25. Norris and Arkin, 71–72.

26. US Department of Defense (2002), 27.

27. "Type 92 Xia," *GlobalSecurity.org,* www.globalsecurity.org/wmd/world/china/type_92.htm, last modified: August 12, 2002; Yihong Zhang, "China's Rising Forces," *Jane's International Defense Review,* vol. 35, no. 8 (August 2002): 37. Several Chinese magazines have recently published pictures of the Xia at sea. Personal correspondence, Dr. Lyle Goldstein and Professor William S. Murray, US Naval War College.

28. The US Department of Defense (2003, 31) report on PRC military power notes that "China is expected to deploy the JL-1 medium-range SLBM aboard the *Xia* SSBN in 2003," suggesting that the Xia's Julang-1 missiles were removed during the overhaul process and have not been reinstalled on the SSBN as of July 2003. Some reports have speculated that the overhaul might permit the Xia to carry the Julang-2 missile when it is eventually deployed. David Miller, *Submarines of the World* (St. Paul, MN: McGraw Hill, 2002), 407.

29. Lewis and Xue, *China's Strategic Seapower,* 115–122; *Jane's Fighting Ships 1993–94* (New York: McGraw Hill, 1993), 110.

30. "Type 94," *GlobalSecurity.org,* www.globalsecurity.org/wmd/world/china/type_94.htm, last modified: August 12, 2002; Zhang, "China's Rising Forces," 37; US Department of Defense (2003), 31.

31. Some reports claim that the JL-2 is capable of carrying up to six warheads in an MRV mode, which could increase China's overall SLBM capability to as many as 576 warheads if six Type 094 SSBNs are deployed. The primary source for these reports is Tung Yi, "Range of Nuclear Warheads Can Cover Europe and America," *Sing Tao Jih Pao* (Hong Kong), January 1, 2001, FBIS CPP20010106000009. However, this report also claims that China already has five Type 092 Xia SSBNs deployed, which greatly weakens its credibility. Due to restrictions on thrust and payload, we believe that the JL-2 is unlikely to carry multiple warheads.

32. China's recent purchase of eight additional Russian Kilo-class submarines suggests that other Chinese submarine programs, such as efforts to develop the indigenous *Song*-class diesel attack submarine, are also encountering serious technical problems. Charles Hutzler, "Deal Shows Weakness of China's Arms Industry—

Buying 8 Russian Subs, Beijing Tries to Redress Some of Sector's Failures," *Wall Street Journal,* June 28, 2002, A11. Also see Lyle Goldstein and William Murray, "Undersea Dragons: China's Maturing Submarine Force," *International Security,* vol. 28, no. 4 (Spring 2004): 161–196.

33. See Kenneth W. Allen, Glenn Krumel, and Jonathan D. Pollack, *China's Air Force Enters the Twenty-First Century* (Santa Monica, CA: RAND, 1995); John Wilson Lewis and Xue Litai, "China's Search for a Modern Air Force," *International Security,* vol. 24, no. 1 (Summer 1999): 64–94.

34. The most recent report, citing remarks by Russian Air Force Commander in Chief Vladimir Mikhaylov, claims Russia is prepared to sell Tu-95/BEAR and Tu-22M3/BACKFIRE bombers to China. See Aleksey Nikolskiy and Vasiliy Kashin, "With No One to Bomb, Russia May Sell its Strategic Aviation to China," *Moscow Vedomosti,* January 14, 2005, FBIS CEP20050114000312. Russia has historically been reluctant to sell China weapons systems that might someday be used against it, so Russian sales of advanced bombers are unlikely.

35. "China's National Defense in 2002," Information Office of the State Council, People's Republic of China, December 2002, www.nti.org/db/china/engdocs/whpandef_2002.htm. This omission may indicate that the Air Force no longer has a nuclear role, or may reflect China's unwillingness to acknowledge the possession of tactical nuclear weapons.

36. Allen and Kivlehan provide a detailed discussion of SMF training activities. The description in this paragraph draws from various Chinese press reports, which tend to stress positive developments. Nonetheless, some general trends can be identified. The authors thank Lora Saalman and Shi-chin Lin for research assistance on this section.

37. Based on Allen and Kivlehan; and "Zhongguo Junxiao Zhaosheng" (Chinese Military Academy Admissions), *Jiefangjun Bao* (*PLA Daily*), www.pladaily.com.cn/item/jxzs/tmp/bkzn/bt.htm.

38. "Langfang Lujun Daodan Xueyuan" (Langfang Army Missile Academy), *Jiefangjun Bao,* www.pladaily.com.cn/item/jxzs/tmp/bkzn/60.htm; "Kongjun Gongcheng Daxue" (Air Force Engineering University), http://edu.xaonline.com/afeu-zhaosheng.html.

39. "Di'er Paobing Gongcheng Xue Yuan" (Second Artillery Corps Engineering Academy), *Jiefangjun Bao,* www.pladaily.com.cn/item/jxzs/tmp/bkzn/31.htm; "Langfang Lujun Daodan Xueyuan"; "Kongjun Gongcheng Daxue."

40. Allen and Kivlehan.

41. "Di'er Paobing Moujidi Jianli Tuguan Jianzi Rencaiku" (A Certain Second Artillery Base Establishes a Local NCO Talent Inventory), *Jiefangjun Bao,* April 6, 2004, 2, www.pladaily.com.cn/gb/pladaily/2004/04/06/20040406001188_zgjs.html.

42. "China's Second Artillery Corps Forms 100-Strong Contingent of Missile Experts," Beijing Xinhua Domestic Service in Chinese, December 27, 2000, FBIS CPP20001227000128.

43. "China's Second Artillery Has About 160 Doctorates," *Xinhua,* April 20, 2004, FBIS CPP20040420000028.

44. "PRC: Second Artillery Corps Regiment Conducts Camouflage Training," *Jiefangjun Bao,* February 15, 2004, 2, FBIS CPP20040223000136; Wu Sulin, "PLA Tactical Missile Forces Live-Fire Exercise," *Shanghai Guoji Zhanwang,* March 1, 2004, 10–15, FBIS CPP20040315000213; Mao Xinhua et al., "Shen Kong Mou Daodan Luduan Zheng Xunlian Zhidao Sixiang de Yi Duan Jingli" (The Experience of a Shenyang Missile Brigade in the Correct Approach to Training), *Jiefangjun*

Bao, June 2, 2002; "PRC Radio on New Breakthrough in Strategic Missile Technology," August 9, 2000, FBIS CPP20000809000111.

45. Feng Jinyuan and Xia Hongqing, "A Certain Second Artillery Base Improves its Mobile Combat Operations Capabilities," *Jiefangjun Bao,* September 3, 2002, FBIS CPP20020903000058; Liu Shuli, "Magic Sword, 'Night Tiger,'" *Hsien-Tai Chun Shih* (*Conmilit*) (Hong Kong), November 11, 2002, 2–3, FBIS CPP20021202000190; "PLA 2nd Artillery Corps Holds Night Fire Missile Training," *Zhongguo Tongxun She* (Hong Kong), August 29, 1999, FBIS CPP19990830000003.

46. Wang Xiaojun and Xia Hongqing, "A Certain Brigade Under the Second Artillery Corps Focuses on Combined Tactical Training Exercises and Program of Training Officers and Soldiers Separately," *Jiefangjun Bao,* January 13, 2004, 2, FBIS CPP20040113000099.

47. Wang Xiaojun and Xia Hongqing, "Logistics Detachments of Certain Base under Second Artillery Corps Achieve Good Training Results Thanks to Application of New Training Program," *Jiefangjun Bao,* September 15, 2002, FBIS CPP20020916000048; Qiao Dexiang et al., "Xiang 'Kuai' Zi Yao Zhandouli" (Enhance Combat Capability Through Speed), *Zhongguo Kongjun* (*Chinese Air Force*), January 2003, 45–47.

48. Yao Changde and He Tianjin, "Our Strategic Missile Unit Greatly Improves Its Surveying and Mapping Capabilities," *Keji Ribao* (Beijing), January 17, 2002, FBIS CPP20020214000048.

49. Liu Yidai and He Tianjin, "Brigade of Second Artillery Corps Actively Improves Means of Training to Quickly Make New Armament Combat Ready," *Jiefangjun Bao*, November 21, 2002, 2, FBIS CPP2002112000027; Dong Jushan and Wu Xudong, "True Story: China's Mysterious Strategic Missile Forces on the Rise," *Guangzhou Ribao,* July 1, 2001, FBIS CPP20010703000044.

50. "Second Artillery Corps' Missile Simulation and Training System Handed over for Use," *Guangzhou Ribao,* February 15, 2001, FBIS CPP20010217000011.

51. Zhang Jihong et al., "Smoke Rises from the Laboratory," *Keji Ribao* (Beijing), December 1, 2001, FBIS CPP20020214000044.

52. A minimum of two submarines are necessary to keep one on operational patrol at all times; the US Navy typically requires three submarines in order to have one operationally deployed at all times.

53. Lin Chong-pin, *China's Nuclear Weapons Strategy* (Lexington, MA: Lexington Books, 1988); Lewis and Hua, 24–25; Li Bin, "The Effects of NMD on Chinese Strategy," *Jane's Intelligence Review,* vol. 13, no. 3 (March 2001): 49–52.

54. Gill, Mulvenon, and Stokes; Avery Goldstein, *Deterrence and Security in the 21st Century: China, Britain, France, and the Enduring Legacy of the Nuclear Revolution* (Stanford: Stanford University Press, 2000), 239–247.

55. Major General Yang Huan, "China's Strategic Nuclear Weapons," in *Chinese Views of Future Warfare,* Michael Pillsbury, ed. (Washington, DC: National Defense University Press, 1997), 131–135.

56. US Department of Defense (2005), 28.

57. See remarks of an anonymous US official in Diamond.

58. US Department of Defense (2005), 28.

59. Lewis and Hua, 28; "US Exports to China 1988–1998: Fueling Proliferation," Wisconsin Project on Nuclear Arms Control, April 1999.

60. US Department of Defense, (2003), 31.

61. Bill Gertz, "China Tests Ballistic Missile Submarine," *Washington Times,* December 3, 2004, A1.

62. Lewis and Xue, *China's Strategic Seapower.*

63. "China's National Defense in 2002" refers to strategic nuclear forces as being under the direct command of "the Central Military Commission (CMC) of the PRC." However the Communist Party organ, also called the Central Military Commission (and with an identical membership to the state CMC), almost certainly has control of Chinese strategic nuclear forces.

64. Federation of American Scientists, "Command and Control," updated June 23, 2000, www.fas.org/nuke/guide/china/c3i.

65. For views of some US officials that missile defense deployments will not affect China's strategic modernization, see Andrea Koppel, "China Denies Military Expansion 'Inevitable,'" September 5, 2001, www.cnn.com/2001/US/09/05/china.us.arms; Michael R. Gordon, "Bush Due to Meet Chinese on Issues Crucial for Ties," *New York Times,* March 19, 2001, 1; "Secretary of Defense Donald Rumsfeld Interview on ABC News Sunday," February 11, 2001, www.defenselink.mil/transcripts/2001/t02122001_t0211abc.html; Peter W. Rodman, *Shield Embattled: Missile Defense as a Foreign Policy Problem* (Washington, DC: The Nixon Center, October 2001), 47–50, www.nixoncenter.org/publications/monographs/shieldembattled.pdf.

66. Alan D. Romberg and Michael McDevitt, eds., *China and Missile Defense: Managing US-PRC Strategic Relations* (Washington, DC: The Henry L. Stimson Center, February 2003); Paul H.B. Godwin and Evan S. Medeiros, "China, America, and Missile Defense: Conflicting National Interests," *Current History,* vol. 99, no. 638 (September 2000): 285–289; Charles Ferguson, "Sparking a Buildup: US Missile Defense and China's Nuclear Arsenal," *Arms Control Today,* vol. 30, no. 2 (March 2000): 13–18.

67. Li Bin, "The Impact of US NMD on Chinese Nuclear Modernization," *Pugwash Online,* April 2001, www.pugwash.org/reports/rc/rc8e.htm.

68. Interviews with Chinese security analysts, Beijing, March 2002; Evan S. Medeiros, *Ballistic Missile Defense and Northeast Asian Security: Views from Washington, Beijing, and Tokyo* (Monterey, CA: Center for Nonproliferation Studies, 2001), www.cns.miis.edu/pubs/eanp/bmdrep/bmd_web.pdf.

69. For summaries of these debates, see Phillip C. Saunders, "New Approaches to Nonproliferation: Supplementing or Supplanting the Regime?" *The Nonproliferation Regime,* vol. 8, no. 3 (Fall–Winter 2001): 123–136; and Charles L. Glaser and Steve Fetter, "National Missile Defense and the Future of US Nuclear Weapons Policy," *International Security,* vol. 26, no. 1 (Summer 2001): 40–92. Also see, "Expounding Bush's Approach to US Nuclear Security: An Interview with John R. Bolton," *Arms Control Today,* vol. 32, no. 2 (March 2002): 3–8, www.armscontrol.org/act/2002_03/boltonmarch02.asp.

70. Yu Qi, "Naoren de Tiaoyue he Bazhu de Tumou" (Annoying Treaty and Hegemonic Attempt), *Jiefangjun Bao,* August 1, 1999, 5.

71. Chinese concerns initially focused on the impact of *Russian* responses to SDI and the overall impact on strategic stability. See Zhuang Qubing, "Meiguo 'Xingqiu Dazhan Jihua' Poxi," (An Analysis of the US Star Wars Program), *Guoji Wenti Yanjiu* (*International Studies*), no. 4 (1984); and Bonnie S. Glaser and Banning N. Garrett, "Chinese Perspectives on the Strategic Defense Initiative," *Problems of Communism,* vol. 35, no. 2 (March–April 1986): 28–44.

72. See Li Bin, "The Effects of NMD on the Chinese Strategy"; Li Bin, Zhao Baogen, and Liu Zhiwei, "China Will Have to Respond," *Bulletin of the Atomic Scientists,* vol. 57, no. 6 (November/December 2001); Dingli Shen, "A Chinese Perspective on National Missile Defense," Institute for Energy and Environmental Research, February 2001, www.ieer.org/latest/shen-ppr.html; Dingli Shen, "What

Missile Defense Says to China," *Bulletin of the Atomic Scientists,* vol. 56, no. 4 (July/August 2000): 20–21, www.thebulletin.org/issues/2000/ja00/ ja00shen_perspective.html; and see He Linshu and Wang Shuhe, "Penetration Measures Against NMD," *Beijing Daodan yu Hangtian Yunzai Jishu* (*Missile and Space Delivery Systems Technology*), June 10, 2002, 23-26, FBIS CPP20021007000146.

73. Mark A. Stokes, "Chinese Ballistic Missile Forces in the Age of Global Missile Defense: Challenges and Responses," in *China's Growing Military Power: Perspectives on Security, Ballistic Missiles, and Conventional Capabilities,* Andrew Scobell and Larry M. Wortzel, eds. (Carlisle, PA: Strategic Studies Institute, US Army War College, September 2002), 107–167; Mike Nartker, "China: New Report Details Chinese Missile Defense Countermeasures," *Global Security Newswire,* September 25, 2002.

74. Author's conversations with Chinese nuclear strategists, 2001.

75. Steven Lee Myers, "US Missile Plan Could Reportedly Provoke China," *New York Times,* August 10, 2000, A1.

76. *Foreign Missile Development and the Ballistic Missile Threat Through 2015,* unclassified summary of a National Intelligence Estimate, Washington, DC: National Intelligence Council, December 2001, www.fas.org/irp/nic/bmthreat-2015.htm.

77. Because the size of the Bush administration's planned BMD system is still unclear, Chinese analysts have focused more on the political intentions behind US BMD deployments rather than the technical capabilities of the initial systems.

78. For a Chinese assessment of possible ways to penetrate a US NMD system, see He Linshu and Wang Shuhe.

79. Li Bin, "The Effects of NMD on the Chinese Strategy."

80. See He Yingbo and Qiu Yong, "THAAD-Like High Altitude Theater Missile Defense: Strategic Defense Capability and Certain Countermeasures Analysis," *Science and Global Security,* vol. 11 (2003): 151–202.

81. China reportedly conducted a DF-21 (CSS-5) test in July 2002 that included dummy warheads to serve as decoys. Bill Gertz, "China Tests Arms Designed To Fool Defense Systems," *Washington Times,* July 23, 2002, A1. One possible exception is the DF-15A, which may incorporate a maneuvering warhead. "CSS-6 (DF-15/M-9)," *Jane's Strategic Weapon Systems,* no. 42 (Surrey, UK: Jane's Information Group, 2005).

82. See He Linshu and Wang Shuhe. For a technical overview of BMD countermeasures, see Andrew M. Sessler et al., *Countermeasures: A Technical Evaluation of the Operational Effectiveness of the Planned US National Missile Defense System* (Boston: Union of Concerned Scientists, 2000), www.ucsusa.org/documents/CM_all.pdf.

83. Phillip C. Saunders, Jing-dong Yuan, Stephanie Lieggi, and Angela Deters, "China's Space Capabilities and the Strategic Logic of Anti-Satellite Weapons," Center for Nonproliferation Studies report, Monterey Institute of International Studies, July 2002, http://cns.miis.edu/pubs/week/020722.htm.

84. Wu Kai, "Dui He Liliang de Sikao" (On Nuclear Forces), *Bingqi zhishi* (*Ordinance Knowledge*), no. 4 (April 2001): 11.

85. See Michael Puttré, "Satellite-Guided Munitions," *Scientific American,* vol. 288, no. 2 (February 2003): 66–73.

86. "US War Game Signals New Arms Race in Space Weaponry in 21st Century," *Jiefangjun Bao,* February 21, 2001, FBIS CPP20010221000091; Teng Jianqun, "You Meijun Taikongzhan Yanxi Suoxiang" (Thoughts Arising from the US Military's Space War Exercise), *Jiefangjun Bao,* February 7, 2001, 9, FBIS CPP20010207000050; Nicholas Berry, "Space War Games and China as Vader's

Empire," *The Weekly Defense Monitor,* vol. 5, no. 5 (February 1, 2001); Jason Sherman, "China Looks Askance at Space War Game," *Defense News,* February 28, 2001, 3, 19.

87. Johnston, "China's New 'Old Thinking'"; Alastair Iain Johnston, "Prospects for Chinese Nuclear Force Modernization: Limited Deterrence versus Multilateral Arms Control," *China Quarterly,* no. 146 (June 1996): 548–576.

88. Johnston, "Prospects for Chinese Nuclear Force Modernization," 555–557.

89. Brad Roberts, Robert A. Manning, and Ronald N. Montaperto, "China: The Forgotten Nuclear Power," *Foreign Affairs,* vol. 79, no. 4 (July/August 2000): 53–63.

90. See "China's Fissile Material Production and Stockpile," *China WMD Database,* Center for Nonproliferation Studies, Monterey Institute for International Studies, www.nti.org/db/china/fmstock.htm; and David Wright and Lisbeth Gronlund, "Estimating China's Production of Plutonium for Weapons," *Science and Global Security,* vol. 11, no. 1 (2003): 61–80.

91. David E. Mosher and Lowell H. Schwartz, "The China and Nuclear Reunion Is Only A Motive Away," *Los Angeles Times,* February 25, 2001.

92. Lewis and Hua, 22; James A. Lamson and Wyn Q. Bowen, "'One Arrow, Three Stars': China's MIRV Program, Part I," *Jane's Intelligence Review,* vol. 9, no. 5 (May 1997): 216–218; and James A. Lamson and Wyn Q. Bowen, "'One Arrow, Three Stars': China's MIRV Program, Part II," *Jane's Intelligence Review,* vol. 9, no. 6 (June 1997): 266–269.

93. Lewis and Hua, 22.

94. This capability was developed in order to launch Motorola's Iridium series of communications satellites. For an example, see "Long March Rocket Lifts 'Experimental Satellite I,' 'Nanostar I' into Space," *Beijing Xinhua Domestic Service,* April 18, 2004, FBIS CPP20040419000003.

95. Federation of American Scientists, "China's Nuclear Weapons: Present Capabilities," last updated May 1, 2001, www.fas.org/nuke/hew/China/ChinaArsenal.html.

96. Director of Central Intelligence, "The Intelligence Community Damage Assessment on the Implications of China's Acquisition of US Nuclear Weapons Information on the Development of Future Chinese Weapons," April 21, 1999, www.nti.org/db/china/engdocs/cia499.htm.

97. We believe China's large foreign currency reserves are sufficient to fund whatever strategic modernization efforts China's leaders deem absolutely necessary, but an economic slowdown could make the leadership more reluctant to devote resources to this purpose.

98. For an assessment of the potential impact of China's strategic modernization on Sino-US political relations, see Phillip C. Saunders, "US-China Relations in a Changing Nuclear Environment," in *Strategic Surprise? US-China Relations in the Early Twenty-First Century,* Jonathan D. Pollack, ed. (Newport, RI: Naval War College Press, 2003), 159–184.

99. Lewis and Xue, *China Builds the Bomb.*

100. Banning Garrett, "The Need for Strategic Reassurance in the 21st Century," *Arms Control Today,* vol. 31, no. 2 (March 2001): 9–14, www.armscontrol.org/act/2001_03/garrett.asp.

101. Glenn Kessler, "US, China Agree to Regular Talks," *Washington Post,* April 8, 2005, A14.

5

Beijing's Perceptions of US Intentions

Ronald N. Montaperto

This chapter focuses on Beijing's overall perceptions of the United States and analyzes the various ways in which they influence Chinese policies on nuclear issues. The objective is twofold: first, to identify and describe Chinese elite impressions and perceptions of Washington's long-term intentions toward China; and, second, to assess the ways in which those perceptions are likely to be manifested in specific decisions about the size and composition of China's nuclear forces, their posture, and Beijing's policies on nuclear weapons proliferation. It is, thus, an effort to enrich the discussion of "hard" issues such as force balance as factors in Chinese decisionmaking by assessing the impact of "soft" political and national interest-related factors on such matters. It is as much about Chinese foreign policy in general as it is about specific decisions on nuclear matters.

The chapter begins with an analysis of elite perceptions based on authoritative, official publications, publications in academic venues, and discussions with Chinese officials over a period of nearly twenty years. The objective is to describe the Chinese view of United States intentions. It then moves to a consideration of the extent to which Chinese opinion considers Washington to be physically and above all politically capable of acting on the basis of its perceptions; that is, it deals with Beijing's assessment of US capabilities. A third section describes Beijing's emerging strategies for dealing with the United States. This is followed by a review of the evolution of Chinese decisions on nuclear matters and an assessment of likely future decisions.

These objectives, however, are more readily described than accomplished. As will become apparent, there is more than one set of perceptual patterns within the Chinese policy community and, despite some commonalities, each has the potential to produce different—and at times conflicting—decisions. In similar fashion, policy discourse in the United States obviously affects Chinese perceptions and, as Brad Roberts notes in his chapter on alternative futures, US experts sometimes do not agree on how to interpret the same sets of data.[1] Finally, Chinese strategic culture contains an imperative to create uncertainty in the minds of real or potential adversaries by shrouding capabilities in secrecy; this inevitably complicates any effort to understand Chinese positions.

US Goals and Objectives: The Quest For Hegemony

There can be little or no doubt that the state of thinking in Beijing ranges from a high level of skepticism to frank apprehension about the United States and its intentions in the longer term. What little positive comment exists is focused on forces and trends that limit US actions rather than on positive factors intrinsic to America itself. Chinese analysts even impute a measure of hypocrisy to Washington's motives, noting that although US leaders speak of establishing democratic governments and market economies as a moral good, the reality amounts to imposing such values on nations against their will.

Chinese analysts take special note of such official documents as the *National Military Strategy*, the *Quadrennial Defense Review (QDR)*, the *Nuclear Posture Review (NPR)*, and the *National Strategy to Combat Weapons of Mass Destruction*, and conclude with apparent certainty that Washington views China as a potential threat. Indeed, in the *QDR* it is strongly suggested that China is the only nation that might rise to challenge United States preeminence.[2]

Concern that China is the target of negative US intentions is reinforced by other developments. For example, there is the reality of deepening US alliance relations with Japan, the perception that Tokyo is rearming, and US efforts to expand access to and secure bases in Central Asia and Southeast Asia.[3] These concerns are further reinforced by perceived developments in US thinking about the nature of its basic military capabilities. Of particular concern in this regard is a new emphasis on ballistic missile defense and precision guided conventional weapons, which in combination with improved nuclear weapons and delivery systems comprise a self-proclaimed new US triad designed to guarantee US security well into the twenty-first century. The new triad is of crucial concern to Beijing because, as has been noted elsewhere in this volume, the projected combination of capabilities would seriously threaten to degrade the effectiveness of Beijing's own ballistic missile force and render China vulnerable to US manipulation. Since Beijing's intercontinental ballistic missile force is a major component of its effort to deter a potential US intervention in the event of a conflict in the Taiwan Straits, Chinese concerns are very real. For Beijing, reunification with Taiwan is a vital national interest and any development that is perceived to limit or negate its freedom of action is bound to affect both its perception of the United States and its decisions on nuclear force structure and posture.[4]

Coping with the Hegemon: US Strengths and Vulnerabilities

The discourse, however, does not end here. China must, after all, continue to safeguard and improve its place in the world and much attention is given to crafting strategies for doing so. Beijing's dilemma can be described as follows: how does a rising nation committed to achieving reunification and a world class level of economic development so order its external relations that it is able to achieve its objectives and not provoke the opposition of a suspicious great power that possesses overwhelming comprehensive national power?[5]

The requirement to craft strategies for resolving China's particular strategic challenge produces a lively discussion among Chinese analysts focused mainly on their perception that the United States is fulfilling the role of global hegemon. Chinese analysts seek to identify conditions that might provide Beijing with certain leverages in conducting relations with Washington. That in turn provokes analysis of US strengths and vulnerabilities.

Accordingly, there is a careful assessment of both the internal and external factors that enhance and/or constrain Washington's policy alternatives. The extremely active discussion includes assessments of the vulnerabilities in America's comprehensive national power and especially its military power, the impact of opposing domestic, political, and economic trends on policy decisions, and the stresses and strains affecting Washington's relations with external powers and international organizations. Additionally, considerable attention is paid to assessing how the priorities and interests of the majority of nations combine to define the climate within the overall international system: basically, do the nations of the world seek peace and stability or something else?

The purpose of the discussion, which is often conducted in direct response to the directives of the Chinese Communist Party (CCP) and governmental authorities, is to identify ways and means by which Beijing can pursue its own policy objectives more effectively. The various positions that emerge form the basis for the process of decisionmaking. It is worth noting, parenthetically, that the level of sophistication and complexity of the discussion has increased markedly in the last decade. Generally speaking, there is little disagreement within the Chinese policy elite about the hegemonic, anti-China orientation of the United States. However, there is noticeably less agreement about Washington's ability to work its will in the international arena. It is these perceived weaknesses and vulnerabilities that provide the basis for Beijing's relatively positive approach to conducting day-to-day relations with Washington. As will be shown, these perceived vulnerabilities and limitations on US freedom of action also have major impact on Chinese policies in the nuclear realm.[6]

Take for example the issue of the United States as global hegemon. For some Chinese analysts, US hegemonism and unilateralism are totally unacceptable, particularly in light of the overwhelming comprehensive national power of the United States. The war in Iraq is viewed as an element of Washington's larger plan to impose its values on a global scale. The effort to democratize the "Greater Middle East" is seen as but the first step in this process.[7]

Proponents of this view have a similar interpretation of the global war on terrorism. Although they are quick to acknowledge the seriousness of the problem and the challenge that separatism and terrorism pose to China itself, they also assert that Washington is using the war on terrorism as a cover under which it can expand its global presence by deploying its forces to the Middle East and Central Asia. The recent call by Beijing (and Moscow) for the removal of US forces from Central Asia undoubtedly is motivated by this concern. Similarly, it is argued that it is strategic rivalry and not solely the desire to spread democracy that accounts for US support for Taiwan. A Taiwan that is separate from the mainland, or worse, independent, not only prevents the completion of the process of Chinese reunification, it also blocks China's rise to its rightful place in the global system. A surprisingly large number of analysts would also argue that an independent Taiwan would provide the US with an "unsinkable aircraft carrier," which when combined with its military deployments in Japan and the Republic of Korea, would provide a link in the chain of containment aimed at China.[8]

And yet, there is another, more nuanced and less pessimistic take on United States unilateralism. According to this view, while Washington's policies are problematic in terms of the pursuit of Chinese national interests, in some ways they do serve Chinese goals. For example, the United States dominance—in East Asia if not in the Middle East—guarantees a measure of political stability sufficient to enable Beijing to concentrate on its most important priority apart from Taiwan, economic development.[9] It is necessary, however, to underscore the fact that the number of Chinese analysts who would endorse this assessment has declined in recent years, as has its impact on policy. Indeed, no small number of analysts would dispute the imputation of any value at all to the US regional presence. There are two reasons for this: first, Beijing is most suspicious about the growing closeness of US relations with Taiwan, especially in the military sphere; and, second, the Chinese are clearly growing more confident of their ability to manage their own interests themselves.

Also, and more important, it must be realized that Chinese analysts believe there are inevitable limits to unilateral action on a global scale. The Chinese perceive that the unilateralist and preemptive aspects of the US war and occupation of Iraq are obviously destabilizing and Washington will continue to pay a high price in terms of its relations with other Muslim countries. It will also have to come to terms with the continuing lack of support from its allies. In the same way, although it is true that the stabilizing US military presence in East Asia threatens China's position in the Taiwan Straits, it is also true that US military intervention in any conflict that might occur between China and Taiwan will stress its alliances and relations with virtually all of the nations of the region. Hence, difficult though the challenge might be for China, the United States faces political (as well as military) vulnerabilities that could be used as points of leverage to limit and constrain Washington's freedom of action.[10]

At the same time, according to this view, the unilateralism of the United States should also be seen as arising as a natural corollary of its overwhelming comprehensive national power. The United States is the overwhelmingly dominant power within the international system and, by definition, dominant powers inevitably control the pulse of international relations. In other words, some element of unilateralism is inevitable and in many ways desirable. Failure to set the international agenda would amount to an abrogation of responsibility. The result would be a diminution of order within the system that would lead to increased levels of instability, if not chaos. Neither of these conditions would be in China's interest. Washington is doing exactly what it is supposed to do and, should its actions impinge upon Chinese interests, Beijing has the means to protect itself.[11]

Questions of distribution of power across the international system and the priorities of the majority of nations engender a similar exchange. With respect to national priorities, official Chinese statements assert that peace and development are the most important trends defining the contemporary international system. On the question of the distribution of power, the official position holds that the world is gradually moving toward a state of multipolarity. It is further argued that this is a positive development since it will prevent the domination of the international system by any one power while ensuring stability and peace based upon the creation of a balance of power.[12]

However, as with the issue of hegemonism and unilateralism, the official view masks the existence of a much more nuanced discussion. There are those who question whether there is a movement toward multipolarity at all. Proponents of this view hold that, although other centers of power are emerging, they do not rise to the status of poles within the international system. Decades will pass before today's big powers can, or will wish to, challenge the preeminence of the United States.[13]

Whether the international system is moving towards multipolarity or not is, therefore, seen by some Chinese analysts as irrelevant. For the foreseeable future at least, Chinese and other national leaders must face the need to manage national policies in a world in which one power, the United States, predominates. The European Union, Russia, India, and China may be able to affect United States behavior in some ways, but none of them will be able by themselves to actually set the global strategic agenda. The reality of an effectively unipolar world will not change in the near to mid term.

Nor is multipolarity necessarily a positive development. The historical, cultural, religious, and strategic rivalries that divide the global system mean that maintaining stability in a multipolar world will require a constantly evolving process of shifting roles and relations that is intrinsically destructive of stability and therefore subversive of peace.[14]

Chinese policymakers, therefore, face the challenge of making decisions based on an assessment of the trade-off between seeking the freedom of action that accrues from a world in which no one power is dominant and accepting at least temporarily the constraints imposed by the need to consider the potentially negative reaction of one overwhelmingly dominant power. The question is: should China try to reshape the world to its advantage by actively challenging and seeking to alter its strategic structure and norms, or is it more effective to work within the reality of the international environment and seek incremental change over a longer period of time?

Both choices obviously involve risk and a certain level of instability. But, it is argued here that the Chinese have chosen the latter course. Whether this choice reflects a deeper change in the ways in which the Chinese policy community conceives and thinks about foreign and national security policy, or whether the choice amounts to little more than a tactical adjustment to see China through a difficult time, remains to be seen.[15] Still, no matter what the case, the choice is directly relevant to the bilateral interaction of China and the United States on nuclear matters.

Living with the United States

During the last three years or so, the content and tone of Beijing's foreign and national security policies in general, and its approach to Washington in particular, have reflected a mixture of elements drawn from both of the positions described above. However, as the 2002 and, perhaps to a lesser extent, the 2004 white papers make clear, Beijing apparently has chosen to work within the system to achieve its objectives.

On the one hand, the intellectual policy discourse reveals deep suspicion and concern that in the longer-term bilateral relations are likely to be difficult if not actually hostile. This is apparent in some Chinese policies. For example, PLA modernization continues apace and it is clear that a major consideration is the need to confront the United States successfully in the event of conflict in the Taiwan Straits. Similarly, although the desired end state remains unclear, and as Phil Saunders and Jing-dong Yuan remind us in this volume, Beijing continues to modernize its strategic nuclear forces, clearly with US capabilities in mind. It should also be noted that as recent events in Hong Kong attest, the Chinese leadership shows no willingness to be more responsive to pressures for greater freedom and openness.

But, on the other hand, the reality of day-to-day interactions at this time clearly indicates willingness to engage actively with the United States and with the Asia Pacific region across a wide spectrum of issues. It is also arguable that Beijing shows a willingness to work actively to prevent disagreement from escalating to a point at which relations are disrupted.[16] This assertion is supported by examination of Chinese behavior with respect to four issues that are crucial in defining the nature of the bilateral relationship: counterterrorism; Taiwan; participation in international and multilateral organizations; and proliferation and arms control.

Terrorism

With respect to the first, Beijing is working actively with Washington to deal with the terrorist threat both within the region and globally. China's leaders understand that since September 11, 2001, countering terrorism has become the highest priority for the United States. Moreover, the leadership has shown itself to be eager to engage in this arena. It will be recalled that then president Jiang Zemin was quick to express Chinese condolences and offer assistance immediately after 9/11.

Significantly, once Washington reciprocated by agreeing to acknowledge the legitimacy of Chinese concern about terrorist activities in Xinjiang, the conditionality of Beijing's support for the US position and strategy abated. Although the Chinese almost certainly expect that their assistance should increase US support for their position on Taiwan, there has apparently been no explicit articulation of such a demand, either publicly or in private. History has demonstrated that Chinese and US claims that the need to cooperate in countering terrorism would provide a basis for redefining the bilateral tie were extreme. With hindsight, however, it is clear that September 11 did mark the beginning of a much-improved atmosphere as well as willingness to cooperate on matters of common concern.

Taiwan

Ever since President Chen Shui-bian's first inaugural address, Beijing's Taiwan policies have continued to be more measured than they had been in the past. Chinese leaders appear to agree that the policies of the past, which alternated between forceful assertion by military means and softer approaches based on economic relations, have failed to arrest what they perceive to be Taiwan's slide towards separatism and independence. In spite of increased saber-rattling after Chen's second inauguration, they have yet to agree on a new approach.

In the meantime, the approach continues to be to remind Taipei of the inevitable negative consequences and costs of a declaration of independence, to affirm the benefits to Taiwan of compromise and flexibility, and to complicate the position of Tawiwan's government by establishing contacts with leaders of the opposition. Beijing would obviously terminate this approach if Taipei were to attempt unilaterally to alter the status quo either by constitutional revision that redefined the sovereignty and territory of the Republic of China or by an outright declaration of independence. The antisecession law adopted by the National

People's Congress in 2005 is an attempt to intensify the pressure on Taipei. Beijing will also continue to increase the pressure on Washington to restrain Chen's actions, an effort that appears thus far to have failed to measure up to Beijing's expectations. This shows that Taiwan will remain one of the questions that are not subject to negotiation and compromise and will remain the one issue that could produce a rupture in relations and even armed conflict between the two nations.[17]

International Organizations

As recently as five years ago, Beijing regarded international organizations as backdrops against which its competition with the United States played out. In the Chinese view, the US used international forums such as the United Nations (UN) to assert its dominance. The Chinese saw their participation as a means of countering that dominance and gaining credit by asserting their concerns and asserting the sovereignty of other developing countries. Multilateral approaches to Asian issues were condemned out-of-hand as devices designed to marginalize Beijing's role in the region.[18] However, in recent years, Beijing has greatly expanded its participation in the Association of Southeast Asian Nations (ASEAN) Regional Forum, instituted the ASEAN +3 discussions, hosted a series of workshops and training sessions focused on economics and terrorism, participated in United Nations peacekeeping operations, and voted for UN Resolution 1441 on Iraq and for acceptance of the UN-brokered Iraqi interim government. More significantly, in a complete break with past practice, Beijing has established a six-party process on the Korean peninsula that might evolve into a permanent organization.[19]

Proliferation and Arms Control

Finally, with respect to proliferation and arms control, the Chinese have turned away from decades of asserting the right of nations to possess nuclear arms and free-riding and begun to participate in and support a range of arms control and nonproliferation regimes. Beijing has ratified the Treaty on Nonproliferation of Nuclear Weapons and the Chemical Weapons Convention. After years of nitpicking about the nature of "inherent capabilities," it agreed to join the Missile Technology Control regime. Recently the Chinese government emplaced a set of regulations designed to control the sale of dual-use technologies. This action was capped by entrance into the Nuclear Suppliers Group.[20]

New Trends in Foreign Policy

These briefly sketched examples are not intended to suggest that the leadership has concluded that China's interests coincide with those of the United States, or that there is a high degree of agreement on international issues. Beijing and Washington will continue to disagree on a wide range of issues, including proliferation and arms control and the structure and posture of their respective nuclear forces. It is, rather, to suggest that Beijing has decided that it is more supportive of Chinese interests to work within the structure and norms of the international system and try to shape regional and global conditions to China's advantage than it is to resist or accept them only grudgingly.[21]

It is also to suggest the emergence of a policy framework in Beijing that allows the leadership to accept or at least settle for outcomes that may be less than ideal, but which do not involve damage to such vital Chinese interests as national reunification (Taiwan), maintaining internal stability, and, of greatest significance, achieving the economic development on which the leadership has staked its continued tenure. Put differently, the ideal is not to be permitted to become the enemy of the acceptable.

There will be no compromise on issues involving sovereignty or the leadership of the Chinese Communist Party. Beyond that, all other problems are to be managed rather than allowed to evolve to the point of conflict. Dealing with WMD and delivery systems proliferation seems clearly to fall within the set of issues marked for engagement, negotiation, and compromise. Whether issues concerning the size and posture of its nuclear forces do or do not remains to be seen.

Considering the purpose of this chapter, it is worth speculating about the rationale that may account for Beijing's present approach. The generally negative perception of the United States has already been described and certain differences in view noted. At this point, it is worth asking whether there is anything about the competition between proponents of different points of view in China that might affect future decisions on nuclear issues. It is also worth inquiring as to why the Chinese government has decided it is possible and desirable not only to maintain stable relations with the United States, but also to work actively to improve them, and how this determination might affect Beijing's decisions on nuclear matters.

First, Chinese leaders correctly judge that the China policies of successive US administrations vary and change in response to internal political circumstances and the influence of external problems. It can be argued that Chinese analysts and practitioners alike have concluded that the perceptions of China held by the present administration are not consistent with those of previous administrations and, moreover, may not be shared by future US governments.

Second, it is also arguable that Chinese officials do not believe that longer-term concerns about China are shared with equal intensity by all sectors within the Bush administration, or that all sectors assign similar priorities to the need to deal with the challenge of China in the first place. For example, especially during the current administration, a wealth of anecdotal evidence supports the view that Chinese military and civilian officials have found the Department of State generally to be more open to proposals for expanded ties than the Department of Defense.[22] While prepared to acknowledge that US thinking about China is measurably more skeptical across the board than has been the case in the past, there is also a recognition that the United States too has hardliners and moderates and that this division provides opportunities to achieve positive results for China on at least some issues of major importance. However, and third, the key to understanding China's approach to its relations with the US lies in the suggestion that Beijing analysts distinguish between US perceptions and intentions on the one hand and US capabilities on the other. Put simply. it is posited here that there is a view in China that, despite its dangerous intentions and its overwhelming military capabilities, the United States is, at this moment in time, incapable of treating China in ways consistent with those suggested in the *QDR*, the *NPR,* and other national strategy documents. To divert energies and resources into containment strategies would produce excessive political, economic, and strategic costs for America and simultaneously detract from the ability to deal with the terrorist threat. Just as the need to create conditions necessary to sustain economic development is the driving force of Chinese foreign policy, so too the foreign policy of the United States is defined by the need to prosecute the global war against terrorism. That struggle is the prism through which Washington currently views the world and nearly all foreign and national security policy decisions are evaluated according to how much or how little they support counterterrorism objectives.

The views of Chinese analysts tend to support the interpretation sketched above. According to the dominant Chinese view, the need to develop and maintain support for the antiterrorist effort constrains US unilateralist impulses. The sequence of events in Iraq is cited as an example of this constraining force. Having encountered difficulties and in the face of only grudging international support, Washington has been forced to modify its policies in order to retain the support of allies and friends. As President Bush's 2005 mission suggests, the US has also found it necessary to restore its relations with NATO and the UN.[23]

A Period of Strategic Opportunity?

At the same time and for similar kinds of reasons, the Bush administration will not wish to be distracted by frictions with China, particularly when Beijing's assistance is required to achieve supervening goals involving the war on terrorism. For example, Beijing's ties with Pakistan and its lack of open opposition to US military deployments in Central Asia are valued by the United States. In the circumstances, containing China would be counterproductive.

Thus, negative perceptions notwithstanding, Beijing's approach to managing relations with the US appears to be based on the following judgments. First, irrespective of whether the international system is moving toward true multipolarity or not, new centers of strategic influence like the European Community, Russia, ASEAN, NATO, and China itself exist and are likely to grow more significant with the passage of time. This will complicate planning for the United States as it will be necessary to consider a wider range of potential reactions before implementing various policies.

More pertinently, and despite notable differences between their comprehensive national power and that of the United States, the new centers will remain willing to adopt policies that are different from Washington's when they judge it to be in their interest to do so. As with Iraq, the Korean Peninsula, and definitely with Taiwan, different definitions of vital national interests will produce policy options that tend to separate Washington from its friends and allies, despite the gravitational pull of shared democratic values. Military strength alone will not guarantee full freedom of action.[24]

Second, according to US estimates contained in the *National Security Strategy* and the *QDR,* Washington acknowledges that some years will pass before China is capable of challenging the United States as a peer competitor. Hence, given its other more immediate priorities, the United States is not likely to threaten the interests or the position of China anytime soon.

In effect, Beijing judges that it faces a period of up to fifteen or even twenty years during which it will be possible to avoid conflict and devote its national energies to developing its economy to a point at which it will be able to hold its own, if not as a true pole within the international system, then at least as a major power in its own right.[25] During the period of strategic opportunity, the objective of Chinese policies should be to shape the international environment in ways that work to China's advantage. This will require securing an economic, political, and strategic base within the region and globally by developing broad and deep ties with other nations, international and regional organizations, and above all by avoiding conflict.[26]

In sum, it seems clear that Washington's economic, political, and strategic importance will guarantee that the United States remains the key element in Beijing's overall strategic calculus. China's leaders will maintain a basic mistrust of US intentions in the longer term but nonetheless continue to keep the relationship stable while seeking opportunities for comprehensive development in order to compete more effectively in the future. This stance will undoubtedly have major implications for Chinese decisions on nuclear matters.

In order to be successful, this effort will require a constant monitoring of US policy guidance documents as well as the content of US policies in certain key—to Beijing—areas to identify any changes in US positions. Two of the most important indicators in Beijing's estimation almost certainly will be United States relations with Taiwan and changes in policies related to nuclear affairs. These will include US antiproliferation policies, the ways in which Washington sizes, structures, and postures its nuclear forces, and the evolution of US nuclear doctrine. With respect to this last, the mix of offensive and defensive capabilities will be of signal importance. Chinese leaders will watch very closely to see how Washington decides to integrate ballistic missile defense systems into its overall strategies.

Nonproliferation and Arms Control

Until the turn of the century, nonproliferation, counterproliferation, and arms control were issues that divided the United States and China. For Beijing, the possession of nuclear weapons was a matter of national sovereignty. Similarly, if any nation chose to exercise its sovereign right to develop a nuclear capability, Beijing felt it should have the latitude to determine for itself whether or not to render assistance by whatever means it considered appropriate. Nor did Beijing express much confidence in efforts at nuclear disarmament or arms control sponsored by the other nuclear powers. Rather, the Chinese preferred to identify themselves with a number of small and middle powers with nuclear ambitions and criticized such proposals and regimes as hypocritical, naked attempts by the United States and the former Soviet Union to maintain their own nuclear preeminence.[27]

A third element in China's past behavior was the practice of conditioning Chinese participation in and support for arms control on reciprocal US, Russian, or UN actions, often in areas that were only tenuously connected to concerns about proliferation. For example, after having transferred certain missile and nuclear technologies to Iran and possibly Iraq, Beijing then withdrew support for the proposed Arms Control Middle East (ACME) process, largely as a response to US refusal to end the sale of weapons to Taiwan. US attempts to influence Chinese transfers of nuclear and missile technology to Pakistan were rebuffed under similar circumstances. All in all, from a US perspective, Beijing's actions in these areas were cynical, self-serving, and downright dishonest.[28]

However, in the last few years, the situation has changed. Nuclear nonproliferation and arms control have emerged as areas in which both sides see benefit and as areas in which both sides should and do cooperate. Beijing has apparently decided that its interests are better served by joining the movement to limit the spread of nuclear arms.[29]

This movement was slow to emerge and the forces behind it were many and varied. Externally, the United States and the former Soviet Union reduced the size of their arsenals to unexpectedly low levels, thus depriving Beijing of its rationale for not joining the process and actually leaving it vulnerable to criticism for not participating in the global arms control agenda. Additionally, the nuclearization of South Asia, the crises involving North Korea, and the emergence of a credible possibility of nuclear (and chemical and biological) weapons of mass destruction falling into the hand of terrorists all served to sensitize the Chinese leadership to the need for corrective measures.

Internally, sectors in Beijing realized that China was unable to influence the international discourse on arms control because it did not have available a cadre of experts with the technical knowledge and ability to hold their own in international circles. During the 1990s, such a cadre emerged and, while many of its leaders continued to hew to the traditional line, others introduced arguments for a course reversal.[30]

The main events in the evolution of Chinese nonproliferation policies have already been sketched and need not be repeated here. It is sufficient to recall that in addition to formal accession to major nonproliferation protocols, Beijing has taken steps to bring its transfers of nuclear and dual-use technologies under control, to put programs already in place on hold, and to exert influence where it can, most notably in Pakistan. It is probable that the centrality to China of positive relations between the US and Pakistan in the context of the need to combat terrorism is responsible for Chinese efforts to persuade Islamabad to be more careful about its transfers of nuclear, missile-related, and dual-use technologies.

China's new stance is directly related to the larger decision to use *this* period of strategic opportunity to strengthen its long-run position both in the region and globally by associating itself with nonproliferation efforts that are welcome in the international community. It also serves Chinese interests in a more immediate sense. Beijing could probably live with a nuclear North Korea but, in the short run, the North Korean program raises the possibility of instability if not actual conflict in an area contiguous with China's borders. Such a development would clearly not serve the interests of a leadership that is committed to maintaining the stable external environment that is essential for continued economic development.

The end result of the combination of internal impulses, external pressures, and perceived Chinese interests will be to diminish and probably remove questions of nonproliferation and arms control from the list of nettlesome problems that will influence the overall Sino-US bilateral relationship. Anti-proliferation initiatives of the United States, particularly as they bear upon concerns about terrorism, will not separate Washington and Beijing. On the contrary, they are likely to receive Chinese backing and support.

Nuclear Force Issues

On the other hand, issues involving nuclear force size, structure, and posture, and the role of ballistic missile defense, are far more complex and hold far more potential for disrupting relations, even allowing for Chinese recognition of the importance of the US tie to their overall goals and objectives. This is because Chinese analysts see Washington's nuclear policies as concrete indicators of US intentions over the longer term. Actual deployments will resolve any lingering ambiguities about gaps between perceived intentions and Washington's ability to implement them. It is also worth noting that US Taiwan policy plays an identical role in Chinese assessments. For Beijing, Taiwan is a matter of sovereignty. In the same way, US nuclear force capabilities, deployments, and the role of missile defense bear directly on national survival.

These issues are, therefore, of transcendent importance and do not fall within the realm of those that are to be managed by compromise, adjustment, or patient acquiescence.[31]

Ending arms sales to Taiwan, however inappropriate and unlikely such a decision would be, would greatly ease Chinese concerns about US regional military deployments as elements of a larger containment strategy. Nuclear weapons policies that allow for Chinese concerns about the survival of their nuclear forces, which also raise major issues of appropriateness and likelihood, would have identical symbolic significance.

Of all the dimensions along which Chinese analysts and officials evaluate US intentions, these two are arguably the most important. Frictions over human rights, the value of the *renminbi,* and the trade deficit will not, in light of the policy framework *now* operating in Beijing, have permanent adverse impact on the relationship. Nuclear weapons policy, on the other hand, could have a very serious impact indeed.

Nuclear Force Issues in China's Calculus of Defense

Generally speaking, there are two major reasons for the existence of China's nuclear forces. First, in a historical sense, the Chinese believe now as they did when the nuclear program began in the late 1950s that a credible nuclear capability is essential to maintaining freedom of action by reducing China's vulnerability to pressures exerted by other nuclear powers. China must be able to prevent nuclear blackmail. Although the end of the Cold War and the major reductions in the forces of the United States and the former Soviet Union and Russia have changed China's nuclear environment, the principle remains the same. The United States and Russia continue to be factors of major consideration. So too, despite Chinese denials, does a nuclear India.

The second relates to the first but is more specific and far more immediate. Among analysts there is undeniably considerable discussion and debate about tactics, various courses of a potential escalation chain, the nature of the final outcome, and even the very utility of nuclear weapons as a deterrent factor in the context of a Taiwan Straits conflict. Despite that discourse, however, Chinese decisionmakers appear to believe that a nuclear weapons capability is an essential component in deterring US military support for Taiwan in the event of such a conflict. Until the issue is settled, therefore, it is necessary for US analysts to treat the nuclear factor as an essential element of planning for contingencies in the Taiwan Straits.[32] Thus, nuclear weapons may prove to be quite relevant to confrontation over Taiwan. It is impossible to assess with any degree of certainty how the nuclear dimension would play out. (See also Ting Wai in this volume for additional analysis on Taiwan.)

On the surface it would seem that the US holds the upper hand owing to its overwhelming nuclear and, since the early 1990s, precision-guided conventional capabilities. However, this assessment fails to recognize that for Beijing, Taiwan is an issue of national identity and, therefore, that Beijing may be willing to bear the costs of conflict, including the considerable costs of a nuclear exchange.

This in turn raises the issue of escalation and its control. Although intuitively it would seem that Washington would be reluctant to use nuclear weapons in the early stages of a conflict due in part to its greater conventional capability and the greater costs incurred in a nuclear exchange, later developments could very well cause the United States to mount conventional attacks on military facilities in the interior of China. The likelihood of such a course would be enhanced if Beijing were to successfully neutralize US regional forces and/or US bases in Japan or the Western Pacific through diplomatic or military means. Finally, there is the issue of ballistic missile defense. Again, intuitively, BMD would seem to work to the advantage of the United States and Taiwan. However, Taiwan—and conceivably US—missile defenses would likely be immediate and primary targets in any conflict, thus raising once again the problem of escalation control.

In any case, it will be recalled that probably for economic and technological reasons, Beijing has never attempted to achieve equivalency of numbers in building its nuclear force. Rather, the Chinese have preferred to achieve deterrence by maintaining a relatively small number of weapons while ensuring by means of cover and concealment that, in the event of a strike against them, a number would survive that would be sufficient to inflict unacceptable damage on the attacker. The corollary of this concept of minimum deterrence is the deliberate rejection of a first strike capability. Survivability is key. The adversary must believe that Beijing can inflict unacceptable damage, or at least not be certain that it cannot.

Whether the Chinese have ever truly believed they possess such a capability or that such a basic notion of minimum deterrence is appropriate to the contemporary strategic environment is a matter of conjecture. Certainly circumstances in Russia and India, US proficiency with precision guided weapons, Washington's announced intention to proceed with deploying missile defense systems, and Beijing's own considerable technological progress would appear to raise questions about the effectiveness of minimum deterrence and also suggest that Beijing possesses the technical means to develop alternative strategies.[33]

This is not to argue that Beijing either has or is planning to shift away from minimum deterrence to something else. Suffice it to say that in addition to showing signs of concern about minimum deterrence, Beijing also shows evidence of doubt about the survivability of its force. Ironically, the Chinese cannot be certain—as they must be—that potential adversaries remain unsure of their ability to locate and destroy all of Beijing's missiles.[34]

It is almost without doubt the concern about the need to maintain survivability and that lack of certainty that drives the nuclear force modernization program that has been in place for nearly two decades. Advances in the capabilities of other powers, and especially the emergence of ballistic missile defense as a major element of nuclear doctrine and strategy, must be compensated for. However, it is impossible to be confident about the ultimate objective. The entry of mobile, solid-fuel IRBMs (intermediate range ballistic missiles) and ICBMs (intercontinental ballistic missiles) along with a new reliance on SRBMs (short range ballistic missiles) with both nuclear and conventional warheads could also suggest a movement toward limited deterrence or even an eventual warfighting capability.[35] (For more on developments in Chinese doctrine, see Evan Medeiros in this volume.)

Thus, it can be said definitively, that China's nuclear modernization program amounts to considerably more than a one-for-one replacement of older weapons with new ones. On the contrary, modernization is directly targeted on one major objective: maintaining a secure second-strike capability. Minimum deterrence continues to hold the attention of Chinese strategists.[36]

Whether Beijing is aiming to perfect a doctrine of minimum deterrence, develop the capability for limited deterrence and warfighting, or something else, the Chinese cannot tolerate any US action that reduces or negates the elements of its strategy. Therefore, what the United States does or does not do with respect to its own nuclear force structure and posture and the ways in which it integrates and deploys defense into its strategy and doctrine will be seen by Beijing as a strong indicator of US intentions over the longer term.

One other factor also needs to be mentioned. If it is certain that ensuring survivability in order to maintain a secure second-strike capability is the goal of Chinese nuclear force modernization, it is equally certain that Beijing's specific intentions will remain shrouded in mystery, at least for a time. This is because of the uncertainty principle.

Because Beijing's strategy requires that an adversary be unable to determine accurately whether or not a first strike has destroyed or neutralized China's ability to launch a second strike, it is not in China's strategic interest to be transparent about most aspects of its nuclear posture and strategy. No amount of strategic dialogue is likely to be sufficient by itself to overcome Beijing's incentives to remain as opaque as possible. This is likely to be a major issue in the future development of bilateral relations.

Conclusion: The Future of Bilateral Nuclear Relations

It is likely that the most important variable in determining the nature of the future nuclear relationship will ultimately involve US decisions on ballistic missile defense, the mix of offensive and defensive components the United States decides to employ, and, most important of all, whether the systems are deployed against China. The size of the force is not likely to be an issue since the apparently continuing focus on minimum deterrence suggests an interest mainly in offsetting rather than matching United States numerical superiority. Then too, China's approach, whether aimed at minimum or limited deterrence, also effectively removes force reduction as a means of managing nuclear differences. Force size is simply not a salient issue.

Logically then, the US has three choices. Washington could choose to implement the strategy some Chinese analysts seem to consider implicit in the *National Security Strategy,* the *NPR,* and the *QDR* and deploy a force that would combine BMD and offensive systems in ways that would effectively deny to China the second-strike capability it holds to be necessary. If this were to happen the cost to bilateral relations could be quite high.

It could be argued that this is essentially the situation at the present time and that, far from declining, the bilateral relationship is actually thriving. In response it can only be suggested that the question of whether or not the BMD systems under consideration will be used to neutralize the Chinese missile force, or if they will be actually deployed against China, has yet to be finally determined. That uncertainty, plus the realization that much time will pass before the system is complete and deployed, would account for any willingness by Beijing to avoid allowing the issue to affect relations negatively at this time. However, should the systems fulfill their technological promise, and especially if they should be integrated with systems in Japan and Taiwan, the impact is likely to be negative in the extreme. The Chinese force modernization program would, albeit with a certain lag time, focus on producing the increased numbers and incorporating the penetration aids that would enable the defeat of the defensive system. It is also possible that the Chinese would develop their nascent MIRV capabilities.

Second, the United States could accept the reality of China's second-strike capability and continue the present arrangement, which amounts to a more or less standard deterrence relationship with Beijing. Such an arrangement would substitute mutual vulnerability for the mutual assured destruction of the Cold War era, but the result would be largely the same. A decision of this kind would clearly serve the interests of the Chinese leadership. Whether it would also serve the interests of the United States was a hotly debated question until the conciliatory imperatives of cooperating in the war on terrorism intervened to moderate the discussion. Indeed, the issue could reemerge in the future if the imperative toward cooperation should cease to apply. Nonetheless, if such a decision were to be made, it would be viewed as a definite political signal that containment is not a US objective. It would also solidify the position of the Chinese leadership and, depending on developments in cross-straits relations, enhance the overall stability of bilateral relations.

Finally, Washington could proceed with plans for a BMD system designed to protect against rogue states and terrorists while maintaining an option to deploy it against China should that be considered necessary at some future time. In a word, the United States could hedge its bets. Hedging, however, would truly be a continuation of the status quo in which Beijing and Washington continue to put aside differences in order to achieve objectives of a higher priority, while continuing subtly to enhance their respective positions and thereby achieve advantage for future competition.[37]

No matter what decision is made, one thing remains clear. Beijing's perceptions of the United States at this time are essentially negative. However, Beijing's perception of its own interests and its assessment of US priorities and capabilities at this time and into the future supervene to prevent a downturn in bilateral relations. China's negative perception of the United States has not affected its decisions on proliferation and arms control policies. Neither has it affected Chinese decisions on matters of force structure, strategy, and doctrine *so far.* Beijing will modernize its nuclear forces irrespective of what course Washington chooses. However, whether force modernization continues to be focused on maintaining an effective minimum deterrent or whether it aims at building new capabilities for inflicting harm on the United States will be influenced by decisions yet to be made by US leaders. Ultimately, Chinese perceptions of the United States and its intentions will have a significant, even defining impact on Chinese decisions on nuclear matters.

Notes

1. See also *Foreign Missile Developments and the Ballistic Missile Threat to the United States Through 2015* (Washington, DC: National Intelligence Council, 1999) and "House Select Committee on US National Security and Military/Commercial Concerns with the People's Republic of China," declassified report issued May 25, 1999.

2. Perusal of the 2001 *Quadrennial Defense Review* supports this interpretation. *Quadrennial Defense Review Report* (Washington, DC: Department of Defense, September 30, 2001), available at www.defenselink.mil/pubs/qdr2001.pdf.

3. "The Choice of China's Diplomatic Strategy," *People's Daily Online,* March 19, 2003, http://English.peopledaily.com.cn.

4. Wang Guosheng and Li Wei, "US Comprehensively Adjusts Nuclear Strategy," *Jiefangjun Bao,* January 30, 2002, FBIS CPP200201300076. This concern was also voiced to the author at a conference convened by Pacific Forum CSIS and the Center for American Studies of Fudan University in January 2002. Indeed, the concern has been a constant feature of discussions with Chinese interlocutors that has only just begun to ameliorate.

5. Comprehensive national power is a uniquely Chinese concept that refers to the ability of a nation to concentrate a wide array of resources in order to achieve successfully its national goals and objectives. Comprehensive national power comprises not only economic and military strength, but also such less objective factors as internal stability and order, social cohesion, institutional strength, and citizen loyalty.

6. The existence of this internal discussion of alternative policies came to light at a discussion during a conference on United States/China relations convened in April 2001 at the Asia Pacific Center for Security Studies in Honolulu, Hawaii. David Finkelstein in *China's New Security Concept: Reading Between the Lines* (Alexandria, VA: Center for Naval Analyses, April 1999) offers a comprehensive overview of this phenomenon at an earlier stage of its development.

7. "Call for Meeting 21st Century Challenge—Comment on US 2002 Defense Report," *People's Daily Online,* August 29, 2002, http://english.peopledaily.com.cn.

8. "Dialog: Focus on US Global Military Deployment," *People's Daily Online,* June 16, 2003, http://English.peopledaily.com.cn.

9. Private communication with Zhuang Jianzhong, Vice Director of the Shanghai Center for PacRim Strategic Studies. This point has been a durable, if never officially expressed, component of Chinese scholarly analysis for more than two decades. Although Washington's active military support of Taiwan has reduced the number of analysts who acknowledge the positive effects of US military deployments in Northeast Asia, it continues to have some resonance.

10. "Factors Hindering US Hegemonic Moves: Analysis," *People's Daily Online,* April 8, 2003, http://English.peopledaily.com.cn.

11. Ye Jicheng, "Beyond Polarization Mentality—Thoughts on China's Diplomatic Strategy," *Guangzhou Nanfang Zhoumo* Internet Version, January 8 and 15, 2004, www.nanfangdaily.com.cn/zm.

12. *China's Diplomacy 2002,* Policy Research Office of the Ministry of Foreign Affairs of the People's Republic of China, 2002; also "FM Slams Unilateralism, Favors Multilateralism," *China Daily,* March 6, 2004, http://www2.chinadaily.com.cn.

13. Ye Jicheng.

14. Ye Jicheng. Admittedly, this view is not widely shared by other Chinese analysts, at least not openly. However, it does reflect accurately the views of scholars and members of the Ministry of Foreign Affairs the author has heard since October 2002.

15. This question is extremely important and deserves careful consideration. However, it remains beyond the scope of this chapter.

16. Evan Medeiros and M. Taylor Fravel, "China's New Diplomacy," *Foreign Affairs* (November/December 2003): 22–35.

17. Private discussions with Ms. Bonnie Glaser.

18. It will be recalled, for example, that until 2002, Beijing refused to participate in multilateral discussions of competing territorial claims in the South China Sea.

19. "China Considers Establishing a Northeast Asia Security Negotiation Conference," *Dong-A Ilbo,* February 25, 2004. Also, Medeiros and Fravel provide an excellent summary of Chinese recent participation in international and multilateral organizations.

20. Medeiros and Fravel.

21. Ibid.

22. This has not always been the case. The author is personally aware that historically, since the opening of military-to-military ties in 1982, the Department of Defense and the military services have been more aggressive about developing relations than the Department of State. The initiatives of then Secretary of Defense William Perry were particularly irksome to State Department counterparts. Just now, the situation appears to have reversed. The Office of the Secretary of Defense is quite skeptical of the value of military relations with the PLA and supports them only grudgingly while the services and the State Department are willing to do somewhat more.

23. Qian Qichen, "US Adjusts Strategy after Sept 11 Attacks," *People's Daily Online,* January 19, 2004, http://English.peopledaily.com.cn.

24. Wu Bayi, "Hot Spots, Bright Points, and Footholds," *Beijing Shijie Jishi,* January 1, 2004, FBIS CPP20040112000206.

25. This is precisely why the issue of Taiwan looms so large in Beijing's thinking. Conflict in the Taiwan Straits, especially if it involved the United States, would wipe out all that Beijing has achieved thus far and delay the process of emergence for a generation.

26. "The Choice of China's Diplomatic Strategy."

27. Robert A. Manning, Ronald N. Montaperto, and Brad Roberts, *China, Nuclear Weapons, and Arms Control: A Preliminary Assessment* (New York: Council on Foreign Relations, 2000).

28. Chinese scholars and some military and civilian officials were quite candid about owning up to the tit-for-tat nature of Beijing's behavior and its direct connection to Washington's military sales to Taipei. The author heard these admissions at a series of meetings in the US and in China during the period 1993–1998 in the context of seeking to find a basis for "engaging" with Beijing. The level of frustration for US interlocutors was extremely high.

29. *China's Non-Proliferation Policy and Measures,* State Council Information Office of the People's Republic of China, December 3, 2003.

30. This is a fascinating story and one that deserves to be written. As reported by Professor Shen Dingli of Shanghai's Fudan University, the movement began among younger academics in Shanghai and Beijing and gradually gained a measure of leadership support. According to Professor Shen, the nuclearization of South

Asia was a major motivating factor. Under the leadership of Ministry of Foreign Affairs Arms Control Department head Sha Zhukang, the public face of the arms control community was extremely conservative. However, that condition has changed in the last two years or so.

31. In numerous discussions with members of the Ministry of Foreign Affairs, members of the PLA, and scholars since 1995, Taiwan and missile defense have consistently been cited as the most important indicators of US intentions. Ending arms sales to Taiwan and either not deploying BMD systems or deploying them in such a way that Chinese forces are not neutralized would be positive signals to Beijing that Washington truly accepts and appreciates what is now sometimes described as China's peaceful rise.

32. Brad Roberts, *China-US Nuclear Relations: What Relationship Best Serves US Interests?* (Washington, DC: Institute for Defense Analyses, 2001). In this work, Roberts carefully explores a range of different possible scenarios and outcomes. The discussion in this chapter relies heavily on his work.

33. Manning, Montaperto, and Roberts.

34. Ibid.

35. Ibid.

36. Roberts (2001).

37. Ibid.

6

The Potential Flashpoint: Taiwan

Ting Wai

Ever since China tested its first nuclear weapon in October 1964, Beijing has been quite vague about its nuclear strategy. Nuclear strategy is often characterized as a "non-strategy," as it is not meant to determine the best methods and techniques of using nuclear weapons under the most ideal conditions. Instead, nuclear strategy is about how to make use of nuclear weapons as an instrument in order to prevent armed conflicts and deter others from resorting to force. Apart from continuously insisting on the no-first-use principle, how does the People's Liberation Army (PLA) perceive the role of nuclear weapons, as well as the functions of the Second Artillery responsible for managing and launching nuclear missiles, particularly in a potential Taiwan conflict involving the United States?

Despite the slow progress and the enormous difficulties encountered during research and development, the People's Republic of China (PRC) has never stopped its process of modernizing its nuclear forces. This chapter aims first of all to give a comprehensive review of the inventory of Chinese nuclear forces, especially in light of a potential Taiwan crisis. However, it is meaningless to give a full account of the different kinds of nuclear forces without linking the hardware component to the "software" of nuclear arms, that is, the nuclear strategy adopted by China. What is then the relationship between the development of new nuclear weapons and the development of the doctrines of nuclear strategy, especially in relation to Taiwan? Would the evolution of new atomic weapons result in a new strategy, or new ways of pondering how to make use of nuclear weapons as a political instrument? Would the successful research and deployment of more lethal and more accurate nuclear missiles enhance deterrence, thus contributing to the evolution of nuclear strategic doctrine? Or, on the contrary, would the modification of nuclear strategy promote advancement in the research and development of new types of nuclear weapons, such as tactical nuclear weapons or neutron bombs, and even facilitate their possible use in a future conflict? In case of an armed conflict with Taiwan, would short-range ballistic missiles (SRBM) carrying conventional or tactical nuclear weapons be used as an instrument of warfare?

No doubt due to the lack of sources from Chinese materials, any research endeavor on Chinese nuclear strategy is extremely difficult. However, an extensive review of Chinese literature is helpful to locate the important topics of debate, as well as the trends of development. It is also possible to find concealed messages. A rather conspicuous picture of Chinese nuclear forces will be revealed as we engage this debate.

Chinese Nuclear Forces: An Inventory

Since the 1980s, China has been laboriously seeking to improve its nuclear deterrence credibility by increasing the quality and survivability of its nuclear arsenal. Significant progress has been made on missile guidance systems; command, control, communications, computers, and intelligence (C4I); the introduction of mobile launch platforms for missiles; the use of solid fuel instead of liquid fuel; increased penetration ability of missiles through planned development of MIRVs (multiple independently targetable reentry vehicles);[1] and the development of a new generation of nuclear-powered submarines with SLBMs (submarine-launched ballistic missiles). These are all effective measures to modernize China's nuclear arsenal.[2] The DF-5 intercontinental ballistic missiles (ICBMs) are considered to be the major force that could launch an attack on the United States. The DF-5s are still propelled by liquid fuel and thus considered to be a "non-ready" force, as fueling would take hours to complete. In addition, the warheads are not "mated," which means they are stored apart from the missiles. Thus the Chinese ICBMs have "no ability to launch on warning. They would be destroyed before they could ever be fueled and launched."[3] However, the DF-5s are considered to be the weapon of last resort in checking and deterring the United States from interfering in any PLA actions against Taiwan.

According to American official sources, the DF-5s are being replaced by the longer range DF-5A.[4] It has also been reported that they would gradually be replaced by the more accurate, mobile, and solid propellant 3-stage DF-31, which has a shorter range of 8,000 km, capable of hitting Alaska, Hawaii, and the western United States. The deployment of the DF-31 will probably start in 2005. An ICBM with an extended range, coded DF-31A, is also designed to achieve a 12,000-km range. It will probably be deployed in the second half of this decade.

The CIA estimates that from 2001 to 2015, the number of warheads deployed against the United States will range from about 75 to 100.[5] This means not only an increase in the number of ICBMs, but also an increase in the number of warheads carried by each missile. Significant progress has been made in MIRV techniques in the last twenty years, and American sources have claimed that MIRVs have been successfully tested and could be operational soon.[6] However, foreign analysts doubt whether the mobile ICBMs or SLBMs are able to launch MIRVs and there is no official Chinese documentary evidence available to shed further light on this issue. It is nevertheless reported in another source that the DF-5s were "modernized in the mid-1980s, fitted with four to six MIRV warheads of 350 kt each."[7] They will be replaced in 2005 by the new generation of ICBMs.

From January 2004 until the presidential election in Taiwan in March 2004, five missile tests were made from the PLA base in Shanxi province. The tests included a DF-31 ICBM, DF-11 and DF-15 SRBMs, as well as a new kind of conventional warhead that is composed of several smaller warheads designed to thoroughly destroy airport runways.[8]

What is more important for China's second-strike nuclear capability is the nuclear-powered ballistic missile submarine (SSBN). The first SSBN of 6,500 tons, named the *Xia* class, which grew out of the so-called 092 plan, joined the navy in 1988 and fired its first SLBM in September that year. The Xia's nuclear deterrent consists of 12 JL (Julang)-I SLBMs, each equipped with a warhead of 250 kt with a range of 1,700 km. Unfortunately for China, the submarine is not fully operational. It has not ventured out far beyond China's regional waters, and appears to be vulnerable to modern antisubmarine devices.[9] Apparently the nuclear reactor and the propulsion systems are in trouble. Despite a four-year overhaul from 1995 to 2000, the submarine is still not fully operational.[10]

Therefore it seems that the PLAN (People's Liberation Army Navy) has been concentrating its energy in designing a new generation of nuclear submarines. There are two efforts under way. Plan 093 aims to design a nuclear-powered attack submarine that is similar to the Soviet *Victor* III class that was designed in the late 1970s. It is predicted that the first 093 submarine will be finished by 2005.[11] Plan 094 aims to construct a new class of nuclear-powered ballistic missile submarines, which are able to carry 12 or 16 of the new JL-II SLBMs, derived from the DF-31, and with a range of up to 8,000 km.[12] Four to six submarines will be built and they are planned to have an operational date of around 2005–2006. It is reported that the first JL-II was launched on June 16, 2005 from the Yellow Sea.[13] The JL-II may be equipped with MIRVs, and up to six independently targetable warheads would be armed.[14] But the CIA believes that equipping the Julang with MIRVs would reduce its range.[15] However, it has also been reported that problems exist with the nuclear reactor and, consequently, "operational deployment of the Project 094 system may be many years away."[16] Analysts in Taiwan believe that the PLAN would fabricate 8 to 12 SSBNs within the 094 project, each of which will be equipped with 18 JL-IIs. The JL-II SLBMs have two types: Type A may bear 3 to 8 warheads, while Type B may bear as many as 11 warheads. The PLA has been successful in fabricating the miniaturized warheads.[17] (For additional details on China's strategic weapons, see Chapter 4 by Phillip Saunders and Jing-dong Yuan in this volume.)

The PLA also has hundreds of SRBMs. Even though these SRBMs are mainly targeted against Taiwan, and are thought to carry conventional weapons, they could be equipped to carry tactical nuclear weapons, to which the PLA has recently been paying particular attention. At present the PLA Second Artillery is equipped with two brigades of 24 DF-15 launchers, with about 100 DF-15 (CSS-6/M-9) missiles with a maximum range of about 600 km. The missile can carry a 350 kt warhead. In addition, the PLA also has two brigades of 32 DF-11A (CSS-7/M-11) launchers, with about 200 missiles directed mainly against Taiwan. The Second Artillery is also equipped with one brigade of 30 DF-7 (CSS-8) launchers. Altogether there are about 450 SRBMs directed against Taiwan.[18] In fact in 2003 the precise figure of 496 SRBMs was given by Taiwan President Chen Shui-bian.[19]

According to officials of the Taiwan regime, the number of SRBMs pointed toward Taiwan keeps on increasing. A senior Taiwan military officer and president of the National Defense University, General Shiah Yang-jou, estimates that the number of missiles has been increasing in a range of 50 to 100 per year. By the year 2005, mainland China is expected to have about 650 missiles aimed at Taiwan. Another estimate by Taiwan strategic analysts is 620 missiles by 2005.[20] The purpose is to threaten Taiwan and to "force surrender out of Taiwan through the operational model of maximum intimidation and minimum loss."[21] These missiles may carry simply conventional warheads, but they might also be equipped with tactical nuclear weapons, including the neutron bomb that the PLA successfully tested in September 1988.

According to Lieutenant General Abe C. Lin, Taiwan's military chief responsible for information and electronic warfare, China has been successful in developing electromagnetic pulse (EMP) bombs and graphite bombs. They are "capable of massively disturbing or paralyzing an adversary's C4ISR [command, control, communications, computers, intelligence, surveillance, and reconnaissance] systems and their weapon systems by means of suddenly creating violent non-nuclear or nuclear electro-magnetic waves."[22] In case of an attack on Taiwan, this weapon would be used in the beginning of a conflict in order to paralyze the electronic systems, radars, and computers of the government and defense forces of Taiwan.[23] In an article recently published in China entitled "How to Destroy the Future Command and Control Systems of the Taiwan Army," it is clearly specified that EMP bombs will be used to strike the command and control systems of Taiwan in a future conflict. The article also reveals that the newly constructed building of the Taiwan Ministry of Defense has been equipped with protective devices against EMP bombs. A military plan to protect key military targets against electromagnetic pulse is also in place.[24] Needless to say, apart from the fourth generation air fighters such as SU-27s and SU-30s, as well as the most modern destroyers acquired from Russia, China's most threatening and intimidating weapons are the increasing numbers of SRBMs pointing toward Taiwan. They could be used to impose a blockade on Taiwan, cut the vital sea links for trade activities, or paralyze the command and control mechanism of the government and the military. Thus they are very useful in greatly damaging the confidence of sensitive Taiwan citizens toward their future.

No-First-Use: Facing the New Reality of Taiwan?

Ever since China exploded its first atomic bomb in October 1964, it has maintained the policy of no-first-use (NFU) as the primordial principle in its formulation of nuclear strategy. China declared it would not use atomic weapons against any non-nuclear states, and would only use atomic weapons to retaliate after a nuclear first strike against China. (For a discussion of NFU in light of China's overall nuclear doctrine, see Chapter 3 by Evan Medeiros in this volume.) According to an article written by a researcher on Chinese arms control policy in the mid-1990s, NFU has always been part of the Chinese strategy of "people's war under modern conditions." First of all, Chinese conventional defense is more significant, while its nuclear deterrence capability is rather limited. This means that due to the small size and quality of Chinese nuclear weapons, they could provide only limited deterrence. Second, Chinese nuclear forces are not deployed to prevent or deter all kinds of wars, only nuclear war. This is different from the nuclear arsenals of the United States, Russia, or even Britain and France, as their nuclear weapons are also used to deter conventional warfare.[25] By all means, China has to ensure that it really possesses the technical capability as well as the intention to retaliate in order to deter against any potential attack or blackmail.

The problem that remains unresolved in Chinese nuclear strategy is that, if its nuclear capabilities were annihilated during a first strike launched by an adversary, what could it use in order to retaliate? It is often argued that after the ICBMs of an adversary have been launched, China would react immediately by launching missiles armed with nuclear warheads. But if the Chinese ICBMs are liquid-propelled like the DF-5, they could not be launched immediately, and China's land-based second-strike capability would be destroyed. If the more credible second-strike ability of the Xia class SSBN was not operational due to technical reasons, then China could not retaliate by using nuclear weapons at all. The "no-first-use" principle suits the "socialist" ethical principle and China has been proud to be consistent regarding this principle for the last four decades. But the above-mentioned dilemma cannot be resolved, given the technical backwardness of the Chinese nuclear forces and the implausibility of China retaliating if attacked by nuclear weapons.

Complicating matters are US efforts at missile defense. Due to the research, development, and eventual implementation of Theater Missile Defense (TMD) and National Missile Defense (NMD) by the United States, it seems that strategic analysts within the PRC have been vigorously debating the possible Chinese reactions to the "defensive shield" provided by anti-missile defenses. Without TMD and NMD, both sides are equipped only with "spears" (nuclear missiles). Since both sides fear retaliation, no one dares to launch a spear against the other, thus resulting in mutual deterrence. When one side is equipped also with a "shield," together with the possession of spears, it will enjoy a strategically superior position in relation to its adversary, as the shield would render the spears almost useless. If China also develops missile defenses, or a shield, it would achieve equal status. But due to the enormous technical difficulties as well as cost, China is not able and would not consider constructing its own shield. What can China do in such circumstances?

Chinese strategic analysts decided to increase the number of missiles and warheads, making it more difficult for the shield to impede penetration. This has been often reiterated by Sha Zukang, the former official responsible for arms control within the Ministry of Foreign Affairs.[26] The chance of penetrating the shield must be greater if the number of missiles together with MIRVs is increased. However, what we are interested in is not the hardware part of the issue. The crucial question is: does the TMD or NMD incite any principal changes in the nuclear strategies of China?

An article written in the year 2000, "The Order of Development of Nuclear Forces of Various Nations in the New Century," depicts the need for changes in Chinese nuclear strategy.[27] The article was apparently written under a pseudonym, but it is noted that the author obtained a doctorate in International Law from Europe. The article insists that China's nuclear weapons serve a defensive purpose, and do not constitute a threat to any country, but it is stressed, in the last part of the paper, that

> among the five nuclear powers, the scope of development of the Chinese nuclear forces is the smallest. . . . [The problem] of Chinese nuclear development is basically the strategic aspect, but not the technical factor. Among all the nuclear powers, the degree of national security of China is relatively low. This is directly related to the fact that China has not formulated a strong nuclear deterrence. . . . China has never announced formally its grand nuclear strategy. Based on China's unilateral announcement that it will never be the first to use nuclear weapons and its very limited scope of nuclear arms, China adopts a low-intensity nuclear strategy. Due to the dual reality of possessing only a small nuclear arsenal and declining to first use its nuclear arms, China's ability to retaliate using nuclear weapons would be very limited. The Chinese nuclear armaments system and the relevant nuclear strategy have arrived at a critical point, and they must be changed in a short period of time. . . . At present, Chinese nuclear warheads are miniaturized and operational, the long-range vehicles system is very mature, and the solid-propellant Dong-Feng missiles with MIRVs have entered into force. What Chinese nuclear weapons need to break through is not the technical aspect but the strategic aspect. China needs to base its strategy on the current challenges that she has to face at present, and the defensive means that she possesses, in order to formulate a new nuclear strategy that could fully adapt to the new forms of national security. If China could rely on her nuclear forces to be the central pillar of national security, formulating a new nuclear strategy thus would enable the nation to possess the relevant nuclear strategic capability, and when Chinese deterrence forces could buttress the national security on an undefeated situation in any circumstances . . . then China could become the main force in world nuclear disarmament.[28]

The message is clear: with a new generation of nuclear weapons, China has to modify its nuclear strategy. The outdated liquid-propellant missiles that needed hours to prepare for launch are gradually being replaced with solid-propellant missiles, which means speed of firing and accuracy are better. MIRVs enable China to attack several targets using one missile, thus increasing their deterrent power. Facing the new challenges from the United States, especially its possible deployment of TMD with the collaboration of Japan and Taiwan, might render Chinese nuclear strike abilities (first strike plus second strike) almost useless. It is not surprising that Chinese analysts are considering the need to transform their nuclear strategy. This is especially true in case of an armed conflict with Taiwan. This is not saying that China would necessarily use nuclear weapons against Taiwan, but it would consider abolishing the no-first-use principle so as to maximize the deterrent effects against possible intervention by the United States. (For more on how missile defense will affect China's nuclear posture, see Brad Roberts in this volume.)

In the past, dating back to the 1960s, Chinese leaders did not use the term deterrence in their discussions regarding the "uses" of nuclear weapons. They thought that if China were attacked, they simply needed the same kind of lethal weapon to retaliate. China has experienced the real threat of surgical attacks against its nuclear forces in the infant stage, in July 1963 from Washington, and in September 1969 from Moscow.[29] But Chinese leaders thought that a small number of nuclear forces to take significant revenge on the enemy's "soft" targets like cities would be enough, as they would provide a kind of "equalizer" effect so as to promote nuclear parity.[30] Since the 1960s until the late 1990s, Chinese official documents did not use the term nuclear deterrence, as this was affiliated with concepts like nuclear threat and nuclear blackmail. Both in 1996 and 1998, China urged the nuclear powers to "abolish their policy of nuclear deterrence."[31]

But in the 2002 White Paper on National Defense, China uses the term deterrence to characterize the use of Chinese nuclear weapons: "Its [Chinese nuclear force's] primary missions are to deter the enemy from using nuclear weapons against China."[32] In the books published by the PLA since the mid-1980s, strategic analysts began to emphasize the deterrent effects of nuclear weapons rather than their actual operational effect. But they also stressed that the Chinese deterrence policy is by nature different from the deterrence policy of the hegemonic states.[33] When Chinese leaders and strategic analysts accept the concept of nuclear deterrence per se, that is to say, nuclear force is used to deter any kind of hostile actions, what will be the nuclear strategy of China then, with its much improved nuclear arsenals facing the NMD and TMD of the United States?

It would seem that the most logical deduction arising from the above analysis would be to abolish the principle of "no-first-use." A 2003 report submitted by the United States Department of Defense has already stipulated that "As China improves its strategic forces, despite Beijing's 'no-first-use' pledge, there are indications that some strategists are reconsidering the conditions under which Beijing would employ theater nuclear weapons against US forces in the region."[34] Here we need to clarify the real meaning of "no-first-use." A recent document from China has specified that "no-first-use" does not mean the launch of nuclear missiles by China after the nation has been attacked, as by then most of the Chinese nuclear forces would have been destroyed by the first strike of the enemy. It categorically means the launch of Chinese nuclear missiles during the early warning period, when it is clear that enemy missiles have been launched toward China but have not yet arrived.[35] However, the liquid-propellant missiles, which need at least several hours to fuel, would be useless for retaliation in such circumstances. Only the mobile, solid-propellant DF-31 would be useful in launching a revenge attack, as it could be fired almost immediately after enemy missiles are launched.

Furthermore, regarding "no-first-use," different sources have demonstrated that the principle is not applicable to Taiwan, as Taiwan is considered a Chinese domestic problem. For instance, one source notes:

> The representatives of the PRC to the arms control negotiations of the United Nations consistently maintain that since Taiwan is an integral part of China, the commitment of "no-first-use" is not applicable. This proves that China adopts an ambiguous nuclear weapon strategy in the area that she deems to be within her sovereignty limit.[36]

A source from Taiwan stresses:

> If Taiwan attempts to become independent and there is intervention from abroad, China would not be reluctant to use tactical nuclear weapons for the sake of defending "territorial integrity." The Chinese journal *Guo Fang Bao (National Defense)* has continuously recommended using nuclear weapons against Taiwan. If the PLA deems it necessary to attack Taiwan by military means, its past commitment on the basic strategy of "no-first-use" or "not using nuclear weapons or threatening to use nuclear weapons against non-nuclear states" would thus be modified. . . . This should be the most threatening action at the psychological level as well as on our political, economic, and military facilities.[37]

This position is further supported by a researcher from Taiwan, Chen Shihmin, who noticed the important statement of Sha Zukang that "the Chinese promise of 'no-first-use' is not applicable to Taiwan as Taiwan is a national territory of China."[38] Though it was pointed out by Tang Jiaxuan, the former foreign minister of China, in August 1999 that China would not use its nuclear armaments against compatriots in Taiwan,[39] Chen Shihmin is legitimate in asking if the Taiwan people refuse to become Chinese compatriots, would Tang's commitment still be applicable to Taiwan? In other words, if Beijing considers that its territory has been occupied by others, would China definitely be the first to use nuclear weapons, to get rid of the invaders? During the Taiwan Straits crisis in spring 1996, when Washington sent two aircraft carriers to the region, General Xiong Guangkai, deputy chief of staff of the PLA, did explicitly ask whether the United States really wanted to protect Taiwan in exchange for the price of the destruction of Los Angeles.[40] The same kind of statement was declared again in May 2000. China clearly stressed that if the United States dared to exercise military actions against China while defending the subversion of Taiwan, Beijing would not hesitate to use nuclear arms to threaten the United States, even though the retaliation from the latter would be terribly disastrous to China.[41] Apparently, China is making use of nuclear weapons to threaten and deter the United States so that the latter is obliged to think very carefully on whether it should intervene in a Taiwan crisis.

An immediate question that arises is: in light of the imbalance in nuclear forces, is this Chinese threat to deter American intervention really credible? The Chinese military authorities are indeed envisaging the possibility of attacking American aircraft carriers. Whether this is done by missiles carrying conventional warheads or tactical nuclear weapons remains unknown. However, at least one thing is certain. Chinese analysts assert that facing the intervention of aircraft carriers, China should "proactively attack" the aircraft carrier task forces, either to destroy them or at least repulse them to 2,000 or 3,000 km from the Chinese coast. For this purpose, using long-range, high-speed, and precision-guided ballistic missiles is preferable to cruise missiles. This is regarded as a "*Shashoujian*" (killer mace) against aircraft carriers and may even produce the deterrent effect.[42] Chinese analysts believe that, faced with the strong will and determination of the Chinese to attack aircraft carriers using precision-guided missiles, the Americans would not dare to intervene. The absence of intervention by US forces would enable the PLA to easily invade Taiwan. However, if US aircraft carriers dared to go to the Taiwan Straits, would China really use precision-guided ballistic missiles to attack them? If United States carriers were attacked using nuclear arms, and Washington decided to retaliate by perhaps attacking PLA military bases in Fujian province, there would be a military crisis for China, and further escalation up the nuclear ladder would become a nightmare for Beijing.

A monumental work on China's national defense edited by General Zhang Wannian, former chief of staff of the PLA, stipulates that in order to make up for the insufficiency of Russia's comprehensive national strength, Russia is increasingly using nuclear weapons as the pillar to revamp its national power. Moscow abolished the commitment of no-first-use in order to deter the negative effects of the eastern enlargement of NATO, to defend national interests and national security, and to maintain its status as a great nation.[43] The French dictum "*dissuasion du faible au fort,*" that is, deterrence of the weak against any hostile actions from the stronger, is well appreciated by Chinese strategic analysts. The Russian abandonment of no-first-use is considered an effective means for the weak to reinforce the equalizer effect that nuclear weapons could provide by increasing the "strategic ambiguity" imposed on the stronger potential enemy. For China, there is a need to show its serious intention to use nuclear weapons in order to make credible the deterrence of the weak against the strong, which means deterrence against any possible US intervention. This explains why Beijing has consistently insisted it will resort to war in case of Taiwan independence, particularly since the March 2004 presidential election in Taiwan.

Significance of Nuclear Weapons in a Taiwan Crisis and Sino-American Relations

The policy of the United States vis-à-vis the division of China is twofold. First, Washington has adopted the so-called one-China policy. Second, it wishes that the cross-straits conflict be resolved by peaceful means. In other words, Washington does not welcome either side resorting to war. The Americans stopped Chiang Kai-shek from sending the Nationalist army to the mainland when China was still suffering from the setback of the Great Leap Forward.[44] By the same token, the United States does not want the PLA to attack Taiwan. Washington assisted Taiwan in acquiring advanced F-16 fighters (150 in total) in 1992 and promised Kidd-class destroyers as well as submarines in 2001, under the two different Bush administrations, in order to balance against the upgraded air and naval forces of China after its acquisition of SU-27 and SU-30 fighters, as well as two Sovremenny-class destroyers. It is believed that a parity of the two forces will ensure a strategic equilibrium that is able to deter the mainland from attacking Taiwan. Nevertheless, in the eyes of Beijing's leaders, assisting the military buildup of Taiwan certainly helps to sustain the division of China. Since Taiwan nationalism is growing, the alleged "prevention" of reunification by the United States would make reunification more and more difficult. So Beijing is caught in a dilemma: either allow Taiwan to continue to develop its nationhood, or risk entering into conflict with the United States if Beijing decides to invade Taiwan.

By all means the United States does not want to see an armed conflict between the mainland and Taiwan, as it would also be caught in a dilemma. If the United States does not intervene, then Taiwan would most probably be "lost" and conquered by China. If the United States intervenes, it will enter into direct conflict with China. Therefore, consistent Washington policy in the last few decades has been to avoid war. Apart from helping Taiwan balance against the military superiority of the PLA, Washington has been pressing Taipei not to talk about or declare independence. In order to maintain "strategic ambiguity," Washington never directly expresses under what circumstances the US military would intervene.

However, since US deployment of TMD could render the PLA's SRBMs against Taiwan less effective, Beijing leaders have to think about how to counter this possibility. Augmenting the number of missiles and, consequently, warheads is the natural reaction, and these démarches have been explicitly announced by Chinese officials.[45] Apart from this, it seems that a debate is going on about whether the nuclear strategy of China needs to be modified. The most reasonable response is to abolish the no-first-use policy, as this will definitely increase the strategic ambiguity Washington has to face. If the PLA determines to attack Taiwan, the deployment of US aircraft carrier battle groups, together with the assistance of supporting Japanese forces and the resistance of Taiwan forces, would be capable of stopping the invasion.[46] The PLA is not in a position to defeat the United States. However, if NFU has been rejected, then Washington's political and military leaders must ponder the possibility that conventional or even tactical nuclear weapons carried by precision-guided missiles would be used by the PLA to attack the aircraft carriers. The US TMD might be able to intercept the Chinese SRBMs, but what would happen if the TMD fails to intercept all? If the Americans hesitate to intervene, or simply do not intervene, fearing further escalation to nuclear war, then the PLA would probably be successful in conquering Taiwan. It is now Beijing's leaders who present strategic ambiguity to Washington. This kind of thinking, if real, might also be a new Chinese reaction to the unilateralism adopted by the Bush administration, which is, in turn, influenced by the "offensive realism" proclaimed by John Mearsheimer.[47] The superpower, the only hegemon, is always afraid of being challenged by a rising power, and Mearsheimer thinks that this rising power, China, might certainly become another hegemon. Thus Washington must preempt and master any apparent hostile actions from the rising hegemon, while China now also wants to preempt the United States from intervening in China's domestic affairs.

In July 2005 a Chinese general, expressing his personal views, noted that China indeed may be willing to use nuclear weapons against the United States in a conflict over Taiwan. General Zhu Chenghu, former deputy director of the Institute for Strategic Studies of China's Defense University, and at present dean of its Defense College, explicitly announced, "If the Americans interfere in the conflict, if the Americans draw their missiles and position-guided ammunition into the target zone on China's territory, I think we will have to respond with nuclear weapons." He further stressed that "the policy [NFU] could be changed and was really only intended to apply to conflicts with non-nuclear states in any case.[48]

It is possible that this new kind of Chinese thinking has aroused serious attention from US strategic analysts. As one analyst makes very clear, the United States should prevent China from deterring it:

> Should China feel compelled to utilize military force against Taiwan, they would seek to deter US intervention, and nuclear threats could be part of their deterrent strategy. The US would need to be free to intervene if our interests so dictated. So our posture with respect to China should aim not only at deterring Chinese use of force against US interests, but more importantly, should have the goal of preventing China from deterring us. This suggests the need for some mix of offenses and defenses, including theater-based nuclear capabilities.[49]

The crucial question is what would happen if Chinese deterrence fails? That is, if the PLA threatens to use precision-guided missiles equipped with tactical nuclear weapons against US aircraft carriers, and if the US Navy still enters a Taiwan conflict, would China really launch its nuclear weapons? If so, that would bring China to the brink of possible nuclear war. If not, China would suffer a humiliating defeat and its attempt to conquer Taiwan would fail. The Chinese want to deter the Americans, while the Americans wish to deter the Chinese and to prevent China from deterring them. This would imply that the United States would use all types of means, including TMD to prevent, and tactical nuclear weapons to retaliate, against Chinese incoming missiles with tactical nuclear warheads. Only a strong determination by Washington would prevent Beijing from deterring the United States. Robert Ross claims that the US enjoys a high degree of superiority that can deter PLA actions:

> The conventional superiority of the US enhances US credibility to intervene in regional conflicts and thus to deter war. . . . The US-China military balance undermines PRC confidence that it can deter US intervention on behalf of Taiwan. . . . China has enough respect for US resolve that US-China asymmetric interests do not appreciatively enhance China's confidence that it can use force without it leading to US intervention.[50]

But, could US superiority really be effective in deterring any Chinese military action? In other words, once Beijing employs force against Taiwan (which means that US deterrence has failed), would the US really react and attack Chinese forces, facing a potential danger of retaliation from the Chinese military, possibly using nuclear weapons? What would happen if the PLA ignores the intruding aircraft carriers, while firing missiles at the outer sea of Taiwan, cutting the sea links and imposing a blockade of the island with its submarines? Would the US intervene and engage Chinese forces?

Current Chinese literature on the "new military revolution" maintains that winning the war does not mean destroying the army of the enemy or occupying territory. It simply means forcing the enemy to submit. In addition, forces should be concentrated not on eradicating the army of the enemy, but on destroying the enemy's command and control systems.[51] If missiles were fired against Taiwan's command and control headquarters in the government and the military, and a blockade were imposed, Taiwan's people could lose confidence in the future of Taiwan rather rapidly, and the government and the military could lose the will to resist. They would then have no choice but to go to the negotiation table.

In any case, deterrence against possible US intervention during an attack against Taiwan has become a primary goal of the PLA. In a significant article on Chinese thinking on nuclear forces, a senior engineer of the Second Artillery, Cheng Zhiren, and a member of the Bureau of the General Chief of Staff, Sang Zhonglin, speak clearly about the "uses" of nuclear force. They attack the idea that the deterrent effects of the nuclear arsenals of a medium nuclear power facing the TMD or NMD of the United States could be reduced to a minimum. They stress that the deterrent effects of nuclear weapons arise from their enormous destructive power. If there is no possibility that they will be used, then they lose their effect, including their deterrent power. Both authors think that this is a weapon of last resort; if using conventional weapons cannot resist the massive attack of the enemy, deploying and using tactical nuclear weapons could make up for the disadvantages caused by weak conventional arms. In other words, tactical nuclear armaments are usable. They also emphasize that using nuclear weapons is not equivalent to nuclear war. It is just another weapon that can be used in a war. In different stages of a war, depending on the circumstances and situation, conventional weapons as well as nuclear weapons could all be used, and nuclear war cannot replace or stop conventional war.[52] This is basically the reason why all nuclear states are researching advances in nuclear weapons, such as miniaturizing warheads, increasing their accuracy, or designing warheads that can penetrate the ground in order to destroy bunkers.

Chinese experts think that the US development of NMD aspires to prevent incoming missiles from entering the United States, but the deeper intention is to deter others from launching a nuclear attack or compel them to abandon the possible use of nuclear weapons. Another aim is to coerce other countries to enter an arms race so that the unbearable cost would wear those countries down. What Chinese strategic analysts are thinking when it comes to penetration of the NMD or TMD is not simply relying on penetration aids such as decoys, chaff, and so on. They are investigating three possible options. First, the use of space-based nuclear attack satellites to launch an attack directly on the United States. Second, the use of SSBNs to launch SLBMs near the coast of the United States. Third, they envisage the possibility of attacking the American military satellites that form part of the NMD.[53] These possible strategies are echoed by Brad Roberts:

> That need (to penetrate ballistic missile defense) points also to the potential utility for China of systems designed to attack the ballistic missile defense system itself—whether direct attack with ASAT on space-based infrastructure, or direct attack on ground-based radars, and/or indirect electronic attack on elements of the C4ISR structure.[54]

In addition, according to Chinese sources, tactical nuclear weapons are becoming more effective and efficient, as their destructive power can now be controlled and limited.[55] China would consider using tactical nuclear weapons if deemed necessary. The neutron bomb, as one of the tactical nuclear armaments that would incur minimum destruction on the infrastructure but maximize the killing of human beings, is considered an "appropriate" weapon in destroying Taiwan military resistance during a possible PLA landing on Taiwan.[56] China succeeded in developing the neutron bomb in 1988.[57]

The neutron bomb is exceptionally useful in killing or at least "paralyzing" the soldiers inside tanks and armored vehicles, due to the effects of gamma rays and neutrons. Neutron bombs are small and can be carried by SRBMs. They can be used to destroy the humans at the airports of the enemy, as well as the naval manpower within warships. After disembarking, when soldiers are proceeding toward cities that are political and economic centers, the defensive side would try to concentrate its forces and consolidate their bases outside the cities in order to wait for occasions to counterattack. In such circumstances, neutron bombs could be very useful in destroying the will to resist of the defendants. It is also argued that, since concentration of the forces of the defensive side is beneficial to the offensive side (as the latter can use neutron bombs to destroy a massive number of defensive soldiers), the defensive side will try to disperse its forces, thus enabling the offensive side to have a smooth and easier debarkation. The determination to use the neutron bomb right from the beginning would thus become a powerful instrument forcing the defensive side to submit. Chinese analysts further note that, when resorting to using neutron bombs, strategic nuclear deterrence is crucially needed to deter other states (that is, the United States) from interfering after the neutron bomb has been used.[58]

Apart from envisaging the use of tactical nuclear weapons, China is also keen on developing more advanced and powerful conventional weapons. It seems that China is impressed by the latest technology of the United States in fabricating those extremely powerful conventional weapons like smart bombs, microwave, and laser weapons. Some of these weapons have been demonstrated in the war of intervention against Iraq in March 2003. They showed an impressive power to destroy underground bunkers. Their explosive power could even be compared to a small tactical nuclear weapon. Moreover, Washington pointed out in the *Nuclear Posture Review* released in January 2002 that it might even consider using small-scale tactical nuclear weapons to hit preemptively the targets of some adversaries, including China and Russia.[59]

Furthermore, the threshold between conventional and nuclear weapons is blurred. The tactical nuclear weapon is considered only to be more powerful than the most powerful conventional weapon.[60] This new way of thinking influences Chinese military thought as well, and

China does not hesitate to accept and learn how to fight a war with tactical nuclear weapons, as well as to develop various kinds of advanced conventional weapons.[61] These weapons, together with a strong will, could be used to carry forward limited but fierce military actions in order to frighten opponents right from the beginning of the conflict, so that the latter have to ask for concessions or compromise. In other words, the PLA seeks to win at the beginning stage of the war, fighting a "small war" to stop a "massive war."[62]

For the sake of fighting a successful war, China has been active in researching and developing new kinds of weapons. The so-called new concept weapon systems include non-lethal weapons, the kinetic energy weapon (electrothermal chemical guns) to intercept high-speed missiles, different kinds of laser weapons, and electromagnetic weapons or radio-frequency weapons that are able to paralyze an enemy's electronic systems.[63] A Chinese source confirms that electromagnetic pulse weapons have been deployed since the mid-1990s, using M-9 and M-11 SRBMs as the carriers.[64] The PLA may even consider "using nuclear weapons as an unconventional attack option" in order to produce a high-altitude electromagnetic pulse. According to the annual report on the PRC's military power for 2004, "China could use high-altitude nuclear bursts to disrupt enemy C4ISR."[65] Their target is evidently Taipei command and control systems. Beijing is also developing anti-satellite (ASAT) weapon systems to attack a space-based ballistic missile defense system. According to Chinese scientists, "intercepting satellites is easier than engaging reentry vehicles."[66] China may well be thinking about employing irregular and asymmetric warfare too.

Conclusion

The PRC started to change its attitude toward arms control agreements in the early 1990s. In order to demonstrate that it seeks to continue integrating into the international community, China acceded to the Nuclear Non-proliferation Treaty (NPT) in 1992, the Chemical Weapons Convention (CWC) and Comprehensive Test Ban Treaty (CTBT) in 1996, and the Zangger Group in October 1997, just one week before President Jiang Zemin's visit to Washington. China is also applying to accede to the Nuclear Suppliers Group (NSG). China wants to prove that it is willing to abide by international norms that are inherent in these international regimes or international institutions, though the international norms are basically products of the ideas, values, worldviews, and culture of the United States. With the advent of the new century, China seems to be satisfied with its positions toward the arms control agreements, and at the same time thinks that the US should also be contented with the démarches of China in abiding by international norms.

But since the start of the Bush administration, Beijing has found itself in an intriguing position. While China in the past was pressed by the United States to join international institutions, and eventually decided to join one after another, now it finds that the United States has started steering away from some of these same institutions. The abrogation of the Anti-Ballistic Missile (ABM) Treaty in 2002, the Senate refusal to ratify the CTBT, and the refusal to join the Kyoto Convention on environment control all demonstrate that the United States is shifting toward a unilateral direction. Washington does not want to be bound or "locked in" by these institutions if they do not suit its national interests. In other words, if Washington thinks that it is not in its interests to join these international regimes, it simply ignores or quits the regimes. So China is very frustrated: when it becomes more receptive toward arms control mechanisms, it finds that now the United States avoids being bound by these agreements. It is now China that wants the United States to abide by these international agreements, as it suits its interests if every nation, in particular the United States, abides by them.[67] Contrary to what many in the West think—that China has ambitions to become a "revisionist" power challenging the status quo of the world order dominated by the United States—one can even say that China has become a status quo power playing a constructive role. On the contrary, the United States has become a "revisionist" power, as it does not want to be bound by some important mechanisms, as illustrated in the behavior of the Bush administration.

What is more, with the implementation of NMD and TMD, the worst scenario for China is Washington launching a first strike against Chinese nuclear forces with China's remaining second-strike missiles intercepted by ballistic missile defenses. In other words, with NMD and TMD in place, China is forced into a strategically inferior position. In the eyes of Chinese analysts, this will certainly promote American hegemony and "neo-interventionism." But in the eyes of Taiwan scholars, this will help Washington to be more resistant to Chinese nuclear blackmail if there is a crisis over Taiwan, thus helping the US government raise the credibility of buttressing the defense of Taiwan.[68]

Nuclear weapons and nuclear strategy are mutually affecting. There is a constant and definite interaction between the two. The development of hardware (nuclear armaments) with more accuracy together with changes in external circumstances (ballistic missile defense plus the

Nuclear Posture Review of the United States) may lead to changes in Chinese nuclear strategy. Suffering from an increasingly inferior position strategically vis-à-vis the United States, in the last few years China has been laboriously searching for the best way to achieve a breakthrough. Missile defenses plus the high-profile unilateralism of the Bush administration, especially the sale of arms to Taiwan, greatly irritate Chinese decisionmakers. In the eyes of Chinese leaders, President Bush's military assistance to Taiwan to a large extent enhances and reinforces President Chen Shui-bian's pro-independence stance, and thus is detrimental to the primordial national interests of China. As a result, China has been very enthusiastic in the research and development of new kinds of conventional weapons, the so-called new concept weapon systems, including different kinds of laser weapons and electromagnetic weapons to paralyze electronic systems of the potential enemy. Beijing is actively developing anti-satellite weapon systems to counterattack the space-based ballistic missile defense system to be designed and deployed by the United States.

What is more important is that Beijing thinks the divergence between a small tactical nuclear weapon and the most powerful conventional weapon is not great. The deterrent power of nuclear weapons comes directly from their enormous destructive power. If they cannot be utilized, then nuclear weapons lose their effect, including their power of deterrence. If conventional weapons cannot achieve their strategic goals, then deploying or even using tactical nuclear weapons could make up for the disadvantages. In other words, Chinese strategic thinkers do not think that nuclear weapons cannot be used. They also make it very clear that using nuclear weapons does not mean automatically a nuclear war. With these ideas in mind, it is not impossible, and quite logical, that Chinese military experts are seriously considering the viability of abolishing their principle of "no-first-use." If abolishing the principle could really succeed in deterring and stopping the US military from intervening in case of a PLA attack against Taiwan, then this suits the strategic interests of China, since the successful reunification of Taiwan by force could then be achieved free of foreign intervention. But this also depends on whether the Chinese military has a real and strong intention to resort to its nuclear capabilities, in case the US military indeed does intervene. The credibility of the Chinese nuclear forces is obviously at stake here.

Though it is difficult to know whether the Chinese authorities would eventually abolish their NFU principle, it is evident that Beijing analysts do not think that using nuclear armaments, particularly tactical weapons, would inevitably lead to a cataclysmic nuclear war. During a hypothetical invasion against Taiwan, if Chinese nuclear forces could credibly deter the US military from taking forceful intervening actions, while at the same time its tactical nuclear weapons (such as the neutron bomb and the EMP bomb) destroy the strong will of resistance of the Taiwan regime at the beginning stage of the crisis, Beijing would be very satisfied.

However, it is clear that what Beijing has in mind is rather to accelerate the research, development, and deployment of a new generation of armaments, in order to create a militarily overwhelming situation that will threaten and frighten the Taiwan regime. With the latter succumbing to pressure from Beijing, it is hoped that Taipei would eventually accept terms for negotiation toward reunification. War is considered only as an instrument to press Taiwan into accepting Chinese conditions. So what Beijing has sought since the Taiwan presidential election in March 2004 is to intensify its actions of "*wengong wubei*" (attack by propaganda and preparation by military means). We will witness stronger political attacks and more intense military exercises in the near future.

Notes

The author is grateful to Dr. Chen Shihmin of National Taiwan University who assisted him in finding useful documents, and the librarian of the Institute of International Relations, National Chengchi University, Taipei, who granted him the right to use their library. He also thanks Wang Wen and Ellen Lai for providing research assistance, and Terence Yeung, who gave useful comments on an earlier draft of the paper.

1. It was reported that China already tested the MIRV in 1987. See Lin Chongpin, *He Ba* (*Nuclear Hegemon*) (Taipei: Students' Publishing, 1999), 435. See also the website of *Shijie Ribao* (*World Daily*), February 8, 2003, quoting from Lin Changsheng and Niu Minshi, "The Construction and Strength of China's ICBM," *Zhonggong Yanjiu* (*Studies of Chinese Communism*) (Taipei), vol. 37, no. 7 (July 2003): 88. According to the CIA, China "encounters significant technical hurdles" in developing a multiple RV capability for its mobile ICBMs and SLBMs. See Robert S. Norris and Hans M. Kristensen, "Nuclear Notebook: Chinese Nuclear Forces, 2003," *Bulletin of the Atomic Scientists,* November/December 2003, 77–80.

2. See Chen Shihmin, *Analyse et Comparison des stratégies nucléaires des puissances nucléaries moyennes: France, Royaume-Uni et Chine* (*Comparative Analysis of the Nuclear Strategies of the Middle Nuclear Powers: France, the United Kingdom, and China*), doctoral dissertation, University of Paris, April 2000, 312.

3. See David Shambaugh, *Modernizing China's Military: Progress, Problems, and Prospects* (Berkeley: University of California Press, 2003), 280.

4. US Department of Defense, *Annual Report on the Military Power of the People's Republic of China 2003,* Report to Congress Pursuant to the FY2000 National Defense Authorization Act, July 28, 2003, 31.

5. See *Foreign Missile Development and the Ballistic Missile Threat through 2015*, unclassified summary of a National Intelligence Estimate (Washington, DC: National Intelligence Council, December 2001), 10.

6. Ibid. See also Mark A. Stokes, "The People's Liberation Army and China's Space and Missile Development: Lessons from the Past and Prospects for the Future," in *The Lessons of History: The Chinese People's Liberation Army at 75*, Laurie Burkitt, Andrew Scobell, and Larry M. Wortzel, eds. (Carlisle, PA: Strategic Studies Institute, US Army War College, July 2003), 221. After the third test of the DF-31 in November 2000, another Chinese source indicated that the DF-31 may carry one nuclear warhead of 1 megaton, or three warheads of 100 kilotons, using MIRV technology. See *Sing Tao Daily* (Hong Kong), December 20, 2000, A15.

7. Robert Hutchinson, *Weapons of Mass Destruction* (London: Weidenfeld and Nicolson, 2003), 99.

8. See *Pingguo Ribao* (*Apple Daily*) (Taiwan version), March 19, 2004, 21.

9. See Chen Shihmin, *Analyse et Comparison des stratégies nucléaires*, 311; and Norris and Kristensen, 78.

10. Shambaugh, 271.

11. See "China Improves the 'Ming' Class Submarine," *Qianlong Junshi* (*Thousand Dragons Military*) online for *Bingqi Zhishi* (*Armaments Knowledge*), February 14, 2001, http://cgi.qianlong.com/mility/bqzs3/DisplayCode.asp?Dataname=Article&Code=20914.

12. Hutchinson, 92–93.

13. *Ta Kung Pao*, June 20, 2005, A4.

14. Shambaugh, 272.

15. Norris and Kristensen, 80.

16. Hans M. Kristensen, "Chinese Nuclear Forces," SIPRI project on Nuclear Technology & Arms Control, *SIPRI Yearbook 2003: Armaments, Disarmament and International Security* (Oxford: Oxford University Press, 2003), http://projects.sipri.se/nuclear/china.pdf.

17. Reported in *Zhongguo Shibao* (*China Times*) (Taipei), March 9, 2004, http://military.china.com/zh_cn/news/568/20040309/11939769.html; see also Han Haichen, *Ershiyi Shiji Zhongguo Haijun* (*21st Century PLA Navy*) (Hong Kong: East-West Cultural Inc., 2000), 156–158.

18. *Military Balance: 2004–2005* (London: International Institute for Strategic Studies, 2004), 170.

19. See *Ming Pao*, Hong Kong, May 14, 2004, A26.

20. See Ye Jincheng, Chen Meihui, and Lu Shijun, "Review and Future Estimation of PLA Force Development," *Guofang Guanli Xuebao* (*Journal of National Defense Management*) (Taipei), vol. 23, no. 2 (November 2002): 62.

21. "The Pursuit of Security: Conversation with General Shiah Yang-jou," *Taiwan Defense Affairs*, vol. 1, no. 2 (Winter 2000/2001): 155–156.

22. See "The First Line of Hyper Warfare: Conversation with Lieutenant General Abe C. Lin," *Taiwan Defense Affairs*, vol. 1, no. 4 (Summer 2001): 133. Lieutenant General Lin is the Director of the Communication Electronic and Informational Bureau, Ministry of National Defense, Taiwan's military chief for information and electronic warfare.

23. See Tai Bingchang and Wang Tao, "On EMP Weapons," *Hangkong Zhishi [Aerospace Knowledge]*, no. 397 (May 2004): 34–35.

24. See Zhu Fei, "How to Destroy the Future Command and Control Systems of the Taiwan Army," *Jianchuan Zhishi [Naval and Merchant Ships]*, no. 296 (April 2004): 12–14.

25. Liu Huaqiu, "Analysis of China's Arms Control Policy," *Xiandai Junshi* (*Contemporary Military*), November 1995, 15.

26. See for instance, Zhu Feng, "The TMD and Cross-Straits Relations: An Analysis on the Extension of TMD to Taiwan by the United States," Research Report 28, Research Center on Cross-Straits Relations, Hong Kong, June 1999.

27. Gao Yan, "The Order of Development of Nuclear Forces of Various Nations in the New Century," *Ta Kung Pao* (Hong Kong), May 3, 2000, A5. *Ta Kung Pao* is the most authoritative newspaper representing official Chinese views in Hong Kong.

28. Ibid.

29. See Zheng Zhiren, "The Five Nuclear Crises of China" (Second Part), November 4, 2004, http://cgi.qianlong.com/mility/bqzs3/DisplayCode.asp?DataName=Article&Code=20616. The author is a senior engineer of the Second Artillery, while the website belongs to the journal *Bingqi Zhishi* (*Armaments Knowledge*).

30. See Zhang Jianzhi and Wang Xiaoxu, "Influence of the Appearance of the Atomic Bomb Toward World Order: In Memory of the 50th Anniversary of the Victory of the Anti-Fascist War," *Jiefangjun Bao* (*PLA Daily*), August 1, 1995, 6. See also Yi Chi, "The Process of the Chinese Development of Nuclear Bombs," at www.gchjs.com/wz/wz232.htm.

31. See Zhu Mingquan, "China's Nuclear Deterrence Policy: Formulation and Development," in *Daguo Weijiao* (*Diplomacy of the Great Powers: Theory, Decision-making and Challenge*), vol. 2, Xiao Jialing and Tang Xianxing, eds. (Beijing: Current Affairs Press, 2003): 566–567.

32. Ibid., 567.

33. Ibid., 568.

34. US Department of Defense (2003), 31.

35. See "China Would Build 12 Super Nuclear Submarines," at http://military.china.com/zh_cn/news/568/20040309/11639769.html.

36. Michael Nacht and Tom Woodrow, "Agenda on Nuclear Arms," in *Strategic Trends in China,* Hans Binnendijk and Ronald N. Montaperto, eds. (Washington, DC: National Defense University, June 1998). This is quoted from the Chinese translation of the book published by Bureau for Translation of History and Politics, Ministry of National Defense, Taiwan, April 1999, 108.

37. See Ye Jincheng, Chen Meihui, and Lu Shijun, 62.

38. See *Zhongguo Shibao* (*China Times*) (Taipei), August 28, 1996, quoted in Chen Shihmin, *Analyse et Comparison des stratégies nucléaires,* 352.

39. Ibid.

40. Ibid., 349.

41. See V.I. Slipchenko, *The Sixth Generation War* (Vecho, 2002), 295. Chinese translation published by Xinhua Publishing House, Beijing, 2004.

42. See Wang Zaigang, "Vanquishing the Aircraft Carrier Task Force: Cruise Missiles, or Ballistic Missiles?" *Jianchuan Zhishi* (*Naval and Merchant Ships*), no. 305 (January 2005): 24–27; see also Yang Zukuai and Wang Zaigang, "How to Develop our Country's Precision-Guided Ballistic Missiles?" *Jianchuan Zhishi* (*Naval and Merchant Ships*), no. 305 (January 2005): 28–30.

43. Zhang Wannian, ed., *Dangdai Shijie Junshi yu Zhongguo Guofang* (*Contemporary World Military and Chinese National Defense*) (Beijing: Military Science Press, 2000), 34.

44. Nancy B. Tucker, *China Confidential* (New York: Columbia University Press, 2001).

45. See Gao Yan; Lin Zhongda, *Zhanqu Feidan Fangyu yu Taihai Anquan* (*TMD: Its Formation and Impact on Taiwan Strait Security*) (Taipei: Taiwan Elite

Press, 2000), 303–321; Zhou Xuehai, *Xinxi Shidai He Junkong* (*Nuclear Arms Control in the Information Age*) (Beijing: Chinese Workers' Press, 2003), 154–156.

46. In February 2005, US and Japanese officials responsible for national defense and foreign policy met in Washington, D.C., and declared that appeasing the Taiwan Straits situation is their "common strategic goal." This was the first time that Tokyo was clearly involved in strengthening deterrence against possible Chinese actions vis-à-vis Taiwan. See "China Is Seriously Concerned with US-Japan Declaration," *Ta Kung Pao*, February 21, 2005, A2; and "US-Japan Declaration Urges Peaceful Resolution to Cross-Straits Relatons," *Hong Kong Economic Journal*, February 21, 2005, 7.

47. See John J. Mearsheimer, *The Tragedy of Great Power Politics* (New York: Norton, 2001).

48. See Danny Gittings, "General Zhu Goes Ballistic," *Asian Wall Street Journal*, July 18, 2005, A13; *Ming Pao*, July 16, 2005; and Joseph Kahn, "Chinese General Threatens Use of A-Bombs if US Intrudes," *New York Times*, July 15, 2005, A8.

49. See Leon Sloss, "Deterrence, Defenses, Nuclear Weapons and Arms Control," *Comparative Strategy*, no. 20 (2001): 438.

50. Robert S. Ross, "Navigating the Taiwan Strait: Deterrence, Escalation Dominance, and US-China Relations," *International Security*, vol. 27, no. 2 (Fall 2002): 65, 68.

51. See Huang Hong, ed., *Shijie Xinjunshi Biange Baogao* (*Report on New Military Revolution of the World*) (Beijing: People's Press, 2004), 298.

52. Wu Jie, "Thinking on Nuclear Forces," April 4, 2001. See the website of *Bingqi Zhishi* (*Armaments Knowledge*), http://cgi.qianlong.com/mility/bqzs3/Display Code.asp?DataName=Article& Code=20931. This article is an interview of Zheng Zhiren and Sang Zhonglin.

53. Ibid.

54. Brad Roberts, *China and Ballistic Missile Defense: 1955 to 2002 and Beyond* (Alexandria, VA: Institute for Defense Analyses, September 2003), 37.

55. See Yu Xiaopeng, *Ershiyi Shiji Zhanzheng Qushi* (*War Trends of the 21st Century*) (Beijing: Xinhua Press, 2002), 165–167.

56. Chang Feng, "The Uses of the Neutron Bomb During the Battle of Debarkation," *Jianchuan Zhishi* (*Naval and Merchant Ships*), no. 295 (March 2004): 12–14.

57. China detonated its first neutron bomb in 1988. This was announced in the Cox Committee Report released in 1999. See Michael Laris, "China Says It Can Build Neutron Bomb," *Washington Post*, July 15, 1999, http://taiwansecurity.org/WP/WP-990715.htm. See also Sam Cohen, "Chinese Nuclear Espionage: Fact or Convenient Fiction?" *Washington Inquirer*, January 25, 1999, http://iraqwar.org/aim1.htm.

58. See Liu Hua, "Reconsidering the Use of Neutron Bombs in a War of Debarkation," *Jianchuan Zhishi* (*Naval and Merchant Ships*), no. 298 (July 2004): 12–14.

59. According to the *Nuclear Posture Review* leaked to the American public in January 2002, the US Department of Defense called for contingency plans for the use of nuclear weapons against specific countries, which include Iraq, Iran, North Korea, Libya, Syria, Russia, and China. An unclassified summary of the Nuclear Posture Review's main themes and recommendations is in Chapter 7. See "Adapting Strategic Forces."

60. See Chen Bojiang et al., eds., *Xin Junshi Geming yu Dandai Zhanzheng Redian Wenti* (*New Military Revolution and Contemporary War Hot Spot Issues*) (Beijing: Chinese Communist Party History Press, 2004), 47–59.

61. A series of articles on how to prepare for a potential war of debarkation have appeared in the journal *Jianchuan Zhishi* (*Naval and Merchant Ships*) since early 2004. These articles are very useful in understanding Chinese thinking concerning the strategies and tactics of fighting such a war, presumably against Taiwan. See An Jing, "Battle of Debarkation under Nuclear Conditions," *Jianchuan Zhishi*, no. 293 (January 2004): 10–12; Han Yang, "Airborne Actions in a War of Debarkation under Nuclear Conditions," *Jianchuan Zhishi*, no. 297 (May 2004): 10–12; Zeng Tai, "Special Actions in a War of Debarkation under Nuclear Conditions," *Jianchuan Zhishi*, no. 299 (July 2004): 22–24; and Shang Lin, "Battle of Strategic Nuclear Reaction," *Jianchuan Zhishi*, no. 300 (August 2004): 22–24.

62. See Zhang Wannian, 90.

63. Ibid., 64; see also US Department of Defense (2003), 37–38.

64. See "Bokai Miwu Kan Zhongguo Zhenshi Heliliang" (Clear the Fog in Order to See China's Real Nuclear Power)," http://fifan.nease.net/chinaarm/chinuclear.htm.

65. See US Department of Defense, *Annual Report on the Military Power of the People's Republic of China*, FY04 Report to Congress on PRC Military Power Pursuant to the FY2000 National Defense Authorization Act (Washington, DC: Department of Defense, May 28, 2004), 52.

66. See Mark A. Stokes, "Chinese Ballistic Missile Forces in the Age of Global Missile Defense: Challenges and Responses," in *China's Growing Military Power: Perspectives on Security, Ballistic Missiles, and Conventional Capabilities*, Andrew Scobell and Larry M. Wortzel, eds. (Carlisle, PA: Strategic Studies Institute, US Army War College, September 2002), 147.

67. See Su Hao, "Issues of Arms Control and Sino-American Relations," *Heping yu Fazhan* (*Peace and Development*) (March 2000): 42–47.

68. This argument is well defended by a Taiwan scholar. See Chen Shihmin, "PRC's Nuclear Force Development and the Evolution of its External Relations in the Cold War Era (1950s to 1980s)," *Zhongguo Dalu Yanjiu* (*Mainland China Studies*), vol. 46, no. 6 (November–December 2003): 49–50.

7

Alternative Futures

Brad Roberts

Preceding chapters in this volume have explored multiple factors bearing on the future of China's nuclear posture, including both domestic and international factors as well as technical and political ones. How will these various factors combine to determine China's nuclear future? Of all the various alternative futures that are plausible, which ones are likely? Given the variety of factors and their often contradictory implications, a simple prediction would seem unwise. Moreover, because China's military culture remains largely closed to outside observers and its nuclear program especially has been shrouded in secrecy, there are likely to be some very significant gaps in the picture of China's policy and thinking depicted in this volume.

Yet some analysts look at all this data and conclude that dramatic departures in China's nuclear posture are nearly impossible; others, surveying essentially the same data, conclude that they are inevitable—and indeed well advanced. A 1999 US National Intelligence Estimate concluded that "by 2015, China is likely to have tens of missiles capable of targeting the United States, including a few tens of more survivable land- and sea-based mobile missiles with smaller nuclear warheads."[1] In contrast, a congressional investigation concluded that China may well be poised for an "aggressive deployment of upwards of 1,000 thermonuclear warheads on ICBMs by 2015."[2] Where does the truth lie?

Rather than beginning with what might be, let us begin with what is. This chapter begins with an exploration of the ongoing modernization of China's strategic forces with the aim of projecting a trajectory of force development (assuming all of the various factors remain equal and that there are no huge surprises hidden behind that veil of secrecy). As argued below, that baseline trajectory aims at continued development of

China's strategic force so that it remains viable for basic strategic purposes in the face of US deployment of ballistic missile defense (BMD). Such continued development suggests something of the changing quantitative and qualitative parameters of China's strategic forces in the years ahead—because qualitative and thus operational improvements to China's forces are an inevitable by-product of modernization (even regardless of the BMD context). The pace at which such modernization is proceeding and will proceed seems likely to be tied directly to Chinese expectations about the pace at which US BMD will proceed into the field.

This chapter then explores departures from this baseline. Notionally, there are two basic departures. One points toward a much more capable force, as China reacts to factors beyond BMD. The other points toward a force even less capable vis-à-vis the United States (but not others).

Then there is a consideration of probabilities: how do these trajectories rate in terms of likelihood? Here various factors are explored. But special prominence is given to the role of US policy and strategy in shaping the thinking of Chinese planners about what capabilities best serve their interests. The chapter closes with a discussion of dissuasion—one of the central tenets of the Bush administration's *Quadrennial Defense Review* (*QDR*) and *Nuclear Posture Review* (*NPR*) and conceived very much with China's nuclear future in mind.[3]

How Will Modernization Change the Force?

By now well established in this volume, particularly in Chapter 4 by Saunders and Yuan, is the fact that China is modernizing its strategic forces. Indeed, China is midstream in a decades-long effort aimed at making improvements to its strategic forces through the development, production, and deployment of follow-on systems to those already in place. Modernization will result in improvements to range, mobility, and accuracy of these missile systems.[4] Where is this modernization program headed? There is no solid publicly available evidence indicating that China has made the basic decisions about the key parameters of its future force—about whether the intercontinental component will remain relatively small in the overall mix, whether new systems will be deployed with multiple warhead capabilities, or whether nuclear capabilities will be given to the theater systems as well. To better understand where Chinese force modernization is headed requires an understanding of the primary concerns driving the effort. These have been well explored in previous chapters but a brief summary is useful here.

Various concerns have motivated China's efforts to improve its strategic forces. To a certain extent modernization is driven simply by concerns about the aging of systems deployed two or three decades ago and reaching the end of their serviceable lives. To a certain extent it is driven by the availability of new technology and expertise from Russia—and by the wealth to acquire both made possible by a more prosperous economy. The availability of more advanced technologies to China's strategic designers and engineers has fueled a general push for higher quality in replacement systems. As already noted, this in itself means some important changes to the operational characteristics of the force. For example, the deployment of road-mobile DF-31 missiles means that warheads will have to be mated to missiles, in a way not currently understood to be the case with the silo-based ICBMs, and this will increase their capacity to quickly alert and ready their forces for launch. A more mobile force that is more ready for launch will also result in improved survivability of the force in scenarios where it is attacked preemptively. Improved capabilities for command, control, communications, computers, intelligence, surveillance, and reconnaissance (C4ISR) will also permit China to move away from a posture premised on absorbing the first blow and to launch on warning, launch under attack, or something analogous. Conversely, improved survivability would reduce pressures to launch on warning. As Paul Godwin has argued, such a move "would be especially attractive if the SSBN (ballistic missile submarine) program was unsuccessful or was cancelled because of costs."[5]

According to one Chinese analysis, the PRC force modernization plan aims at certain specific improvements in force operational characteristics. One is to reduce the vulnerability of strategic missiles to first strike by reducing their size and shifting to solid-fueled systems. Another is to increase the mobility of the overall force, "while also adding to their stealthiness during launch and flight. Other planned improvements include methods for hardening missiles to survive a nuclear attack and to reduce the pre-launch and mid-course vulnerability. Another key task for China's missile forces is to increase their accuracy, as well as their ability to penetrate strategic defenses."[6]

Thus, China's force will grow more capable even if it does not increase numerically. Its future force will be more alert (because the warheads will travel with mobile systems), better able to survive preemptive attack, more capable of launch under attack, more accurate, more capable of penetrating or overwhelming US defenses, and more threatening to US allies in the region.

The Impact of Ballistic Missile Defense

But the modernization of China's strategic forces is driven by factors beyond those noted above. Two additional factors stand out as especially salient. One is mounting concern about the effectiveness of the force. Force effectiveness is measured in terms of the ability to survive preemptive strike and deliver warheads to targets in a manner consistent with operational and strategic plans. The survivability criterion is especially important for a force postured on the no-first-use doctrine, as discussed in greater detail in the chapters in this volume by Medeiros and Ting.

This concern about effectiveness has been considerably magnified by the second major concern: the shift in focus from Russia to the United States among Chinese military planners. With the end of the Cold War and the collapse of the Soviet Union, China's leaders worry less about invasion from its north and west and more about the United States and the possibility of confrontation over Taiwan. Especially after the Taiwan crisis of 1996, when the United States deployed aircraft carriers to show support for Taiwan at a time of PRC missile firings across the strait, Chinese planners have had to contemplate a serious possibility that the effort to use military means to complete reunification with Taiwan would bring direct military confrontation with the United States and thus also possible US strategic operations (both offense and defense) against China's strategic forces.

Over the last decade, as policymakers in both Washington and Beijing began to see the deployment of ballistic missile defenses by the United States as likely if not inevitable, Chinese officials and academic experts became increasingly vocal in their opposition to such deployments. They have raised multiple concerns. First and foremost was the perceived threat of BMD to the viability of the Chinese deterrent force. Second, they were concerned about the impact of US withdrawal from the Anti-Ballistic Missile (ABM) Treaty on international arms control and strategic stability. Third, they predicted a new round of nuclear proliferation in response to a more assertive United States and even arms racing in outer space. Fourth, they feared that US BMD deployments would consolidate US hegemony, free it from the balance of power, and thus precipitate greater instability and conflict—and renewed coercion of Beijing. (See Chapter 5 by Ronald N. Montaperto in this volume for a discussion of the Chinese view of US hegemony.) Thus some Chinese officials and experts predicted dramatic departures in Chinese military thinking and, together with their Russian counterparts, hinted at potentially dramatic departures in force deployments.[7]

US policymakers generally have sought to disavow any connection between BMD and PRC force modernization. For example, the Bush administration has argued that "China is already engaged in a substantial effort to modernize its strategic nuclear forces, which are currently capable of striking the United States. We do not believe our deployment of limited missile defenses should lead Beijing to further accelerate or expand its buildup of strategic nuclear forces."[8] Similarly, Clinton administration officials argued: "Whether or not we proceed with national missile defense, China's nuclear forces would expand in a way that would make this system less threatening to China."[9] Indeed, Washington should not let Beijing blame it for every new deployment. But US BMD is hardly irrelevant to *how* China modernizes its forces. Indeed, it seems likely to have a direct effect on the Chinese modernization effort.

Somewhere between the arrival of the new Bush administration in January 2001 and formal US withdrawal from the ABM Treaty eighteen months later, the Chinese government gave up on its effort to persuade Washington not to proceed with BMD. Actual US withdrawal on June 18, 2002, was noted only by a spokesman of the Ministry of Foreign Affairs, with a statement expressing regret at the end of the treaty and hope that the United States would act "prudently" on the issue.[10] Beijing's quiet acquiescence to the act of withdrawal itself was a striking contrast to the energetic criticism of China's disarmament ambassador, Sha Zukang, and others in the preceding years. What accounts for this shift in Chinese policy and strategy? Various factors appear to have been at work.

One was the sense of growing crisis that gripped China's America watchers in the early months of the Bush administration. In 2001, some of their worst fears seemed to be coming true, as President Bush offered an unconditional promise of protection to Taipei (later "clarified" to add a condition or two) and Pentagon planners deemed a certain unnamed rising power in Asia to be the likely next peer competitor of the United States.[11] It is useful to recall that the 2000 presidential election featured in part a debate about whether the Clinton administration had been too deferential toward Russia and China.[12] The EP-3 crisis signaled to them the potential for a sudden deterioration of bilateral relations into confrontation and even potentially war.

President Bush's call in the wake of the September 11 attacks to "choose sides" provided an opportunity for Chinese President Jiang

Zemin to try to move bilateral relations onto a new footing. Since then steady progress has been made in restoring or initiating bilateral dialogues on strategic stability, nonproliferation, regional security issues, and of course the war on terrorism. China has also received a steady stream of visitors from the Bush administration, including the president himself, carrying the message embodied in the summer 2001 White House statement on BMD: that BMD is not about China and should not result in major alterations to China's ongoing modernization of its nuclear forces.[13]

Also during this period the informal Track Two dialogues involving Chinese and US experts and officials participating in their private capacities contained ever fewer of the harsh exchanges on BMD that had become frequent in the 1990s. The following Chinese commentary is illustrative of this shift in tone:

> With the dawning of the 21st century, especially considering the 9/11 attack, the world entered a new post-post cold war age. International relations in this age will perhaps be featured by the mixture of cooperation and confrontation but with cooperation as the main theme. Although missile defense will affect the strategic balance among the big powers, they can try to find a way out and make various compromises and reach a new balance for they need cooperation more than they need confrontation. So the problems caused by missile defense can be solved more easily than at any other time under the new international circumstances. . . . Another important factor is that there does exist the threat of missile proliferation and one cannot exclude the possibility of future nuclear weapon attack by terrorists. So the US is justified in inventing and deploying limited missile defense. The world perhaps will come to the new terms and consensus with the US on this over time.[14]

Another factor in China's calculus must have been growing acceptance of the fact that Sino-Russian partnership in confronting the United States would not prove effective in preventing US deployments. Throughout the second half of the 1990s Beijing and Moscow had found increasingly common cause in preventing US pursuit of national missile defenses and also withdrawal from the ABM Treaty. Sino-Russian strategic consultations intensified with the arrival in Washington of the Bush administration, with a summit in July 2001. But in Banning Garrett's assessment, many Chinese had come to see "NMD as inevitable and believe that the opposition of Russia and China will at best delay the US deployment decision."[15] Some Chinese experts spoke informally of the failure of a decade's effort "to stiffen the Russian spine" and of "the inevitable sell-out" by Moscow as it tilted toward Washington and away from Beijing. Russian proposals for a joint Russian-US anti-missile system and Russian suggestions that its experts were prepared to cooperate with the United States to develop nuclear interceptors for US BMD systems only aggravated these Chinese sentiments.[16]

Signaling the changing tenor of Chinese BMD statements, Ambassador Sha was replaced as director general of the Department of Arms Control and Disarmament by a man of a more traditional diplomatic style, Ambassador Liu Jieye. Indeed, this came amidst a larger transition in the Chinese leadership. In autumn 2002 the 16th Congress of the Chinese Communist Party formalized a wide-ranging turnover in Chinese leadership and the emergence of a new generation evidently committed to the maintenance of positive relations with the United States as a top priority.[17] This reinforced the more pragmatic political line on BMD.

But political acquiescence by Beijing to the inevitability of US ballistic missile defense does not necessarily equate with passivity in China's response. Indeed, adjustments to China's military posture and foreign policy were often threatened in the period of full court press against BMD under Ambassador Sha. But which ones are likely? China cannot afford politically and otherwise to lose confidence in the effectiveness of its forces—their ability to perform essential missions in likely scenarios—and thus seems certain to work very hard to adapt its strategic posture to ensure their continued effectiveness as US BMD capabilities reach the field. There should be no doubt on these matters—Chinese views have been clear and consistent. Moreover, this follows directly from the apparently central role of ballistic missiles in China's emerging concepts of how to fight and win regional wars under high-tech conditions.[18]

But what responses specifically should be expected? And how might they differ from what might have occurred regardless of US BMD and as a result of ongoing Chinese modernization? The Chinese government has provided no official or unofficial statements on this question. It has not even described in any detail the modernization program now under way—an obviously essential bit of information if we are to understand the departures from the baseline that might be driven by US BMD. Thus all we can do is speculate, hopefully on an informed basis, drawing on what we can understand or reasonably infer about China's options. In considering those options, it is useful to distinguish between quantitative and qualitative adjustments.

Quantitatively, the possibility exists that China could respond to US BMD with a substantial increase in its deployed forces. The CIA predicts an increase over the next decade from roughly 20 to between 75 and

100 nuclear warheads deployed atop missiles able to reach the United States.[19] This might be achieved by increasing the number of warheads deployed on individual missiles. For many years China has had the capability to deploy multiple reentry vehicles (MRVs) atop its larger missiles. Its ability to deploy multiple lighter warheads that are also independently targetable (MIRVs) is somewhat uncertain, given doubts about the impact of the nuclear test moratorium and Chinese adherence to the Comprehensive Test Ban Treaty on its warhead development and certification effort. But a buildup of deployed forces could also rely instead on an increase in missiles and launchers. Of course, some mix of these approaches is also possible—more missiles, more launchers, and more warheads per missile.

Qualitatively, the need to penetrate ballistic missile defenses suggests in addition increased reliance on penetration aids such as decoys, chaff, and maneuverable warheads. That need points also to the potential utility for China of systems designed to attack the ballistic missile defense system itself—whether direct attack with anti-satellite attack (ASAT) on space-based infrastructure, or direct attack on ground-based radars and/or indirect electronic attack on elements of the C4ISR structure. These qualitative improvements to Chinese forces as required to meet the BMD challenge are separate from the previously noted qualitative improvements driven by modernization per se.

These arguments so far focus on the impact on Chinese force planning of US BMD systems designed to protect the territory of the United States—what through the 1990s was called national missile defense (NMD). But what about the deployment of missile defenses in East Asia to protect US forces, bases, and allies—what used to be called theater missile defense (TMD)? There is some uncertainty about how China would respond to the introduction of theater missile defense in the Asia-Pacific region. There have been many official Chinese statements suggesting that the transfer of TMD to Taiwan would precipitate a major crisis. But there have also been hints from Chinese experts that some modes of deployment may be more tolerable to the Chinese than others. Thus actual Chinese responses are difficult to predict. Although there has been some discussion of possible countermeasures to US NMD, there seems to be far less in the open Chinese literature about the development of military capabilities to defeat TMD. Instead, articles in Chinese military publications tend to discount the effects of TMD on the military situation in the Taiwan Straits, arguing that it will not substantially improve Taiwanese defensive capabilities.[20] Nevertheless, the Chinese military has already undertaken a substantial buildup of its theater ballistic missile force—reportedly on the way to 600–800 total deployed missiles.

The bulk of Chinese commentary has suggested a modest response to BMD, largely based on two arguments. The first is simply that China has no need for anything more than a very modest force structure. China apparently has assumed that a maximum of 20 warheads delivered on the United States is sufficient for its purposes—more specifically, that the prospect of 20 warheads so delivered ought be sufficient to induce US restraint in any confrontation with China. Moreover, it has apparently assumed that even if faced with a preemptive nuclear strike, the fraction of warheads surviving attack ought to suffice—witness the absence of its own BMD systems to protect those few silo-based missiles. Indeed, its leaders seem to calculate that by holding even one US city hostage to attack China can induce the United States not to bring its full power to bear for the defense of Taiwan.[21] Thus few Chinese analysts seem to see any need to meet US BMD deployments with anything more than roughly parallel countervailing deployments—essentially letting BMD pace the growth of China's intercontinental missile force as Beijing acts to maintain the status quo ante.

The second argument in the Chinese debate is that doing more than this could in fact be counterproductive—dangerously so. By this view, a large force buildup could play right into the hands of Americans who might hope that missile defense can be used on China the way Star Wars was used on the Soviet Union—as a ruse to cause excessive military spending that threatens the regime. In the words of Chinese analyst Xia Liping:

> China will not participate in a nuclear arms race with the United States. Firstly, it is unnecessary for China, because China only wants to maintain its minimum capability of retaliatory counterattack. Secondly, China still remembers the lessons of the former Soviet Union. Thirdly, China will be focused on its internal economic development for a long time.[22]

Hence many Chinese analysts have actively promoted "a middle way" for China's response to BMD that balances efforts to increase the survivability of China's ICBM force with the deployment of penetration aids.[23] In the words of one recent authoritative Chinese text, "the basis of the nuclear strategy of China is the containment of nuclear war, not on winning a nuclear war."[24] One influential Chinese analyst, Li Bin, has elaborated a set of principles that should guide such a middle way:

- The approaches China takes should be feasible in helping defeat the US NMD.
- Some of the approaches should be visible to the United States.
- The approaches should be affordable and not constitute a financial burden on China.
- The approaches should be moderate and not increase perceptions of a "China threat" in other countries.
- Decisionmakers will prefer approaches that are compatible with each other.
- Some precautionary approaches are needed.
- Approaches based on challenging technology could obtain more support.[25]

In summary, the baseline trajectory for China's force modernization is defined by the following basic parameters. The first is modernization for its own sake—because it can and must as its deployed systems age. The second is expansion of the intercontinental component of the missile force so that it can successfully retaliate through the US BMD shield. The third is to do so at a pace that matches but does not exceed US BMD deployments—so as not to be the excuse for an even larger and more capable missile defense to come.

Within this trajectory, what mix of force options is China most likely to choose? This is a question that cannot be answered in the abstract. It requires more information than currently available about the confidence of China's scientists and engineers in different technical solutions, the cost consequences of different choices, the bureaucratic politics that inevitably play a role in such decisions, and the willingness of China's leaders to favor one "solution" and its advocates over others.

Departures from the Baseline

What if Chinese leaders were somehow to conclude that this baseline does not serve China's interests? What if pacing US BMD deployments to maintain the status quo ante is no longer seen as sufficient to their ends? Is this a realistic possibility? How might this come to pass? What implications might it have for China's nuclear future?

The possible point of departure for an alternative trajectory begins with China's understanding of the dynamics of a possible confrontation over Taiwan involving both conventional war with US forces and the effort of both sides to manipulate the other by casting a nuclear shadow over the crisis, as discussed in this volume by Ting Wai.[26] As argued above, China's modest force structure seems to suggest that its planning is informed by the belief that US restraint can be induced by the threat of Chinese ability to inflict relatively modest damage on US targets. How might this assumption begin to change? Let us consider three factors.

The first is the impact of defense transformation as being pursued by Secretary of Defense Donald Rumsfeld (and as pursued in earlier variants by his recent predecessors). Over the last decade Chinese analysts and planners have hoped to gain the tools of success in "local wars under high-tech conditions" by purchasing advanced systems and technology on the global market. The 2004 Chinese defense white paper devotes considerable emphasis to achievement of "the RMA [revolution in military affairs] with Chinese characteristics." There seems little evidence that Chinese planners believe they can somehow catch up with the United States and field a conventional force capable of besting the United States anywhere, anytime; instead, some Chinese experts do apparently believe that selective acquisition of RMA capabilities will enable them, in combination with other changes to Chinese forces, to meet the requirements of defeating the United States in a limited war over Taiwan.[27]

But defense transformation holds out the prospect of the United States leap-frogging even further ahead, as China falls even further behind. Chinese military doctrine puts great emphasis on "maintaining control of the overall situation," defined as preservation of central authority, national unity, and momentum toward main tasks.[28] But as one Chinese analyst put it in private conversation, "how long did Saddam have control of the overall situation once US bombs started to fall on Baghdad?" How well can the PLA expect to perform against the revolutionary developments in US capabilities foreshadowed in military operations in Afghanistan and Iraq? The RMA may be opening up the gap between US and PRC forces faster than the PLA can close it.

Defense transformation has short-term aspects in addition to these longer-term ones. The 2001 *Quadrennial Defense Review* precipitated a redeployment of US naval and air strike assets in the Pacific, as well as changes to the ways in which carrier battle groups are readied for deployment, in order to strengthen the capacity of US military forces to cope with contingencies requiring prompt response—such as a Taiwan contingency.[29] Such changes to the US military posture must accentuate PLA concerns about how to exercise decisive leverage over Taipei in the window before the arrival of major US military assets—a window that is closing further as a result of these changes.

A second factor bearing on the future of Chinese thinking about a Taiwan crisis under the nuclear shadow relates to America's strategic personality. Chinese confidence in their ability to induce restraint by the United States through nuclear threats seems to have been strongly informed by the so-called Somalia syndrome—the perception that America is a casualty-averse society that is unwilling to spend blood or treasure in defense of anything but vital interests. US behaviors post–9/11 must call this comfortable assumption into question. The national commitment to vanquish enemies at "the crossroads of tyranny and technology" and to "eliminate gathering threats" has been followed by wars to remove two regimes (in Afghanistan and Iraq) and by US leadership of a nearly global coalition against Al-Qaida. Americans have been willing to spend blood and treasure for these purposes; we have proven willing to take casualties—and to inflict them. As one Chinese observer commented in private discussion, "the number of Americans who died on 9/11 is roughly equal to the number of people that would die if the PLA were to sink an aircraft carrier—and what the United States has done in response sends a very strong message to the Chinese military."

The Chinese are also learning something important and uncomfortable about their assumption of asymmetric stakes in Taiwan. To this point, their belief that the threat of a few casualties can induce a lot of US restraint seems to be informed by a belief that the stakes of China and the United States are asymmetric—that China's stakes are vital but those of the United States are less so. Here again, US behavior after 9/11 must call this comfortable assumption into question. Chinese commentators are increasingly appreciative of the ways in which US values guide US strategic choices. Again in private conversation, a Chinese observer has argued: "America has its own version of the Brezhnev doctrine—the commitment to use force to protect the values of its revolution abroad. Your stake in Taiwan may be much higher than we tend to believe—because it will involve your reputation in your eyes as the guardian of democracy." It may also be that any effort to use WMD to coerce or attack the United States would create interests for the United States that few Chinese analysts have so far understood.[30]

The third factor is the so-called new triad. The Bush administration's *Nuclear Posture Review* of 2003 argued for a reconceptualization of the instruments of strategic power.[31] The "old triad" of nuclear strike forces (bombers, land-based missiles, and sea-based missiles) was submerged intellectually into a larger three-part construct. One element of this construct focuses on strike forces—both nuclear and non-nuclear. The second focuses on defense—both active defenses against missile attack and passive ones. The third focuses on infrastructure—as a tool for maintaining existing deterrent capabilities but also for dissuading potential future competitors with the capacity of the United States to out-compete any adversary. A key objective of the *NPR* is to reduce reliance on nuclear weapons by increasing reliance on conventional strategic weapons and protection methods.

Most Chinese commentary on the *NPR* focused on the fact that China was reportedly mentioned as one of a handful of specific targets and on the potentially damaging consequences of what Chinese experts perceived as a renewed emphasis on nuclear warfighting.[32] The following Chinese commentary is illustrative:

> The result of the US nuclear strategy adjustment will increase the possibility of the use of nuclear weapons and enable the United States to use nuclear weapons in a flexible and selective manner in a real war, thereby lowering the "nuclear threshold." . . . Due to US deployment of an anti-missile system, refusal to ratify the CTBT, unilateral development of a "metal shield" (sic) for itself and pursuit of an absolute security of itself, it will inevitably make countries in the world lose the sense of relative security, lead to an even grimmer world security situation, and could further worsen nuclear proliferation.[33]

But what developments in US operational capabilities does the *NPR* portend for the Taiwan scenario? Of course it promises the improved BMD capabilities of such long concern to Beijing and that, once fielded, will help to reduce the risks to the United States and Taiwan of defending against Chinese attack. But it promises more than BMD. The *NPR* holds out the promise of dramatically improved conventional strategic strike capabilities and the possibility that the United States will gain and work hard to keep the ability to successfully preempt against the entire Chinese ICBM and SLBM force by non-nuclear means. The PLA is already working hard to remedy the vulnerability of its forces to preemption—and its solution may well now look much further away. Americans often do not appreciate the long shadow that successful conventional preemption casts over China's view of the credibility of its nuclear deterrent. If the United States can eliminate China's strategic deterrent while inflicting only very limited casualties as might be possible by non-nuclear means, how credible would be China's threat to inflict nuclear punishment on US cities, perhaps at some much later time? The *NPR* also promises improved nuclear strike capabilities against hard and deeply buried targets (HDBT), which is certain to be seen in China as a rising concern given huge Chinese investments in underground tunneling. Lastly the *NPR* promises advanced intelligence, surveillance, and reconnaissance (ISR) tools which, if successfully applied against China, could strip away the veil of secrecy that masks China's strategic programs—and enable US preemption.

Add these three factors together and the result for the Chinese military planner cannot be a happy one. If all of these capabilities mature as the Bush administration intends, China's military would likely perceive itself as in a terrible box. With US global strike forces not days or weeks but minutes or hours away, Taipei is unlikely to capitulate quickly to Chinese military pressure. Failing to induce capitulation, the PRC would find that the burden of escalation falls on it, not the United States; thus, it would face a choice between backing down and escalating. Any escalation by nuclear means could be well met by the United States with the envisioned posture—meaning with conventional strikes eliminating many air and naval assets essential to the PLA mission. Any attacks on US bases and allies in the East Asian theater might then be well met by missile defenses, thus likely having the effect of strengthening rather than weakening allied resolve. If decisionmakers in Beijing come to see their grip on power at risk in a losing battle over Taiwan and again opt for escalation, the United States could well conclude that, in the endgame, it must seriously degrade China's conventional and strategic forces so that China cannot pose such threats again any time soon. For China this must be an especially alarming prospect, calling into question the possibility of returning to the status quo ante after a military confrontation it deems necessary to teach the right lesson to the United States and Taiwan. In this scenario, China is the first user of nuclear weapons, possibly the second user, but also the loser. This prospect can hardly be reassuring to Chinese planners.

Faced with this prospect, how might Chinese planners begin to think differently about their nuclear requirements? There seems little reason to think that they might opt to seek a force that has parity with the United States in terms of overall numbers and counterforce warfighting capabilities. This is unlikely not least because of the strong conviction among many Chinese experts, noted above, that the United States duped the Soviet Union into spending itself into oblivion through the charade of the Reagan administration's Strategic Defense Initiative. Rather, it is conceivable that Chinese planners might make changes to the state of the overall balance that aim at restoring confidence in China's ability to survive and indeed prevail in limited nuclear war—i.e., in its ability to inflict costs on the United States and in its ability to protect its own forces from preemption. There seems little reason to think that China might opt to move into a long-term competitive arms race with the United States to achieve these purposes. Again, the Soviet example is a powerful one for them. Rather, Chinese planners might conclude that they need to race for some fixed period of time—roughly conceived here as a deadline before the full fruits of the new triad and defense transformation are available to the United States—so as to press its advantages over Taiwan while those advantages remain.

What might this actually entail programmatically? For China's strategic strike forces, the drive to field sea-based systems, including those for conventional cruise missile attack, might be accelerated, along with more rapid improvements in the ability of Chinese forces to locate and promptly strike US forces at sea. China has also made impressive investments in both active and passive defenses against missile attack and these could be brought to a higher level of readiness and capability.[34] Indeed, one of the simplest "fixes" to the vulnerability of China's existing ballistic missile force would be deployment of BMD of its own (probably nuclear tipped, on the Soviet/Russian model). Given its considerable concerns about US strategic advantages in outer space, China might also move to field space attack and space control assets in quantities sufficient to its purposes. The result would be a strategic posture overall much more capable against the risks of US preemption and deployed in sufficient quantities to pose very substantial risks to the United States, its operational forces, and its allies.

If the baseline trajectory of Chinese force modernization is defined as pacing US BMD, this departure trajectory can be defined as racing the new triad—not in perpetuity, but to the field, and to a moment of crisis over Taiwan.

But What If This Is "Too Hard?"

There are good reasons to think that this effort to race the emerging US strategic posture might be seen as "too hard" by decisionmakers in China. It would be costly, in terms of both financial and manpower resources. It is not obvious that the existing infrastructure for the production of missiles, warheads, and the necessary fissile materials would be capable of sustaining force structure increases beyond certain modest steps. It is highly likely that big buildups in China's strategic posture would generate even deeper concerns among its neighbors about its future geopolitical ambitions and, with that, deeper resistance to Chinese projects and deeper attachments to the United States.

Arguably the largest obstacle to a dramatic departure in Chinese force planning is in the political realm. To choose robust competition with the United States in the strategic military realm would have far-reaching consequences for China's various other interests—a positive political relationship with the United States and its allies, ready access to global technologies and investments, and a peaceful international environment allowing it to focus inwardly. If China's leaders choose not to compete with the United States in this realm at least for the medium-term future, is there another choice they might make other than falling further and further behind?

US experts typically do not appreciate the extent to which Eurasian concerns factor in the Chinese strategic calculus. Americans interested in matters nuclear tend to think about the US-PRC balance whereas Chinese analysts interested in matters nuclear tend to think about the multipolar Eurasian landscape, in which the United States figures prominently but hardly exclusively. China's interest in nuclear security and stability encompasses not just the relationship with the United States but also Russia and India, as well as the various states of East Asia with robust latent nuclear capabilities (principally Japan and South Korea, but also Indonesia and Australia, among others). Indeed, over the five decades of China's strategic programs, the vast majority of resources have been focused on the development of capabilities for the Eurasian theater. China would be modernizing and increasing its strategic power even in the absence of developments in the US-PRC relationship.

Surveying this Eurasian landscape, Chinese experts are quick to note Russia's steep decline—but also its future potential. Moreover, they note that Russia's strategic, economic, and political decline comes at a time of China's economic and political rise. Accordingly, some Chinese political figures argued in the late 1990s—largely in private—that China's interests would be well served by conspicuously stepping into Russia's place as "the second nuclear power" on the global scene and the top nuclear power in Eurasia.[35] In their view, this might be useful to China for signaling its return to its rightful global place after two centuries of eclipse, for eliciting deference "due" the Middle Kingdom, for dissuading potential challengers, and for enticing the United States to engage it in global policy questions.

From a programmatic perspective, how might this be accomplished? The core notion would be a buildup of modern, intermediate-range nuclear forces that are deployed so as to visibly demonstrate numerical superiority vis-à-vis Russia, India, and the breakout capabilities China projects for Japan and Korea. The point would not be to repeat the Soviet choices of the 1950s and 1960s to compete for superiority over the United States; instead, the point would be to posture for superiority over all others in Eurasia. It would leave to a later time the possibility of renewed strategic offense/defense competition with the United States—on the argument that it looks "too hard" for now.

In sum, the future of China's strategic forces can be conceived along three alternative trajectories. One is the baseline trajectory defined simply as a linear projection forward of the existing posture but with incremental improvements in a manner largely dictated by US BMD. The second is a departure trajectory along which China seeks maximum strategic leverage before the United States fully realizes the advantages of defense transformation and the new triad by racing to certain specific new capabilities. The third is a departure trajectory that sets aside for now the question of competing with the United States and focuses instead on signaling China's arrival as the world's second nuclear power, in clear ascendance over Russia.

Assessing Likelihood

How likely is China to pursue one or another of these paths? Chinese officials and experts have strong opinions on this matter—based on the very limited sampling of opinion by this author. They adamantly express their conviction that China is now on and will remain on the first trajectory. They tend to disparage the third trajectory (though some acknowledge a modest debate in the late 1990s). And they discount the second trajectory by saying that China has learned from the Soviet Union's mistake and will never fall into an arms race with the United States (which isn't quite the point). But in a system as closed as theirs, it is impossible to gauge whether the facts on the ground correspond to their reported beliefs.

From the US national security perspective, the core question is whether China is likely to abandon the "pacing" baseline for a "sprint" to some medium-term advantage. US interests would not be served well by a Chinese choice to abandon the baseline for "the world's second nuclear power," especially as China's buildup would be threatening to US friends and allies and would likely generate unwelcome developments in Russia's force posture.[36] But let us focus here on the relative likelihood of moving to the competitive trajectory. Consider first the possible incentives to abandon the baseline trajectory.

China's actual reactions to US defense transformation and to the new triad will ultimately be shaped by their expectations about the potential dynamics of crisis and war with the United States. For lack of a better term, this is China's deterrence calculus. To the extent China's leaders perceive the risks of war as low and the operational capabilities of US forces to be unimpressive in time of war, then changes to the US strategic posture seem likely to have little impact on China's deterrence calculus. But if they believe that the risks of war are rising or high and if they believe that the US seeks and will gain meaningful strategic dominance at all important escalation levels in conflict, then the impact seems likely to be much more significant.

A key factor in China's deterrence calculus must be its reading of US intentions as it infers them from US choices about how to field its new military capabilities. The central question here has been and remains whether the United States intends to field a missile defense so postured as to effectively negate China's deterrent force—or so postured as to have minimal effects on China's force while having strong effect on the emerging missile forces of hostile, rogue states.

There is a good argument that Chinese leaders remain unpersuaded by the professed US commitment not to field defensive systems explicitly aimed at denying China a credible second-strike capability. Chinese analysts have expressed deep skepticism that the "limited defense" promised by the Clinton and Bush administrations will not, in timelines relevant to Chinese force modernization, emerge in the end as a "thicker" defense. Americans must understand the long time-horizons that inform China's investment policies and strategic posture. The DF-31 missile, for example, has been in development for more than two decades. Chinese experts find it virtually impossible to believe that the United States will stop at some initial, limited capability. Indeed, they fully expect the kind of open-ended pursuit of BMD stated as the Bush administration's intended path. China can also find a great deal of evidence in the US political debate suggesting that thin defenses are merely a prelude to thicker defenses, perhaps sooner, perhaps later, but in any case a decade or two hence. And whatever reassurances they might have heard from Bush, Clinton, and then Bush administration representatives about the nature of Washington's commitment to a limited defense, the Chinese have also heard a steady dose of expert opinion from Moscow and elsewhere reiterating the long-held view that the United States will never stop in the effort to construct the maximally effective defense within its reach once it heads down that path. By not foreclosing this option, the United States seems unwittingly to confirm the worst suspicions among Chinese experts and analysts of US strategic intentions. The deep and widely held conviction that the United States is a rogue superpower committed to the full, unilateral exploitation of its power advantages to pursue its values and interests unbalanced by another major power or coalition of powers seems likely to fuel big departures in the behavior of China (and others).

But suppose this conviction passes. Suppose that Chinese experts and planners were to be persuaded that the will does not now and may not ever exist in Washington to posture US BMD in a way that does deep harm to China's strategic posture. Unfortunately, the pressures to abandon the baseline do not automatically disappear. Think of what is required in a game of chess—an understanding of the next moves and the possible moves after next. Suppose China reacts to US BMD as described in the baseline trajectory and undertakes countervailing deployments. These will not pass unnoticed in Washington, where they may change the political climate of debate about BMD and China. Future policymakers in Washington may opt to thicken a limited defense into something more meaningful against the modernizing Chinese force. Anticipating those possible moves, how should China act now? As one Chinese academic, Zhen Huang, has argued:

> Most likely, [China's] program will involve responses to US missile defenses by increasing force levels so as to restore China's minimum deterrence. The problem is, this would still make the Chinese nuclear force develop into an embryonic limited deterrent at the strategic level . . . For the purpose of reconstructing minimum deterrence, China is not only required to keep improving the survivability of its nuclear forces through measures such as camouflage of deployment sites, development of solid propellant, and acquisition of mobile delivery systems, as well as improvements in C4ISR (command, control, communication, computer, intelligence, surveillance, and reconnaissance) capabilities. More critically, it is required to develop effective means to penetrate US missile defense structure so as to strike at least some major cities. It is in this connection that China's nuclear force is likely to move to an initial limited deterrence capability at the strategic level.[37]

Thus the deployment of modernized systems by China could help to precipitate changes in Chinese military doctrine and in foreign threat perception that themselves could lead to a further evolution of the PRC-US strategic balance in ways that would lead to a more competitive strategic relationship. A more competitive strategic relationship seems likely to do damage to the political and economic relationships.

This understanding of the incentives to abandon the baseline trajectory must be balanced with an understanding of the constraints on doing so. It seems likely that there is a certain category of responses to US BMD that can be made without substantial new investments, and another class that would require additional large outlays of funds. Uploading a few warheads onto existing delivery systems or roughly doubling the existing force of ICBMs would obviously involve a far smaller expenditure than a buildup entailing the production of large numbers of new nuclear warheads, new fissile material, new long-range delivery systems in large numbers, new command and control infrastructures, and the associated bases and personnel. China has spent additional funds on strategic force modernization in recent years but its continued macroeconomic difficulties and the competing demands generated by the intended modernization of conventional forces may impair the ability of strategic planners to gain the resources they desire.

Moreover, as argued above, that leadership must weigh costs beyond the purely fiscal. A major buildup would damage Beijing's efforts to construct more cooperative relations with its neighbors, not least by reinforcing their fears of an emerging China threat. It could help to consolidate an image of China in the minds of Americans and others that it is an enemy state bent on confrontation and hegemony. One Asian expert has described an "asymmetrical security dilemma," deriving an argument from the academic literature analyzing the ways in which states' efforts to make themselves more secure by increasing their military strength ends up making them less secure because of the responses their new military power engenders. He argues:

> As China's strategic nuclear posture has become a sensitive litmus test for China's strategic intentions concerning the US, the structural requirement for Beijing to minimize the security dilemma effect may have served as an added factor causing the delay of China's strategic force modernization and its significant expansion.[38]

In considering this mix of incentives and constraints, we must recognize also some basic uncertainties in the outsider's understanding of China's real options. One of these uncertainties is the state of China's own efforts to develop a ballistic missile defense system. Chinese deployment of BMD around its own missile forces would seem to offer a conceptually straightforward remedy to the problems of survivability that seem to face its forces. As noted above, there is evidence of long-running Chinese interest in such a system and of research and development efforts. Potentially, ten-to-fifteen-year programs begun in the early to mid-1990s can be expected to pay dividends in the next few years. On the other hand, development programs for the modernized follow-on systems to missiles originally deployed in the Chinese force have typically run at least a decade or two before deployment actually commenced. Moreover, China's defense industrial establishment has encountered many difficulties translating the ambition for advanced technology military systems into deployed operational capability.[39] One ready fix to the challenges of deploying conventionally tipped ballistic missile defenses would be interim (or permanent) deployment of nuclear-tipped interceptors. Again, this would follow the model of the Soviet and US approaches of the 1960s (and the current Russian BMD system). But there is no evidence to suggest actual Chinese preparations in this regard.

The other basic uncertainty relates to the impact of the nuclear test moratorium and Comprehensive Test Ban on China's ability to field new generation warheads. Those warheads would be lighter and thus more readily lend themselves to deployment in multiple numbers atop current and future delivery systems. The test moratorium seems likely to have prevented certification of this new warhead.[40] If this understanding is false, or if the Chinese have been otherwise able to satisfy themselves as to the efficacy of the new design, then China will have a ready ability to field large numbers of new warheads. An end to the test moratorium would presumably have a similar result.

Dissuasion

Largely unnoticed so far in the US debate about China's nuclear future are the intentions of the Bush administration to shape China's understanding of the costs and benefits of choosing to depart from the baseline to compete with the United States—intentions wrapped up in the word "dissuasion."

Dissuasion has its roots in the 2001 *Quadrennial Defense Review*. There for the first time the Bush administration set out its notion of the means and ends of US power. Its authors argued that the United States has four primary strategic objectives: to assure friends and allies that they remain secure, to dissuade potential adversaries from choosing the path of confrontation, and to deter and defeat enemies. As argued there:

> Well targeted strategy and policy can . . . dissuade other countries from initiating military competitions. The United States can exert such influence through the conduct of its research and development, test, and demonstration programs. It can do so by maintaining or enhancing advantages in some key areas of military capability.[41]

The president echoed this theme in his *National Security Strategy* of a year later:

> We are attentive to the possible renewal of patterns of great power competition. . . . Our forces will be strong enough to dissuade potential adversaries from pursuing a military build-up in hopes of surpassing, or equaling, the power of the United States.[42]

Significantly for the dissuasion notion, the *Quadrennial Defense Review* preceded the *National Security Strategy* by more than a year. A great deal had changed in the interim—not least, as a result of the attacks of 9/11. The *QDR* puts emphasis on dissuasion as a means of demotivating potential adversaries, whereas the *NSS* puts emphasis on dissuasion as a means of motivating cooperation and "deepening partnership." As the president's cover letter to the *NSS* argued:

> Today, the international community has the best chance since the rise of the nation-state in the seventeenth century to build a world where great powers compete in peace instead of continually prepare for war. Today, the world's great powers find ourselves on the same side—united by common dangers of terrorist violence and chaos. The United States will build on these common interests to promote global security. We are also increasingly united by common values.[43]

Whether and how it might be possible to posture US military forces to dissuade China from choosing to depart the baseline trajectory for a course of strategic competition remains an open question. This will require tailoring deployment of the emerging new triad and of the transforming conventional force in specific ways. They must be "strong enough" to signal to China that it cannot out-compete the United States to any decisive military advantage. But they must not be so strong as to be seen by the Chinese as denying China the benefits of US cooperation and partnership. Presumably this obliges the United States to exercise some form of restraint in exchange for Chinese restraint. But this proposition will be hotly resisted by those Americans who see in China the return of a peer adversary and thus, also, military confrontation with China as inevitable. Yet this is precisely the problem for which dissuasion is intended.

Conclusion

Because China alone among the nuclear weapon states provides almost no official information on the disposition and modernization plans for its nuclear forces, China's nuclear future is largely a mystery to analysts outside China—and inside as well. Many alternatives have been discussed. This volume utilizes some of the best available information and thinking to peer beyond the veil of secrecy. There is much evidence, analysis, and opinion to support the notion that China will long remain on the baseline trajectory postulated here—a baseline that will lead China to some significant quantitative and qualitative improvements to its strategic forces. But in a system as closed and secretive as China's, there is good reason to think that the truth may lie elsewhere. The incentives for departures from the baseline have begun to take shape, but so too have the disincentives. To this outsider, the real hard choices that lie ahead for Chinese decisionmakers seem as yet to have emerged only in dim outline.

China will not make its nuclear future alone. To be sure, the essential strategy and investment decisions will be made in Beijing. But there is much that the United States can do to shape the choices before China. Our security interest in avoiding unnecessary conflict, and our political and economic interests in deeper cooperation and partnership, point to the urgency of thinking through the requirements of dissuasion.

Notes

The views expressed here are the author's and should not be attributed to the Institute for Defense Analyses or George Washington University.

1. *Foreign Missile Developments and the Ballistic Missile Threat to the United States through 2015* (Washington, DC: National Intelligence Council, 1999), 5.

2. "House Select Committee on US National Security and Military/Commercial Concerns with the People's Republic of China," declassified report issued May 25, 1999.

3. This chapter draws on several related pieces of work written by the author at the Institute for Defense Analyses. The author is grateful to IDA and to the Defense Threat Reduction Agency, the Office of the Secretary of Defense, and the Defense Intelligence Agency for their support for these projects. Publications from which some of the following arguments are drawn include Brad Roberts, *China-US Nuclear Relations: What Relationship Best Serves US Interests?* (Alexandria, VA: Institute for Defense Analyses [hereafter IDA], 2001); *China and Ballistic Missile Defense: 1955 to 2002 and Beyond* (Alexandria, VA: IDA, 2003); *Tripolar Stability: The Future of Relations Among the United States, Russia, and China* (Alexandria, VA: IDA, 2002); and *American Primacy and Major Power Concert: A Critique of the 2002 National Security Strategy* (Alexandria, VA: IDA, 2002). This work also draws on "China, Dissuasion, and the New Triad" (project summary briefing of February 2004).

4. This section draws from Roberts, *China-US Nuclear Relations,* A4-A8. See also Robert Manning, Ronald Montaperto, and Brad Roberts, *China, Nuclear Weapons, and Arms Control: A Preliminary Assessment* (New York: Council on Foreign Relations, 2000) for further elaboration of many of these points and for a detailed set of references and citations related to Chinese force modernization.

5. Paul H.B. Godwin, "Potential Chinese Responses to US Ballistic Missile Defense," in *China and Missile Defense: Managing US-PRC Strategic Relations,* Alan D. Romberg and Michael McDevitt, eds. (Washington, DC: Henry L. Stimson Center, 2003), 69. Godwin's analysis draws extensively on a set of five options for China's future strategic force as sketched out in Manning, Montaperto, and Roberts.

6. Hongxun Hua, "China's Strategic Missile Programs: Limited Aims, Not 'Limited Deterrence,'" *Nonproliferation Review* (Winter 1998), 65.

7. This summary and the immediately following sections are drawn from Roberts, *China and Ballistic Missile Defense.*

8. "Administration Missile Defense Papers," July 11, 2001, available at www.whitehouse.gov.

9. Erik Eckholm, "China Says US Missile Shield Could Force an Arms Buildup," *New York Times,* May 11, 2000, 1.

10. "GM Spokesman: China 'Regretful' at Expiration of ABM Treaty," *Xinhua,* June 18, 2002, FBIS CPP20020618000166.

11. The *Quadrennial Defense Review* makes reference to "a rising peer adversary in Asia" without mentioning China by name.

12. See for example Peter Rodman, "The World's Resentment: Anti-Americanism as a Global Phenomenon," *National Interest* (Summer 2000), 33–41.

13. Administration emissaries included Assistant Secretary of State James Kelly in May 2001 immediately following the president's May 1 BMD speech and again in October 2001; Assistant Secretary of State Avis Bohlen in December 2001 immediately prior to the formal notification of intent to withdraw from the treaty; and Assistant Secretary of Defense Peter Rodman in September 2002. President Jiang then visited President Bush in Crawford, Texas.

14. Zhuang Jianzhong, "Missile Defense and Big Power Relations," conference paper, Shanghai Center for PacRim Strategic Studies, Shanghai, January 2002.

15. Banning Garrett, "Chinese Perspectives on the US, Taiwan, NMD, and Sino-Russian Relations," unpublished trip report, January 7–13, 2001.

16. John M. Donnelly, "Russia Wants to Work with US on Nuclear-Tipped Missile Defenses," *Defense Week,* July 8, 2002, 2. Yan Guoqun, "Analyzing US 'Nuclear Explosion Interception' Plan," *Jiefangjun Bao,* June 5, 2002, 9, FBIS CPP20020605000060.

17. Thomas Christensen, "The Party Transition: Will it Bring a New Maturity in Chinese Security Policy?" *China Leadership Monitor,* no. 5 (Winter 2003): 3–19. See also Virginia Monken, *China's New Leadership and a Taiwan Confrontation: Implications for Deterrence,* IDA Document D-2869 (Alexandria, VA: IDA, 2003).

18. On this topic see, for example, Linchen Wang, "The Use of Ballistic Missiles and its Influence on Local Warfare," translated manuscript, date and place of publication unknown.

19. *Foreign Missile Developments and the Ballistic Missile Threat to the United States through 2015* (1999).

20. See, for example, "Interview with Xiao Longxu, Senior Engineer, Second Artillery Corps Research Institution," originally appearing in *Jiefangjun Bao, Zhongguo Xinwen She,* August 26, 1999, FBIS OW2608153999; Zhang Jian, "How Can TMD Serve as a Protective Umbrella for Splitting the Motherland?" *Sing Tao Jih Pao,* June 21, 2001, A32, FBIS CPP20010621000041; Zhang Jian and Li Nien-t'ing, "The Inadequate Warning System Makes it Difficult for Taiwan to Counter Mainland China's Missiles," *Sing Tao Jih Pao,* June 21, 2001, A32, FBIS CPP20010621000041; and "Military Expert Believes TMD Cannot Save Li Teng-hui," *Zhongguo Xinwen She,* September 10, 1999, FBIS OW2209045699.

21. See Chas Freeman, "Did China Threaten to Bomb Los Angeles?" March 22, 2001, at www.ceip.org/npp.

22. Xia Liping, "China's Nuclear Policy and Nuclear Disarmament," unpublished research paper of autumn 2002, 11. Xia is director and professor of the Center for International Strategic Studies at the Shanghai Institute for International Studies. Hongxun Hua echoes these conclusions in the previously cited work. See also Li Bin, Zhao Baogen, and Liu Zhiwei, "China Will Have to Respond," *Bulletin of the Atomic Scientists,* vol. 57, no. 6 (November/December 2001), 25–28.

23. Li Bin et al.

24. From "The Strategic Use and Development of the Second Artillery in the New Period," translated manuscript, date and place of publication unknown.

25. Li Bin, "The Impact of US NMD on Chinese Nuclear Modernization," *Pugwash Online,* April 2001, www.pugwash.org/reports/rc/rc8e.htm.

26. For a further discussion of such a confrontation, especially of differing US and PRC notions of possible escalation dynamics, see Roberts, *China-US Nuclear Relations.*

27. Mark Stokes, *China's Strategic Modernization: Implications for the United States* (Carlisle Barracks, PA: Strategic Studies Institute, US Army War College, 1999).

28. For more on this theme see Laurie Burkitt, Andrew Scobell, and Larry M. Wortzel, eds., *The Lessons of History: The Chinese People's Liberation Army at 75* (Carlisle Barracks, PA: Strategic Studies Institute, 2003).

29. The *QDR* can be found at www.defenselink.mil.

30. For a discussion of the ways in which adversary use of WMD would create powerful new interests for the United States in asymmetric conflicts, see Brad Roberts, "Rethinking How Wars Must End: NBC War Termination Issues and Major Regional Contingencies," in *The Coming Crisis: Nuclear Proliferation, US Interests, and World Order,* Victor Utgoff, ed. (Cambridge, MA: MIT Press, 1996), 245–278.

31. An unclassified version of the *NPR* has not been prepared at this writing. An unclassified summary of its main themes and recommendations can be found in chapter 7, "Adapting Strategic Forces," of the *Annual Report of the Secretary of Defense to the President and Congress, 2002* (Washington, DC: US Government Printing Office, 2002).

32. See, for example, Yan Xuetong cited in "US-Taiwan Military Relations and China's Security," summarizing comments made at a March 11, 2002, session of the Qinghua Foreign Affairs Forum, FBIS CPP20020411000188, April 1, 2002. Yan is professor and director of the Institute of International Studies at Qinghua University. See also Tian Jingmei, "The Bush Administration's Nuclear Strategy and Its Implications for China's Security," an unpublished working paper of the Center for International Security and Cooperation, Stanford University, March 2003. The author is an associate professor at the Arms Control Research Division of the Institute of Applied Physics and Computation Mathematics in Beijing.

33. Wang Guosheng and Li Wei, "US Comprehensively Adjusts Nuclear Strategy," *Jiefangjun Bao,* January 30, 2002, FBIS CPP2002013000076.

34. For more on this theme, see Roberts, *China and Ballistic Missile Defense,* and Stokes, *China's Strategic Modernization.*

35. To the best of my knowledge these views have not appeared in print but they have been reported in private conversation by authoritative sources.

36. Roberts, *Tripolar Stability.*

37. Zhen Huang, "China's Strategic Nuclear Posture by 2010: Minimum or Limited Deterrence? Likely Impact of US Missile Defense," paper prepared for the

8th ISODARCO-Beijing Seminar on Arms Control, Beijing, China, October 14–18, 2002.

38. Ibid.

39. Evan A. Feigenbaum, *China's Techno-Warriors: National Security and Strategic Competition from the Nuclear to the Information Age* (Stanford, CA: Stanford University Press, 2003).

40. Zhen, 8.

41. *Quadrennial Defense Review, 2001.*

42. *National Security Strategy, 2002.*

43. See the presidential cover letter accompanying the *National Security Strategy,* available at www.whitehouse.gov.

Bibliography

"Adapting Strategic Forces." *Annual Report of the Secretary of Defense to the President and Congress, 2002.* Washington, DC: US Government Printing Office, 2002.

"Administration Missile Defense Papers." July 11, 2001. www.whitehouse.gov.

Allen, Kenneth. "PLA Second Artillery Organizational Structure." *Chinese Military Update,* vol. 1, no. 7 (January 2004): 1–5.

Allen, Kenneth, and Maryanne Kivlehan. "Implementing PLA Second Artillery Doctrinal Reforms." In *China's Revolution in Doctrinal Affairs: Emerging Trends in the Operational Art of the Chinese People's Liberation Army.* James Mulvenon and David M. Finkelstein, eds., Arlington, VA: The CNA Corporation, 2005, 149–204.

Allen, Kenneth W., Glenn Krumel, and Jonathan D. Pollack. *China's Air Force Enters the Twenty-First Century.* Santa Monica, CA: RAND, 1995.

An Jing. "Battle of Debarkation under Nuclear Conditions." *Jianchuan Zhishi* (*Naval and Merchant Ships*), no. 293 (January 2004): 10–12.

Arkin, William M., Robert S. Norris, and Joshua Handler. *Taking Stock: Worldwide Nuclear Deployments 1998.* Washington, DC: Natural Resources Defense Council Nuclear Program, 1998.

Ball, Desmond. "US Strategic Forces: How Would They Be Used?" *International Security,* vol. 7, no. 3 (Winter 1982–1983): 31–60.

Battilega, John. "Soviet Views of Nuclear Warfare: The Post–Cold War Interviews." Unpublished manuscript. Denver: Science Applications International Corporation, n.d.

"Behind the Mask," *Economist,* March 20–26, 2004: Special Section on A Survey of Business in China, 3.

Berry, Nicholas. "Space War Games and China as Vader's Empire." *The Weekly Defense Monitor,* vol. 5, no. 5 (February 1, 2001).

Betts, Richard K. *Nuclear Blackmail and Nuclear Balance.* Washington, DC: Brookings Institution, 1987.

"Bokai Miwu Kan Zhongguo Zhenshi Heliliang" (Clear the Fog in Order to See China's Real Nuclear Power). http://fifan.nease.net/chinaarm/chinuclear.htm.

Bolt, Paul J., and Carl N. Brenner. "Information Warfare Across the Taiwan Strait." *Journal of Contemporary China,* vol. 13, no. 38 (February 2004): 129–150.

Burkitt, Laurie, Andrew Scobell, and Larry M. Wortzel, eds. *The Lessons of History: The Chinese People's Liberation Army at 75.* Carlisle Barracks, PA: Strategic Studies Institute, 2003.

Burles, Mark, and Abram N. Shulsky. *Patterns in China's Use of Force.* Santa Monica, CA: RAND, 2000.

Burns, John F. "India Defense Chief Calls US Hypocritical." *New York Times,* June 18, 1998, A6.

Burr, William, and Jeffrey T. Richelson. "A Chinese Puzzle." *Bulletin of the Atomic Scientists,* vol. 53, no. 4 (July/August 1997): 42–47. www.thebulletin.org/issues/1997/ja97/ja97richelson.html.

———. "Whether to 'Strangle the Baby in the Cradle': The United States and the Chinese Nuclear Program, 1960–64." *International Security,* vol. 25, no. 3 (Winter 2000/01): 54–99.

"Call for Meeting 21st Century Challenge—Comment on US 2002 Defense Report." *People's Daily Online,* August 29, 2002. http://English.peopledaily.com.cn.

Central Intelligence Agency. "China." *World Factbook.* www.cia.gov/cia/publications/factbook/geos/ch.html.

Chang Feng. "The Uses of the Neutron Bomb During the Battle of Debarkation." *Jianchuan Zhishi* (*Naval and Merchant Ships*), no. 295 (March 2004): 12–14.

Chang, Gordon H. "To the Nuclear Brink: Eisenhower, Dulles, and the Quemoy-Matsu Crisis." In *Nuclear Diplomacy and Crisis Management.* Sean M. Lynne-Jones, Steven E. Miller, and Stephen Van Evera, eds. Cambridge, MA: MIT Press, 1990, 200–227.

Chase, Michael, and Evan S. Medeiros. "China's Evolving Nuclear Calculus: Modernization and the Doctrinal Debate." In *A Revolution in Doctrinal Affairs.* David Finkelstein and James Mulvenon, eds. Santa Monica, CA: RAND, forthcoming.

Chen Bojiang et al., eds. *Xin Junshi Geming yu Dandai Zhanzheng Redian Wenti* (*New Military Revolution and Contemporary War Hot Spot Issues*). Beijing: Chinese Communist Party History Press, 2004.

Chen Haoling. *Junshi Kexue Wenxian Xinxi Jiansuo Zhinan* (*Research Guide for Military Science Documents and Information*). Beijing: Junshi Kexue Chubanshe, 2000.

Chen Shihmin. *Analyse et Comparison des stratégies nucléaires des puissances nucléaries moyennes: France, Royaume-Uni et Chine.* (*Comparative Analysis of the Nuclear Strategies of the Middle Nuclear Powers: France, the United Kingdom, and China*). Doctoral dissertation. University of Paris, April 2000.

———. "PRC's Nuclear Force Development and the Evolution of its External Relations in the Cold War Era (1950s to 1980s)." *Zhongguo Dalu Yanjiu* (*Mainland China Studies*) (Taipei), vol. 46, no. 6 (November–December 2003): 29–57.

"Chen Supports Legal Settlement of Election Disputes." *Hong Kong AFP,* in Foreign Broadcast Information Service (FBIS), April 24, 2004. FBIS CPP20040424000069.

Chen Xiaogong. *Junbei Kongzhi yu Guoji Anquan Shouce* (*Arms Control and International Security Handbook*). Beijing: World Affairs Press, 1998.

Cheng Feng and Larry Wortzel. "PLA Operational Principles and Limited War: The Sino-Indian War of 1962." In *Chinese Warfighting: The PLA Experience Since 1949.* Mark A. Ryan, David M. Finkelstein, and Michael A. McDevitt, eds. Armonk, NY: M.E. Sharpe, 2003, 173–197.

"China." In *Deadly Arsenals: Tracking Weapons of Mass Destruction.* Joseph Cirincione with Jon B. Wolfsthal and Miriam Rajkumar. Washington, DC: Carnegie Endowment for International Peace, 2002, 141–163.

"China Considers Establishing a Northeast Asia Security Negotiation Conference." *Dong-A Ilbo,* February 25, 2004.

"China Database." Nuclear Threat Initiative online. www.nti.org/db/china/sac.htm.

"China Improves the 'Ming' Class Submarine." *Qianlong Junshi* (*Thousand Dragons Military*) online, for *Bingqi Zhishi* (*Armaments Knowledge*), February 14, 2001. http://cgi.qianlong.com/mility/bqzs3/DisplayCode.asp?Dataname=Article&Code=20914.

"China Is Seriously Concerned with the US-Japan Declaration." *Ta Kung Pao,* February 21, 2005, A2.

"China Would Build 12 Super Nuclear Submarines." http://military.china.com/zh_cn/news/568/20040309/11639769.html.

China's Diplomacy 2002. Policy Research Office of the Ministry of Foreign Affairs of the People's Republic of China, 2002.

"China's Fissile Material Production and Stockpile." *China WMD Database.* Center for Nonproliferation Studies, Monterey Institute for International Studies. www.nti.org/db/china/fmstock.htm.

"China's National Defense in 2000." Beijing: Information Office of the State Council, People's Republic of China, October 2000. www.china.org.cn/e–white/2000/.

"China's National Defense in 2002." Beijing: Information Office of the State Council, People's Republic of China, December 2002. http://www.nti.org/db/china/engdocs/whpandef_2002.htm.

China's National Statement of Security Assurances. Beijing: Information Office of the State Council, People's Republic of China, April 5, 1995. www.nti.org/db/china/engdocs/npt0495a.htm.

China's Non-Proliferation Policy and Measures. Beijing: Information Office of the State Council, People's Republic of China, December 3, 2003.

"China's Second Artillery Corps Forms 100-Strong Contingent of Missile Experts." Beijing Xinhua Domestic Service, December 27, 2000. FBIS CPP20001227000128.

"China's Second Artillery Has About 160 Doctorates." *Xinhua,* April 20, 2004. FBIS CPP20040420000028.

"Chinese Nuclear Forces 2003." *Bulletin of the Atomic Scientists,* vol. 59, no. 6: 77–80. www.thebulletin.org/issues/nukenotes/nd03nukenote.html.

"The Choice of China's Diplomatic Strategy." *People's Daily Online,* March 19, 2003.

Christensen, Thomas. "China, the US-Japan Alliance, and the Security Dilemma in East Asia." *International Security,* vol. 23, no. 4 (Spring 1999): 49–80.

———. "The Party Transition: Will it Bring a New Maturity in Chinese Security Policy?" *China Leadership Monitor,* no. 5 (Winter 2003): 3–19.

———. *Useful Adversaries: Grand Strategy, Domestic Mobilization, and Sino-American Conflict.* Princeton, NJ: Princeton University Press, 1996.

Cirincione, Joseph, with Jon B. Wolfsthal and Miriam Rajkumar. *Deadly Arsenals: Tracking Weapons of Mass Destruction.* Washington, DC: Carnegie Endowment for International Peace, 2002, 141–163.

Cody, Edward, and Philip P. Pan. "China Rejects Taiwan's Proposal for DMZ." *Washington Post,* February 12, 2004, A26. www.washingtonpost.com/wp–dyn/articles/A31785-2004Feb11.html.

Cohen, Sam. "Chinese Nuclear Espionage: Fact or Convenient Fiction?" *Washington Inquirer,* January 25, 1999. http://iraqwar.org/aim1.htm.

Cole, Bernard. *The Great Wall at Sea: China's Navy Enters the 21st Century.* Annapolis, MD: Naval Institute Press, 2001.

"CSS–6 (DF–15/M–9)." In *Jane's Strategic Weapon Systems,* no. 42. Surrey, UK: Jane's Information Group, 2005.

DeFrancis, John. *ABC Chinese-English Comprehensive Dictionary.* Honolulu: University of Hawaii Press, 2003.

"DF–31." *Global Security.org*. www.globalsecurity.org/wmd/world/china/df–31.htm.

"Dialog: Focus on US Global Military Deployment." *People's Daily Online,* June 16, 2003.

Diamond, Howard. "Chinese Strategic Plans Move Forward with Missile Test." *Arms Control Today,* vol. 29, no. 5 (July/August 1999). www.armscontrol.org/act/1999_07-08/chija99.asp.

Dibb, Paul. "China's Strategic Situation and Defense Priorities in the 1980s." *The Australian Journal of Chinese Affairs,* no. 5 (January 1980): 97–115.

"Di'er Paobing Gongcheng Xue Yuan" (Second Artillery Corps Engineering Academy). *Jiefangjun Bao* (*PLA Daily*). www.pladaily.com.cn/item/jxzs/tmp/bkzn/31.htm.

"Di'er Paobing Moujidi Jianli Tuguan Jianzi Rencaiku" (A Certain Second Artillery Base Establishes a Local NCO Talent Inventory). *Jiefangjun Bao* (*PLA Daily*), April 6, 2004, 2. www.pladaily.com.cn/gb/pladaily/2004/04/06/20040406001188_zgjs.html.

Director of Central Intelligence. "The Intelligence Community Damage Assessment on the Implications of China's Acquisition of US Nuclear Weapons Information on the Development of Future Chinese Weapons." April 21, 1999. www.nti.org/db/china/engdocs/cia499.htm.

Dong Jushan and Wu Xudong. "Zhongguo Shenmi Zhanlue Daodan Budui Jueqi Jishi" (True Story: China's Mysterious Strategic Missile Forces on the Rise). *Guangzhou Ribao,* July 1, 2001. FBIS CPP20010703000044.

Donnelly, John M. "Russia Wants to Work with US on Nuclear-Tipped Missile Defenses." *Defense Week,* July 8, 2002, 2.

Dreyer, June Teufel. *China's Political System.* 4th ed. New York: Pearson Longman, 2004.

Eckholm, Erik. "China Says US Missile Shield Could Force an Arms Buildup." *New York Times,* May 11, 2000, 1.

"Erpao Daodan Moni Xunlian Xitong Jiaofu Shiyong" (Second Artillery Corps' Missile Simulation and Training System Handed Over for Use). *Guangzhou Ribao,* February 15, 2001. FBIS CPP20010217000011.

"Expounding Bush's Approach to US Nuclear Security: An Interview with John R. Bolton." *Arms Control Today,* vol. 32, no. 2 (March 2002): 3–8. www.armscontrol.org/act/2002_03/boltonmarch02.asp.

"Factors Hindering US Hegemonic Moves: Analysis." *People's Daily Online,* April 8, 2003.

Federation of American Scientists. "China's Nuclear Weapons: Present Capabilities." Updated May 1, 2001. www.fas.org/nuke/hew/China/ChinaArsenal.html.

——— "Chinese Missile Facilities." www.fas.org/nuke/guide/china/facility/missile.htm.

——— "Command and Control." Updated June 23, 2000. www.fas.org/nuke/guide/china/c3i.

Feigenbaum, Evan A. *China's Techno-Warriors: National Security and Strategic Competition from the Nuclear to the Information Age.* Stanford, CA: Stanford University Press, 2003.

Feng Jinyuan and Xia Hongqing. "Di'er Paobing Mou Jidi Zengqiang Jidong Zuozhan Nengli" (A Certain Second Artillery Base Improves its Mobile Combat Operations Capabilities). *Jiefangjun Bao* (*PLA Daily*), September 3, 2002. FBIS CPP20020903000058.

Ferguson, Charles. "Sparking a Buildup: US Missile Defense and China's Nuclear Arsenal." *Arms Control Today,* vol. 30, no. 2 (March 2000): 13–18.

Ferguson, Charles D., Evan S. Medeiros, and Phillip C. Saunders. "Chinese Tactical Nuclear Weapons." In *Tactical Nuclear Weapons: Emergent Threats in an Evolving Security Environment.* Brian Alexander and Alistair Millar, eds. London: Brassey's, 2003.

Finkelstein, David M. *China Reconsiders Its National Security.* Alexandria, VA: Center for Naval Analyses, December 2000.

———. *China's New Security Concept: Reading Between the Lines.* Alexandria, VA: Center for Naval Analyses, April 1999.

———. *Hearing on Military Modernization and the Cross-Strait Balance, Testimony before US China Economic and Security Review Commission.* US Congress, February 6, 2004.

Finkelstein, David M., and Maryanne Kivlehan, eds. *China's Leadership in the 21st Century: Rise of the Fourth Generation.* Armonk, NY: M.E. Sharpe, 2003.

Finkelstein, David M., and James Mulvenon, eds. *A Revolution in Doctrinal Affairs.* Santa Monica, CA: The RAND Corporation, forthcoming.

"The First Line of Hyper Warfare: Conversation with Lieutenant General Abe C. Lin." *Taiwan Defense Affairs,* vol. 1, no. 4 (Summer 2001): 125–143.

"FM Slams Unilateralism, Favors Multilateralism." *China Daily,* March 6, 2004.

Foreign Missile Development and the Ballistic Missile Threat through 2015. Washington, DC: National Intelligence Council, 2001. www.fas.org/irp/nic/bmthreat–2015.htm.

Foreign Missile Developments and the Ballistic Missile Threat to the United States Through 2015. Washington, DC: National Intelligence Council, 1999.

Fravel, Taylor. "The Evolution of China's Military Strategy: Comparing the 1987 and 1999 Editions of *Zhanlue Xue.*" Paper presented at RAND-CNA meeting on "The Revolution in Doctrinal Affairs." December 2002.

Freedman, Lawrence. *The Evolution of Nuclear Strategy.* New York: St Martin's Press, 1981.

———. "The First Two Generations of Nuclear Strategists." In *Makers of Modern Strategy.* Peter Paret, ed. Princeton, NJ: Princeton University Press, 1986, 735–778.

Freeman, Chas. "Did China Threaten to Bomb Los Angeles?" *Proliferation Brief* 4, no. 4, March 22, 2001. www.ciaonet.org/pbei/ceip/frc01.

Gao Rui. *Zhanluexue* (*The Science of Military Strategy*). Beijing: Junshi Kexue Chubanshe, 1987.

Gao Yan. "The Order of Development of Nuclear Forces of Various Nations in the New Century." *Ta Kung Pao* (Hong Kong), May 3, 2000, A5.

Garrett, Banning. "Chinese Perspectives on the US, Taiwan, NMD, and Sino-Russian Relations." Unpublished trip report, January 7–13, 2001.

———. "The Need for Strategic Reassurance in the 21st Century." *Arms Control Today,* vol. 31, no. 2 (March 2001): 9–14. www.armscontrol.org/act/2001_03/garrett.asp.

Gertz, Bill. "China Tests Arms Designed To Fool Defense Systems." *Washington Times,* July 23, 2002, A1.

———. "China Tests Ballistic Missile Submarine." *Washington Times,* December 3, 2004, A1.

Gill, Bates, and Michael O'Hanlon. "China's Hollow Military." *National Interest,* no. 56: 55–62.

Gill, Bates, James Mulvenon, and Mark Stokes. "China's Strategic Rocket Forces: Transition to Credible Deterrence." In *The People's Liberation Army as Organization,* Reference Volume v1.0. James C. Mulvenon and Andrew N.D. Yang, eds. Arlington, VA: RAND, 2002, 517–530. www.rand.org/publications/CF/CF182.

Gittings, Danny. "General Zhu Goes Ballistic." *Asian Wall Street Journal,* July 18, 2005, A13.

Gittings, John. *The World and China.* London: Oxford University Press, 1967.

Glaser, Bonnie S., and Banning N. Garrett. "Chinese Perspectives on the Strategic Defense Initiative." *Problems of Communism,* vol. 35, no. 2 (March–April 1986): 28–44.

Glaser, Charles L., and Steve Fetter. "National Missile Defense and the Future of US Nuclear Weapons Policy." *International Security,* vol. 26, no. 1 (Summer 2001): 40–92.

"GM Spokesman: China 'Regretful' at Expiration of ABM Treaty." *Xinhua,* June 18, 2002. FBIS CPP20020618000166.

Godwin, Paul H.B., "Potential Chinese Responses to US Ballistic Missile Defense." In *China and Missile Defense: Managing US-PRC Strategic Relations.* Alan D. Romberg and Michael McDevitt, eds. Washington, DC: Henry L. Stimson Center, 2003, 61–71.

Godwin, Paul H.B., and Evan S. Medeiros. "China, America, and Missile Defense: Conflicting National Interests." *Current History,* vol. 99, no. 638 (September 2000): 285–289.

Goldstein, Avery. *Deterrence and Security in the 21st Century: China, Britain, France, and the Enduring Legacy of the Nuclear Revolution.* Stanford, CA: Stanford University Press, 2000.

Goldstein, Lyle, and William Murray. "Undersea Dragons: China's Maturing Submarine Force." *International Security,* vol. 28, no. 4 (Spring 2004): 161–196.

Gordon, Michael R. "Bush Due to Meet Chinese on Issues Crucial for Ties." *New York Times,* March 19, 2001, 1.

Gray, Colin S. *Modern Strategy.* Oxford: Oxford University Press, 1999.

Gu Dexin and Niu Yongjun. *Heyouling De Zhengdong—Ershishiji Hewenti Huihu Yu Sikao* (*Rumblings of the Nuclear Specter: Looking Back at and Considering the Nuclear Problem in the 20th Century*). Beijing: Guofang Daxue Chubanshe, 1999.

Gurtov, Melvin, and Byong-Moo Hwang. *China Under Threat.* Baltimore: Johns Hopkins University Press, 1980.

———. *China's Security: The New Roles of the Military.* Boulder, CO: Lynne Rienner, 1998.

Halperin, Morton H. *China and the Bomb.* New York: Praeger, 1965.

———. "Chinese Nuclear Strategy: The Early Post-Detonation Period." *Asian Survey,* vol. 5, no. 6: 271–279.

Han Haichen. *Ershiyi Shiji Zhongguo Haijun* (*21st Century PLA Navy*). Hong Kong: East-West Cultural Inc., 2000.

Han Yang. "Airborne Actions in a War of Debarkation under Nuclear Conditions." *Jianchuan Zhishi* (*Naval and Merchant Ships*), no. 297 (May 2004): 10–12.

Hassig, Khadong Oh. "Northeast Asian Strategic Security Environment." Defense Threat Reduction Agency Study, August 2001. www.dtra.mi/about/organization/asian.pdf.

He Linshu and Wang Shuhe. "Penetration Measures Against NMD." *Beijing Daodan yu Hangtian Yunzai Jishu* (*Missile and Space Delivery Systems Technology*), June 10, 2002: 23–26. FBIS CPP20021007000146.

He Yingbo and Qiu Yong. "THAAD-Like High Altitude Theater Missile Defense: Strategic Defense Capability and Certain Countermeasures Analysis." *Science and Global Security,* vol. 11 (2003): 151–202.

"House Select Committee on US National Security and Military/Commercial Concerns with the People's Republic of China." Declassified report issued May 25, 1999.

Hsu, Jacky, and Shi Jiangtao. "Taipei Says Its Forces Could Hit the Three Gorges Dam, But Do Not Plan To." *South China Morning Post,* June 10, 2004.

Hu Guangzheng, ed. *Zhongwai Junshi Zuzhi Tizhi Bijiao Jiaocheng* (*Comparison of Chinese and Foreign Military Organizational Systems*). Beijing: Junshi Kexue Chubanshe, 1999.

Hua, Hongxun. "Viewpoint: China's Strategic Missile Programs: Limited Aims, Not 'Limited Deterrence.'" *Nonproliferation Review* (Winter 1998): 60–68. http://cns.miis.edu/pubs/npr/vol05/52/hua52.pdf.

Huang Hong, ed. *Shijie Xinjunshi Biange Baogao* (*Report on New Military Revolution of the World*). Beijing: People's Press, 2004.

Hutchinson, Robert. *Weapons of Mass Destruction.* London: Weidenfeld & Nicolson, 2003.

Hutzler, Charles. "Deal Shows Weakness of China's Arms Industry—Buying 8 Russian Subs, Beijing Tries to Redress Some of Sector's Failures." *Wall Street Journal,* June 28, 2002, A11.

"Interview with Xiao Longxu, Senior Engineer, Second Artillery Corps Research Institution." *Jiefangjun Bao* (*PLA Daily*), *Zhongguo Xinwen She,* August 26, 1999. FBIS OW2608153999.

"Jiang Zemin Defines Position of China's Strategic Nuclear Weapons." *Tai Yang Bao* (Hong Kong), July 17, 2000. FBIS CPP20000717000021.

"Jing Zhiyuan Promoted to Commander of PLA Second Artillery Corps." *Taipei Chung-Kuo Shih-Pao,* January 17, 2003. FBIS CPP20030117000028.

Johnson, Seymour. "China Seeks Technology for Next-Generation Missiles." *Jane's Missiles and Rockets,* vol. 3, no. 5 (May 1999).

Johnston, Alastair Iain. "China's New 'Old Thinking': The Concept of Limited Deterrence." *International Security,* vol. 20, no. 3 (Winter 1995/96): 5–42.

———. *Cultural Realism: Strategic Culture and Grand Strategy in Chinese History.* Princeton, NJ: Princeton University Press, 1998.

———. "Prospects for Chinese Nuclear Force Modernization: Limited Deterrence versus Multilateral Arms Control." *China Quarterly,* no. 146 (June 1996): 548–576.

———. "Some Thoughts on Chinese Nuclear Deterrence." Paper prepared for workshop on Chinese military doctrine, CNA Corporation, February 2, 2000.

———. "Thinking About Strategic Culture." *International Security,* vol. 19, no. 4 (Spring 1995): 32–64.

Junshixue Yanjiu Huigu yu Zhanwang (*Military Academic Research Review and Prospects*). Beijing: Academy of Military Sciences Press, 1995.

Kahn, Joseph. "Chinese General Threatens Use of A-Bombs if US Intrudes." *New York Times,* July 15, 2005, A8.

Kane, Thomas M. "Dragon or Dinosaur: Nuclear Weapons in a Modernizing China." *Parameters,* vol. 33, no. 4 (Winter 2003–2004): 98–113.

Kang Jianbin et al. "GPS in Ballistic Missile Guidance Instrument Error Separation." *Daodan yu Hangtian Yunzai Jishu* (*Ballistic Missiles and Space Launch Technology*), February 2002. FBIS CPP20020722000254.

Kerbel, Josh. "Thinking Straight: Cognitive Bias in the US Debate about China." *Studies in Intelligence,* vol. 48, no. 3 (2004): 27–35.

Kessler, Glenn. "US, China Agree to Regular Talks." *Washington Post,* April 8, 2005, A14.

"Kongjun Gongcheng Daxue" (Air Force Engineering University). http://edu.xaonline.com/afeu–zhaosheng.html.

Koppel, Andrea. "China Denies Military Expansion 'Inevitable.'" *CNN,* September 5, 2001. www.cnn.com/2001/US/09/05/china.us.arms/.

Kristensen, Hans M. "Chinese Nuclear Forces." SIPRI Project on Nuclear Technology & Arms Control. *SIPRI Yearbook 2003: Armaments, Disarmament and International Security.* Oxford: Oxford University Press, 2003. http://projects.sipri.se/nuclear/china.pdf.

Kristensen, Hans M. and Joshua Handler. "Appendix 10A: World Nuclear Forces." *SIPRI Yearbook 2002: Non-Proliferation, Arms Control, Disarmament.* Oxford: Oxford University Press for the Stockholm International Peace Research Institute, 2002, 552–557.

Lamson, James A., and Wyn Q. Bowen. "'One Arrow, Three Stars': China's MIRV Program, Part I." *Jane's Intelligence Review,* vol. 9, no. 5 (May 1997): 216–218.

———. "'One Arrow, Three Stars': China's MIRV Program, Part II." *Jane's Intelligence Review,* vol. 9, no. 6 (June 1997): 266–269.

"Langfang Lujun Daodan Xueyuan" (Langfang Army Missile Academy). *Jiefangjun Bao* (*PLA Daily*). www.pladaily.com.cn/item/jxzs/tmp/bkzn/60.htm.

Laris, Michael. "China Says It Can Build Neutron Bomb." *Washington Post,* July 15, 1999. http://taiwansecurity.org/WP/WP–990715.htm.

Larkin, Bruce D. *Nuclear Designs.* New Brunswick, NJ: Transaction Publishers, 1996.

Lewis, John Wilson, and Hua Di. "China's Ballistic Missile Programs: Technologies, Strategies, Goals." *International Security,* vol. 17, no. 2 (Fall 1992): 5–40.

Lewis, John Wilson, and Xue Litai. *China Builds the Bomb.* Stanford, CA: Stanford University Press, 1988.

———. "China's Search for a Modern Air Force." *International Security,* vol. 24, no. 1 (Summer 1999): 64–94.

———. *China's Strategic Seapower: The Politics of Force Modernization in the Nuclear Age.* Stanford, CA: Stanford University Press, 1994.

———. "Strategic Weapons and Chinese Power: The Formative Years." *China Quarterly,* no. 112 (December 1987): 541–554.

Li Bin. "Are US Nuclear Weapons Aimed at China?" *Shijie Zhishi,* April 1, 2002: 16–17.

———. "The Effects of NMD on Chinese Strategy." *Jane's Intelligence Review,* vol. 13, no. 3 (March 2001): 49–52.

———. "The Impact of US NMD on Chinese Nuclear Modernization." *Pugwash Online,* April 2001. www.pugwash.org/reports/rc/rc8e.htm.

———. "Saving Arms Control." *Beijing Review,* April 18, 2002.

Li Bin, Zhao Baogen, and Liu Zhiwei. "China Will Have to Respond." *Bulletin of the Atomic Scientists,* vol. 57, no. 6 (November/December 2001): 25–28.

Li Fumin and Li Dunsong. "A Brief Account of the Growth and Development of Our Country's Strategic Missile Troops." *Junshi Shilin* (*Military History*), no. 5 (1988): 51.

Li Jijun. "Traditional Military Thinking and the Defensive Strategy of China." Address at the United States National War College. *Letort Paper,* no. 1, August 29, 1997.

Li Jutai, ed. *Zhongguo Hewuqi Shiyan Zhuizong* (*Tracing China's Nuclear Weapon Tests*). Beijing: Long March Press, 2000.

Lin Changsheng and Niu Minshi. "The Construction and Strength of China's ICBM." *Zhonggong Yanjiu* (*Studies of Chinese Communism*) (Taipei), vol. 37, no. 7 (July 2003): 80–90.

———. "Re-examining China's Nuclear Strategy." *Zhonggong Yanjiu* (*Studies of Chinese Communism*) (Taipei), vol. 37, no. 12 (December 2003): 67–79.

Lin Chong-pin. *China's Nuclear Weapons Strategy: Tradition Within Evolution.* Lexington, MA: Lexington Books, 1988.

———. *He Ba* (*Nuclear Hegemon*). Taipei: Students' Publishing, 1999.

Lin Zhongda. *Zhanqu Feidan Fangyu yu Taihai Anquan* (*TMD: Its Formation and Impact on Taiwan Strait Security*). Taipei: Taiwan Elite Press, 2000, 303–321.

Liu Hongji and Luo Haixi. *Guofang Lilun* (*Theory on National Defense*). Beijing: National Defense Press, 1996.

Liu Hua. "Reconsidering the Use of Neutron Bombs in a War of Debarkation." *Jianchuan Zhishi* (*Naval and Merchant Ships*), no. 298 (July 2004): 12–14.

Liu Huaqiu. "Analysis of China's Arms Control Policy." *Xiandai Junshi* (*Contemporary Military*), November 1995: 15–18.

Liu Shuli. "Shenjian Ye Laohu" (Magic Sword, 'Night Tiger'). *Hsien-Tai Chun Shih* (*Conmilit*) (Hong Kong), November 11, 2002, 2–3. FBIS CPP20021202000190.

Liu Yidai and He Tianjin. "Di'er Pao Bing Moulu Jiji Gaijin Xunlian Shouduan Xin Zhuangbei Kuai Su Xinggcheng Zhan Douli" (Brigade of Second Artillery Corps Actively Improves Means of Training to Quickly Make New Armament Combat Ready). *Jiefangjun Bao* (*PLA Daily*), November 21, 2002, 2. FBIS CPP20021120000027.

"Long March Rocket Lifts 'Experimental Satellite I,' 'Nanostar I' into Space." Beijing Xinhua Domestic Service, April 18, 2004. FBIS CPP20040419000003.

Manning, Robert A., Ronald N. Montaperto, and Brad Roberts. *China, Nuclear Weapons, and Arms Control: A Preliminary Assessment.* New York: Council on Foreign Relations, 2000.

Mao Xinhua et al. "Shen Kong Mou Daodan Luduan Zheng Xunlian Zhidao Sixiang de Yi Duan Jingli" (The Experience of a Shenyang Missile Brigade in the Correct Approach to Training). *Jiefangjun Bao* (*PLA Daily*), June 2, 2002.

Mearsheimer, John J. *The Tragedy of Great Power Politics.* New York: Norton, 2001.

Medeiros, Evan S. *Ballistic Missile Defense and Northeast Asian Security: Views from Washington, Beijing, and Tokyo.* Monterey, CA: Center for Nonproliferation Studies, 2001. www.cns.miis.edu/pubs/eanp/bmdrep/bmd_web.pdf.

———. "A Cultural Evolution: The Development of China's Arms Control and Nonproliferation Community." In *Integrating a Rising Power into Global Nonproliferation Regimes: US-China Negotiations and Interactions on Nonproliferation, 1980–2001.* Unpublished doctoral dissertation, 2002.

Medeiros, Evan S., and M. Taylor Fravel. "China's New Diplomacy." *Foreign Affairs* (November/December 2003): 22–35.

Medeiros, Evan S., and Phillip C. Saunders. *Building a Global Strategic Framework for the 21st Century: Report from the Fourth US-China Conference on Arms Control, Disarmament and Nonproliferation.* Monterey, CA: Center for Nonproliferation Studies, 2002. www.cns.miis.edu/cns/projects/eanp/research/uschina4/4thconf.pdf.

The Military Balance 2002–2003. London: Oxford University Press for the International Institute for Strategic Studies, 2002.

The Military Balance 2003–2004. London: Oxford University Press for the International Institute for Strategic Studies, 2003.

The Military Balance 2004–2005. London: Oxford University Press for the International Institute for Strategic Studies, 2004.

"Military Expert Believes TMD Cannot Save Li Teng-hui." *Zhongguo Xinwen She,* September 10, 1999. FBIS OW2209045699.

Miller, David. *Submarines of the World.* St. Paul, MN: McGraw Hill, 2002.

Ming Pao (Hong Kong), May 14, 2004, A26.

Monken, Virginia. *China's New Leadership and a Taiwan Confrontation: Implications for Deterrence.* IDA Document D-2869. Alexandria, VA: Institute for Defense Analyses, August 2003.

Mosher, David E., and Lowell H. Schwartz. "The China and Nuclear Reunion Is Only A Motive Away." *Los Angeles Times,* February 25, 2001.

Mulvenon, James. "Chinese and Mutually Assured Destruction: Is China Getting Mad?" In *Getting MAD: Nuclear Mutual Assured Destruction, Its Origins and Practice.* Henry D. Sokolski, ed. Carlisle, PA: Strategic Studies Institute, US Army War College, November 2004, 234–260.

———. "Jiang Controls the Gun?" *China Leadership Monitor* 5. www.chinaleadershipmonitor.org/20031/jm.html.

Myers, Steven Lee. "US Missile Plan Could Reportedly Provoke China." *New York Times,* August 10, 2000, A1.

Nacht, Michael, and Tom Woodrow. "Agenda on Nuclear Arms." In *Strategic Trends in China.* Hans Binnendijk and Ronald N. Montaperto, eds. Washington, DC: National Defense University, June 1998.

Nartker, Mike. "China: New Report Details Chinese Missile Defense Countermeasures." *Global Security Newswire,* September 25, 2002.

Nathan, Andrew J., and Bruce Gilley. *China's New Rulers: The Secret Files.* New York: New York Review of Books, 2002.

Nikolskiy, Aleksey, and Vasiliy Kashin. "With No One to Bomb, Russia May Sell its Strategic Aviation to China." *Moscow Vedomosti,* January 14, 2005. FBIS CEP20050114000312.

Norris, Robert, and William Arkin. "NRDC Nuclear Notebook: Chinese Nuclear Forces, 2001." *Bulletin of the Atomic Scientists,* vol. 57, no. 5 (September/October 2001): 71–72.

Norris, Robert S., and Hans M. Kristensen. "Nuclear Notebook: Chinese Nuclear Forces 2003." *Bulletin of the Atomic Scientists,* vol. 59, no. 6 (November/December 2003): 77–80. www.thebulletin.org/issues/nukenotes/nd03nukenote.html.

"Nuclear Weapons Database: Chinese Nuclear Delivery Systems." Center for Defense Information. www.cdi.org/issues/nukef&f/database/chnukes.html#h6.

Pan Zhengqian, ed. *Guoji Caijun yu Junbei Kongzhi* (*International Disarmament and Arms Control*). Beijing: National Defense University Press, 1996.

Pillsbury, Michael. *China Debates the Future Security Environment.* Washington, DC: National Defense University Press, 2000.

Pingguo Ribao (*Apple Daily*) (Taiwan version). March 19, 2004, 21.

"PLA 2nd Artillery Corps Holds Night Fire Missile Training." *Zhongguo Tongxun She* (Hong Kong), August 29, 1999. FBIS CPP19990830000003.

Pollack, Jonathan. "The Future of China's Nuclear Weapons Policy." In *Strategic Views from the Second Tier.* John C. Hopkins and Wiexing Hu, eds. New Brunswick, NJ: Transaction Publishers, 1995.

"PRC Radio on New Breakthrough in Strategic Missile Technology." August 9, 2000. FBIS CPP20000809000111.

"PRC: Second Artillery Corps Regiment Conducts Camouflage Training." *Jiefangjun Bao* (*PLA Daily*), February 15, 2004, 2. FBIS CPP20040223000136.

"The Pursuit of Security: Conversation with General Shiah Yang–jou." *Taiwan Defense Affairs,* vol. 1, no. 2 (Winter 2000/2001): 140–157.

Puttré, Michael. "Satellite-Guided Munitions." *Scientific American,* vol. 288, no. 2 (February 2003): 66–73.

Qian Qichen. "US Adjusts Strategy after Sept 11 Attacks." *People's Daily Online,* January 19, 2004.

Qiao Dexiang et al. "Xiang 'Kuai' Zi Yao Zhandouli" (Enhance Combat Capability through Speed). *Zhongguo Kongjun* (*Chinese Air Force*), January 2003: 45–47.

Quadrennial Defense Review Report. Washington, DC: Department of Defense, September 30, 2001. www.defenselink.mil/pubs/qdr2001.pdf.

Report of the Select Committee on US National Security and Military/Commercial Concerns with the People's Republic of China. US House Report 105-851, 1999. http://www.access.gpo.gov/congress/house/hr105851/.

Roberts, Brad. *American Primacy and Major Power Concert: A Critique of the 2002 National Security Strategy.* Alexandria, VA: Institute for Defense Analyses, 2002.

———. *China and Ballistic Missile Defense: 1955 to 2002 and Beyond.* Alexandria, VA: Institute for Defense Analyses, September 2003.

———. *China-US Nuclear Relations: What Relationship Best Serves US Interests?* Washington, DC: Institute for Defense Analyses, 2001.

———. "East Asia." In *Arms Control: Cooperative Security in a Changing Environment.* Jeffrey A. Larsen, ed. Boulder, CO: Lynne Rienner, 2002, 253–267.

———. "Rethinking How Wars Must End: NBC War Termination Issues and Major Regional Contingencies." In *The Coming Crisis: Nuclear Proliferation, US Interests, and World Order.* Victor Utgoff, ed. Cambridge, MA: MIT Press, 1996, 245–278.

———. "Tripolar Stability: Relations Among the United States, Russia, and China." Alexandria, VA: Institute for Defense Analyses, September 2002. www.ida.org/IDAnew/Tasks/TripolarStability.pdf.

Roberts, Brad, Robert Manning, and Ronald Montaperto. "China: The Forgotten Nuclear Power." *Foreign Affairs,* vol. 79, no. 4 (July/August 2000): 53–63.

Rodman, Peter. *Shield Embattled: Missile Defense as a Foreign Policy Problem.* Washington, DC: The Nixon Center, October 2001, 47–50. www.nixoncenter.org/publications/monographs/shieldembattled.pdf.

———. "The World's Resentment: Anti-Americanism as a Global Phenomenon." *National Interest* (Summer 2000): 33–41.

Romberg, Alan D., and Michael McDevitt, eds. *China and Missile Defense: Managing US-PRC Strategic Relations.* Washington, DC: The Henry L. Stimson Center, February 2003.

Ross, Robert S. "Navigating the Taiwan Strait: Deterrence, Escalation Dominance, and US-China Relations." *International Security,* vol. 27, no. 2 (Fall 2002): 48–85.

Ryan, Mark A. "Early Chinese Attitudes Toward Civil Defense Against Nuclear Attack." *Australian Journal of Chinese Affairs*, no. 21 (January 1989): 81–109.

Ryan, Mark A., David M. Finkelstein, and Michael A. McDevitt. *PLA Warfighting.* Armonk, NY: M.E. Sharpe, 2003.

Sagan, Scott, et al. "The Madman Nuclear Alert: Secrecy, Signaling, and Safety in October 1969." *International Security,* vol. 27, no. 4 (2003): 150–183.

Saunders, Phillip C. "New Approaches to Nonproliferation: Supplementing or Supplanting the Regime?" *The Nonproliferation Regime,* vol. 8, no. 3 (Fall–Winter 2001): 123–136.

———. "US-China Relations in a Changing Nuclear Environment." In *Strategic Surprise? US-China Relations in the Early Twenty-First Century.* Jonathan D. Pollack, ed. Newport, RI: Naval War College Press, 2003, 159–184.

Saunders, Phillip C., and Jing-dong Yuan. "China's Strategic Force Modernization: Three Scenarios and Their Implications for the United States." Center for Nonproliferation Studies Paper. Monterey Institute of International Studies, 2003.

Saunders, Phillip C., Jing-dong Yuan, Stephanie Lieggi, and Angela Deters. "China's Space Capabilities and the Strategic Logic of Anti-Satellite Weapons." Center for Nonproliferation Studies Web Report. Monterey Institute of International Studies, July 2002. http://cns.miis.edu/pubs/week/020722.htm.

Scobell, Andrew. *China and Strategic Culture.* Carlisle, PA: Strategic Studies Institute, 2002.

"Second Artillery Corps (SAC)." Center for Nonproliferation Studies, 2003. www.nti.org/db/china/sac.htm.

"Second Artillery Corps' Missile Simulation and Training System Handed over for Use." *Guangzhou Ribao,* February 15, 2001. FBIS CPP20010217000011.

"Secretary of Defense Donald Rumsfeld Interview on ABC News Sunday." February 11, 2001. www.defenselink.mil/transcripts/2001/t02122001_t0211abc.html.

Sessler, Andrew M., et al. *Countermeasures: A Technical Evaluation of the Operational Effectiveness of the Planned US National Missile Defense System.* Boston: Union of Concerned Scientists, 2000. www.ucsusa.org/documents/CM_all.pdf.

Shambaugh, David. *Modernizing China's Military: Progress, Problems, and Prospects.* Berkeley: University of California Press, 2003.

Shang Lin. "Battle of Strategic Nuclear Reaction." *Jianchuan Zhishi* (*Naval and Merchant Ships*), no. 300 (August 2004): 22–24.

Shen Dingli. "A Chinese Perspective on National Missile Defense." Institute for Energy and Environmental Research online, February 2001. www.ieer.org/latest/shen–ppr.html.

———. "What Missile Defense Says to China." *Bulletin of the Atomic Scientists,* vol. 56, no. 4 (July/August 2000): 20–21. www.thebulletin.org/issues/2000/ja00/ja00shen_perspective. html.

Sherman, Jason. "China Looks Askance at Space War Game." *Defense News,* February 28, 2001, 3, 19.

Shi Yan. "Creation and Development of China Second Artillery Corps." *Junshi Shilin* (*Military History*), no. 6 (1989): 48.

Singh, Jaswant. "Against Nuclear Apartheid." *Foreign Affairs,* vol. 77, no. 5 (September/October 1998): 41–52.

Slipchenko, V.I. *The Sixth Generation War.* Beijing: Xinhua Publishing House, 2004.

Sloss, Leon. "Deterrence, Defenses, Nuclear Weapons and Arms Control." *Comparative Strategy,* no. 20 (2001): 435–443.

Snyder, Jack. *The Soviet Strategic Culture: Implications for Nuclear Options.* Report R-2154-AF. Santa Monica, CA: RAND, 1977.

Sokov, Nikolai. "Russian Ministry of Defense's New Policy Paper: The Nuclear Angle." Monterey, CA: Center for Nonproliferation Studies, n.d. http://cns.miis.edu.

"Spokesman Answers a Question on US News Report that China Has Become a Target of US Nuclear Weapons." Chinese Foreign Ministry website, March 11, 2002.

Stokes, Mark. *China's Strategic Modernization: Implications for the United States.* Carlisle, PA: Strategic Studies Institute, US Army War College, 1999.

———. "Chinese Ballistic Missile Forces in the Age of Global Missile Defense: Challenges and Responses." In *China's Growing Military Power: Perspectives on Security, Ballistic Missiles, and Conventional Capabilities.* Andrew Scobell and Larry M. Wortzel, eds. Carlisle, PA: Strategic Studies Institute, US Army War College, September 2002, 107–167.

———. "The People's Liberation Army and China's Space and Missile Development: Lessons from the Past and Prospects for the Future." In *The Lessons of History: The Chinese People's Liberation Army at 75.* Laurie Burkitt, Andrew Scobell, and Larry M. Wortzel, eds. Carlisle, PA: Strategic Studies Institute, US Army War College, July 2003, 193–249.

Su Hao. "Issues of Arms Control and Sino-American Relations." *Heping yu Fazhan* (*Peace and Development*) (March 2000): 42–47.

Sugiyama, Hiroyuki. "China Successfully Tests Multi-Warhead Missiles." *Yomiuri Shimbun,* February 8, 2003. FBIS JPP20030207000154.

Sun Tzu. *The Art of War.* Translated by Lionel Giles. http://classics.mit.edu/Tzu/artwar.html.

Swaine, Michael, and Ashley Tellis. *Interpreting China's Grand Strategy: Past, Present, and Future.* Santa Monica, CA: RAND, 2000. www.rand.org/publications/MR/MR1121/.

Tai Bingchang and Wang Tao. "On EMP Weapons." *Hangkong Zhishi* (*Aerospace Knowledge*), no. 397, May 2004: 34–35.

Tanner, Murray Scot. "Hu Jintao's Succession." In *China's Leadership in the 21st Century: Rise of the Fourth Generation.* David Finkelstein and Maryanne Kivlehan, eds. Armonk, NY: M.E. Sharpe, 2003, 45–65.

Teng Jianqun. "You Meijun Taikongzhan Yanxi Suoxiang" (Thoughts Arising from the US Military's Space War Exercise). *Jiefangjun Bao* (*PLA Daily*), February 7, 2001, 9. FBIS CPP20010207000050.

Tian Jingmei. "The Bush Administration's Nuclear Strategy and Its Implications for China's Security." Unpublished working paper. Center for International Security and Cooperation, Stanford University, March 2003.

Tracking the Dragon: National Intelligence Estimates on China During the Era of Mao, 1948–1976. Washington, DC: National Intelligence Council, October 2004.

"Treaty Between the United States of America and the Russian Federation on Strategic Offensive Reductions." *Arms Control Today,* vol. 32, no. 5 (June 2002): 9–11. www.armscontrol.org/act/2002_06/docjune02.asp.

Tucker, Nancy B. *China Confidential.* New York: Columbia University Press, 2001.

Tyler, Patrick E. "As China Threatens Taiwan, It Makes Sure US Listens." *New York Times,* January 24, 1996, A3.

"Type 92 Xia." GlobalSecurity.org. Updated August 12, 2002. www.globalsecurity.org/wmd/world/china/type_92.htm.

"Type 94." GlobalSecurity.org. Updated August 12, 2002.

Urayama, Kori. "China Debates Missile Defense." *Survival* (Summer 2004): 123–142.

US Department of Defense. *Annual Report on the Military Power of the People's Republic of China 2002.* July 12, 2002. www.defenselink.mil/news/Jul2002/d20020712china.pdf.

———. *Annual Report on the Military Power of the People's Republic of China 2003*. July 28, 2003. www.defenselink.mil/pubs/20030730chinaex.pdf.

———. *Annual Report on the Military Power of the People's Republic of China 2004*. May 28, 2004. www.defenselink.mil/pubsd20040528PRC.pdf.

———. *The Military Power of the People's Republic of China 2005*. July 2005. www.defenselink.mil/news/Jul2005/d20050719china.pdf.

"US Exports to China 1988–1998: Fueling Proliferation." Wisconsin Project on Nuclear Arms Control, April 1999. An executive summary is available at www.wisconsinproject.org/pubs/reports/1999/execsumm.html.

"US-Japan Declaration Urges Peaceful Resolution of Cross-Straits Relations." *Hong Kong Economic Journal,* February 21, 2005, 7.

"US-Taiwan Military Relations and China's Security." Comments at March 11, 2002, Qinghua Foreign Affairs Forum, April 1, 2002. FBIS CPP20020411000188.

"US War Game Signals New Arms Race in Space Weaponry in 21st Century." *Jiefangjun Bao* (*PLA Daily*), February 21, 2001. FBIS CPP20010221000091.

Wang Baocun. *Shijie Xin Junshi Geming* (*World's New Military Revolution*). Beijing: People's Liberation Army Press, 1999.

Wang Guosheng and Li Wei. "US Comprehensively Adjusts Nuclear Strategy." *Jiefangjun Bao* (*PLA Daily*), January 30, 2002. FBIS CPP200201300076.

Wang Hongqing and Zhang Xingye, eds. *Zhanyixue* (*The Science of Military Campaigns*). Beijing: Guofang Daxue Chubanshe, May 2000.

Wang Linchen. "The Use of Ballistic Missiles and its Influence on Local Warfare." Translated unpublished paper, n.d.

Wang Wenrong, ed. *Zhanluexue* (*The Science of Military Strategy*). Beijing: Guofang Daxue Chubanshe, 1999.

Wang Xiaojun and Xia Hongqing. "Di'er Paobing Mou Jidi Baozhang Fen Dui Jie Gang Lu Xun Xiao Yi Hao" (Logistics Detachments of Certain Base under Second Artillery Corps Achieve Good Training Results Thanks to Application of New Training Program). *Jiefangjun Bao* (*PLA Daily*), September 15, 2002. FBIS CPP20020916000048.

———. "Di'er Paobing Moulu Dingzhe Hecheng Zhua Fenxun" (A Certain Brigade Under the Second Artillery Corps Focuses on Combined Tactical Training Exercises and Program of Training Officers and Soldiers Separately). *Jiefangjun Bao* (*PLA Daily*), January 13, 2004, 2. FBIS CPP20040113000099.

Wang Zaigang. "Vanquishing the Aircraft Carrier Task Force: Cruise Missiles, or Ballistic Missiles?" *Jianchuan Zhishi* (*Naval and Merchant Ships*), no. 305 (January 2005): 24–27.

Wei Qiyong, Qin Zhijin, and Liu Erxun. "Analysis of Changing Emphasis in US Military Strategy." *Daodan yu Hangtian Yunzai Jishu* (*Missile and Aerospace Delivery Technology*), August 10, 2002.

Wright, David, and Lisbeth Gronlund. "Estimating China's Production of Plutonium for Weapons." *Science and Global Security,* vol. 11, no. 1 (2003): 61–80.

Wu Bayi. "Hot Spots, Bright Points, and Footholds." *Beijing Shijie Jishi*, January 1, 2004. FBIS CPP20040112000206.

Wu Jie. "Thinking on Nuclear Forces." *Bingqi Zhishi* (*Armaments Knowledge*) online, April 4, 2001. http://cgi.qianlong.com/mility/bqzs3/DisplayCode.asp?DataName=Article&Code=20931.

Wu Kai. "Dui He Liliang De Sikao" (Military Experts Discuss Nuclear Capability). *Bingqi Zhishi* (*Ordnance Knowledge*), no. 4, April 2001.

Wu Peng and Si Shilei. "Study of Consequences of Attacks on Nuclear and Chemical Facilities." *Guofang,* September 15, 2002, 19–20, FBIS CPP20021210000140.

Wu Rui and Li Bin. "The Impact of US Nuclear Policies on China—A Political Perspective." Paper presented at Conference on Northeast Asian Security: A Mixture of Traditional and Untraditional Security, Beijing, China, April 2–3, 2004. http://learn.tsinghua.edu.cn/homepage/2000990313/4042.htm.

Wu Sulin. "PLA Tactical Missile Forces Live-Fire Exercise." *Shanghai Guoji Zhanwang,* March 1, 2004, 10–15. FBIS CPP20040315000213.

Xia Liping. "China's Nuclear Policy and Nuclear Disarmament." Unpublished research paper. Center for International Strategic Studies, Shanghai Institute for International Studies, Autumn 2002.

Xue Litai. "The Evolution of China's Nuclear Strategy." In *Strategic Views from the Second Tier.* John C. Hopkins and Weixing Hu, eds. New Brunswick, NJ: Transaction Publishers, 1995.

Xue Xinglin, ed. *Zhanyi Lilun Xuexi Zhinan* (*Campaign Theory Study Guide*). Beijing: Guofang Daxue Chubanshe, 2001.

Yan Guoqun. "Analyzing US 'Nuclear Explosion Interception' Plan." *Jiefangjun Bao* (*PLA Daily*), June 5, 2002, 9. FBIS CPP20020605000060.

Yang Huan. "China's Strategic Nuclear Weapons." In *Chinese Views of Future Warfare.* Michael Pillsbury, ed. Washington, DC: National Defense University Press, 1997, 131–135.

Yang Ruxue. "The Second Artillery's Application of Deterrence in Hi-Tech War." Unpublished manuscript, n.d.

Yang Zukuai and Wang Zaigang. "How to Develop our Country's Precision-Guided Ballistic Missiles?" *Jianchuan Zhishi* (*Naval and Merchant Ships*), no. 305 (January 2005): 28–30.

Yao Changde and He Tianjin. "Wo Zhanlue Daodan Bu Dui Cehui Nengli Da Zeng" (Our Strategic Missile Unit Greatly Improves Its Surveying and Mapping Capabilities). *Keji Ribao* (Beijing), January 17, 2002. FBIS CPP20020214000048.

Yao Youzhi and Peng Guangqian, eds. *Zhanluexue* (*The Science of Military Strategy*). Beijing: Junshi Kexue Chubanshe, 2001.

Ye Jicheng. "Beyond Polarization Mentality—Thoughts on China's Diplomatic Strategy." *Guangzhou Nanfang Zhoumo* Internet Version, January 8 and 15, 2004. www.nanfangdaily.com.cn/zm.

Ye Jincheng, Chen Meihui, and Lu Shijun. "Review and Future Estimation of PLA Force Development." *Guofang Guanli Xuebao* (*Journal of National Defense Management*) (Taipei), vol. 23, no. 2 (November 2002): 55–68.

Yi Chi. "The Process of the Chinese Development of Nuclear Bombs." www.gchjs.com/wz/wz232.htm.

Yi Tung. "Range of Nuclear Warheads Can Cover Europe and America." *Sing Tao Jih Pao* (Hong Kong), January 1, 2001. FBIS CPP20010106000009.

You Ji. *The Armed Forces of China.* New York: I.B. Tauris Publishers, 1999.

Yu Qi. "Naoren de Tiaoyue he Bazhu de Tumou" (Annoying Treaty and Hegemonic Attempt). *Jiefangjun Bao* (*PLA Daily*), August 1, 1999, 5.

Yu Xiaopeng. *Ershiyi Shiji Zhanzheng Qushi* (*War Trends of the 21st Century*). Beijing: Xinhua Press, 2002.

Zeng Tai. "Special Actions in a War of Debarkation under Nuclear Conditions." *Jianchuan Zhishi* (*Naval and Merchant Ships*), no. 299 (July 2004): 22–24.

Zhang Jian. "How Can TMD Serve as a Protective Umbrella for Splitting the Motherland?" *Sing Tao Jih Pao,* June 21, 2001, A32. FBIS CPP20010621000041.

Zhang Jian and Li Nien–t'ing. "The Inadequate Warning System Makes it Difficult for Taiwan to Counter Mainland China's Missiles." *Sing Tao Jih Pao,* June 21, 2001, A32. FBIS CPP20010621000041.

Zhang Jianzhi and Wang Xiaoxu. "Influence of the Appearance of the Atomic Bomb Toward World Order: In Memory of the 50th Anniversary of the Victory of Anti–Fascist War." *Jiefangjun Bao* (*PLA Daily*), August 1, 1995, 6.

Zhang Jihong et al. "Shiyanshi Liqi Xiaoyan" (Smoke Rises from the Laboratory). *Keji Ribao* (Beijing), December 1, 2001. FBIS CPP20020214000044.

Zhang Qinde and Dai Xu, eds. *Xiandai Guofang Dadian* (*Encyclopedia of Modern National Defense*). 3 vols. Beijing: Central Documentation Press, 1999.

Zhang Shu Guang. *Deterrence and Strategic Culture: Chinese-American Confrontation, 1949–1958.* Ithaca, NY: Cornell University Press, 1992.

Zhang Wannian, ed. *Dangdai Shijie Junshi yu Zhongguo Guofang* (*Contemporary World Military and Chinese National Defense*). Beijing: Military Science Press, 2000.

Zhang Yihong. "China's Rising Forces." *Jane's International Defense Review,* vol. 35, no. 8 (August 2002): 37.

Zhanyixue Yanjiu (*Research on the Science of Military Campaigns*). Beijing: Guofang Daxue Chubanshe, 1997.

Zhao Xijun, ed. *Shezhan* (*Deterrence Warfare*). Beijing: Guofang Daxue Chubanshe, May 2003.

Zhen Huang. "China's Strategic Nuclear Posture by 2010: Minimum or Limited Deterrence? Likely Impact of US Missile Defense." Paper prepared for the 8th ISODARCO-Beijing Seminar on Arms Control, Beijing, China, October 14–18, 2002.

Zheng Jun. "Chinese Nuclear Forces and Nuclear Strategy." May 4, 2002. http://cgi.qianlong.com/mility/bqzs3/DisplayCode.asp.

Zheng Zhiren. "The Five Nuclear Crises of China" (Second Part). November 4, 2004. http://cgi.qianlong.com/mility/bqzs3/DisplayCode.asp?DataName=Article&Code=20616.

"Zhongguo Junxiao Zhaosheng" (Chinese Military Academy Admissions). *Jiefangjun Bao* (*PLA Daily*). www.pladaily.com.cn/item/jxzs/tmp/bkzn/bt.htm.

Zhongguo Shibao (*China Times*) (Taipei), March 9, 2004. http://military.china.com/zh_cn/news/568/20040309/11939769.html.

Zhou Jianguo. "Nuclear Strategy of Bush Administration Moving Gradually from Deterrence to Actual Combat." *Jiefangjun Bao* (*PLA Daily*), March 18, 2002.

Zhou Xuehai. *Xinxi Shidai He Junkong* (*Nuclear Arms Control in the Information Age*). Beijing: Chinese Workers' Press, 2003.

Zhu Fei. "How to Destroy the Future Command and Control Systems of the Taiwan Army." *Jianchuan Zhishi* (*Naval and Merchant Ships*), no. 296 (April 2004): 12–14.

Zhu Feng. "The TMD and Cross-Straits Relations: An Analysis on the Extension of TMD to Taiwan by the United States." Research Report 28, Research Center on Cross-Straits Relations, Hong Kong, June 1999.

Zhu Ming. "Be Prepared To Use Nuclear Weapons—Logic of 'Absolute Security.'" *Jiefang Ribao,* March 12, 2002.

Zhu Mingquan. "China's Nuclear Deterrence Policy: Formulation and Development." In *Daguo Weijiao* (*Diplomacy of the Great Powers: Theory, Decision-making and Challenge*). Vol. 2. Xiao Jialing and Tang Xianxing, eds. Beijing: Current Affairs Press, 2003, 529–570.

———. "From Emphasis on the Warfighting Value of Nuclear Weapons to Emphasis on the Deterrence Value of Nuclear Weapons." In *Meiguo Wenti Yanjiu* (*Studies on American Problems*). Vol. 2. Ni Shixiong and Liu Yuntao, eds. Beijing: Current Affairs Press, 2002, 71–114.

———. "What Factors Deter US Attack on China?" In *Daguo Weijiao* (*Diplomacy of the Great Powers: Theory, Decisionmaking and Challenge*). Vol. 1. Xiao Jialing and Tang Xianxing, eds. Beijing: Current Affairs Press, 2003, 251–288.

Zhuang Jianzhong, "Missile Defense and Big Power Relations." Conference paper, Shanghai Center for PacRim Strategic Studies, Shanghai, January 2002.

Zhuang Qubing. "Meiguo 'Xingqiu Dazhan Jihua' Poxi" (An Analysis of the US Star Wars Program). *Guoji Wenti Yanjiu* (*International Studies*), no. 4 (1984).

Ziemke, Carolyn. *Strategic Personality and the Effectiveness of Nuclear Deterrence.* Document D-2537. Alexandria, VA: Institute for Defense Analyses, November, 2000.

Zuberi, Matin. "Soviet and American Technological Assistance and the Pace of Chinese Nuclear Tests." *Strategic Analysis,* vol. 24, no. 7. http://cioanet.org/olj/sa/sa_oct00zum01.html.

The Contributors

Paul J. Bolt is a professor of political science at the United States Air Force Academy. He has taught at Zhejiang University and Baicheng Normal College in the People's Republic of China, as well as the University of Illinois. Dr. Bolt is the author of *China and Southeast Asia's Ethnic Chinese: State and Diaspora in Contemporary Asia* and is a co-editor of *American Defense Policy*. He is also the author of numerous articles on Asian issues.

Christine A. Cleary is currently a graduate student at The Fletcher School, Tufts University. She anticipates graduating with a Master of Art, Law, and Diplomacy, having focused on International Security Studies and East Asia.

Evan S. Medeiros is a political scientist at The RAND Corporation, a nonprofit research institute. He specializes in research on China's foreign and national security policies, US-China relations, and Chinese defense issues. During 2000, he was a visiting fellow at the Institute of American Studies at the China Academy of Social Sciences (CASS) in Beijing and an adjunct lecturer at China's Foreign Affairs College. He travels to Asia frequently and speaks, reads, and writes Mandarin Chinese.

Ronald N. Montaperto is a consultant on Asian affairs. Formerly he was dean of academics at the Asia-Pacific Center for Security Studies and the senior research professor at the National Defense University. In his distinguished career, he has served as a faculty member in the Political Science Department at Indiana University-Bloomington, Director of East Asian Studies at Indiana University, the Henry L. Stimson Chair of

Political Science at the US Army War College, and the Chief of Estimates for China at the Defense Intelligence Agency. He frequently has appeared as a guest analyst of Chinese and Asian affairs and was a professional lecturer in political science at the George Washington University. He has published four books as well as numerous articles on Asia security issues, Chinese foreign and national security policies, and Chinese domestic politics.

Brad Roberts is a member of the research staff at the Institute for Defense Analyses in Alexandria, Virginia, with expertise on the proliferation and control of weapons of mass destruction. He also serves as an adjunct professor at George Washington University, as chairman of the research advisory council of the Chemical and Biological Arms Control Institute, and as a consultant to Los Alamos National Laboratories. He is also a member of the board of directors of the United States Committee of the Council for Security Cooperation in the Asia Pacific (CSCAP). Prior to joining IDA in 1995, he was editor of *The Washington Quarterly* and a member of the research staff at the Center for Strategic and International Studies, Washington, DC.

Phillip C. Saunders has been a senior research professor at the National Defense University's Institute for National Strategic Studies since January 2004. He previously worked at the Monterey Institute of International Studies, where he served as director of the East Asia Nonproliferation Program at the Center for Nonproliferation Studies from 1999 to 2004 and taught courses on Chinese politics, Chinese foreign policy, and East Asian security. Dr. Saunders has conducted research and consulted on East Asian security issues for Princeton University, the Council on Foreign Relations, RAND, and the National Committee on US-China Relations. Dr. Saunders served as an officer in the United States Air Force from 1989–1993, working on Asian security issues at the Pentagon. He has published numerous articles on China and Asian security in numerous journals. He speaks Mandarin Chinese and has traveled throughout East Asia.

Ting Wai, formerly a research fellow at the Institute of Southeast Asian Studies, Singapore, is now an associate professor at the Department of Government and International Studies, Hong Kong Baptist University. His research interests include Chinese domestic politics and foreign policies, and theories of international relations. He has published widely in Chinese, English, and French on Chinese diplomacy, Sino-American relations, Indochina problems, Chinese regionalism, Mainland China-Hong Kong relations, and the external relations and international status of Hong Kong.

Albert S. Willner, a colonel in the United States Army, is Chief, Liaison Affairs Section at the American Institute in Taiwan. Prior to this assignment he served as an assistant professor in the Department of Social Sciences at the United States Military Academy, West Point, New York. As an aviator and China foreign area officer, he has also served in a variety of assignments throughout the United States, Hong Kong, and Germany.

Jing-dong Yuan is a senior research associate at the Center for Nonproliferation Studies and teaches Chinese politics and Northeast Asian security and arms control at the Monterey Institute of International Studies. He has had research and teaching appointments at Queen's University, York University, the University of Toronto, and the University of British Columbia, where he was also a recipient of the prestigious Izaak Killam Postdoctoral Research Fellowship. He was a visiting research scholar at the Cooperative Monitoring Center at Sandia National Laboratories before he joined the Center for Nonproliferation Studies in summer 1999. Dr. Yuan's research focuses on Asia-Pacific security, global and regional arms control and nonproliferation issues, US foreign policy, and China's defense and foreign policy. He writes extensively, and his publications have appeared in numerous journals and books.

Index

About the Book

In the face of significant changes in the contemporary geopolitical environment, China's longstanding policy of maintaining a minimal nuclear stockpile may also be shifting. *China's Nuclear Future* provides a comprehensive overview of both the evolution of China's nuclear policy and the strategic implications of current developments.

The authors examine a full range of issues, from China's rising economic fortunes to the impact of the US-led war on terror. Their assessment of the drivers and constraints that are transforming China's nuclear posture is key to understanding not only the country's possible nuclear futures, but also the broader issue of its role in world politics.

Paul J. Bolt is professor of political science at the US Air Force Academy. **Albert S. Willner,** Colonel, US Army, taught in the Department of Social Sciences at the US Military Academy in 2000–2004; at present, he is pending assignment as the Chief, Liaison Affairs Section at the American Institute in Taiwan.